# SAVAGE SCENE

*The Life and Times of James Kirker, Frontier King*

James Kirker, accompanied by four of his faithful Shawnees, looks down into Colonel Doniphan's camp from a rim high above the Rio Grande. *Courtesy of the artist José Cisneros*

# SAVAGE SCENE

---

The Life and Times of
## JAMES KIRKER
*FRONTIER KING*

---

by
William Cochran McGaw

HASTINGS HOUSE, PUBLISHERS

New York

*TO FRED HEITFELD*

Copyright © 1972 by William C. McGaw

Library of Congress Catalog Card Number: 76-38962

ISBN: 8038-6712-3

Published simultaneously in Canada by Saunders of Toronto, Ltd., Don Mills, Ontario

Designed by Al Lichtenberg
Printed in the United States of America

Library of Congress Cataloging in Publication Data

McGaw, William C.
   Savage scene.

   Bibliography: p.
   1. Kirker, James, 1793–1852 or 3.   2. Indians of North America—Southwest, New—History.   3. Southwest, New—History.   I. Title.
F800.K52M3   917.8'03'20924   [B]   76-38962
ISBN 0-8038-6712-3

# PREFACE

People have said for more than a hundred years that some-body should write a book about Jim Kirker. One author, Mayne Reid, did just that—while Kirker was still alive in 1851—but Reid's book was pure fiction. Entitled *The Scalp Hunters; or Romantic Adventures in Northern Mexico,* the book in no way portrayed Kirker's real life but Reid did spell his name cor-rectly, which is more than can be said for two articles written by Matt Field and appearing in the New Orleans *Picayune* in late February and early March of 1840. Field praised Jim Kir-ker's bravery, exalted his Indian-fighting ability and told how Kirker had made a contract with a Mexican governor to rid the earth of every single Apache for $100,000. Field, however, spelled Jim's name *Kurker.*

"The most famous scalp hunter was James Kirker, written down in Spanish records as Santiago Querque," was the opinion given by J. Frank Dobie in his book, *Apache Gold and Yaqui Silver,* first published in 1928. Dobie went on to tell of a lost gold mine Kirker and his men found in the Sierra Madre foot-hills, and a few years later Leland Sonnichsen took up the topic in *The Story of Roy Bean, Law West of the Pecos.* In his research on Bean, Dr. Sonnichsen discovered that Roy's sister-in-law, Petra, was Kirker's daughter. He also learned that Kir-ker's occupation was "selling Apache scalps to the Mexican government," and concluded that "there might be a story there if anybody were left to tell it."

Arthur Woodward wrote a biographical note on Jim Kirker for the *1934 Annual of the Historical Society of South-ern California,* and in 1951 William H. Hutchinson related in

*Westways* magazine how Jim was thrown some fifty feet into the air in October 1850 when the steamer *Sagamore* blew up at the San Francisco docks.

In recent years several references have appeared in historical publications concerning Kirker's adventures, one of which was an article in the *New Mexico Historical Review* written by Ralph A. Smith, professor of history at Abilene (Texas) Christian College, titled "Apache Plunder Trails Southward, 1831–1840," in which Jim Kirker is prominently mentioned.

It was about nine years ago that Howard Bryan, a writer of early-day events for the Albuquerque *Tribune,* told me about coming across numerous references to Kirker. Howard wondered why such a ubiquitous character had never been the subject of a biography and suggested this might be a project to pursue. Subsequently, I dug up enough material for a column I was then writing for the El Paso *Herald-Post.* His career so interested me that I began devoting more and more time to research on Kirker's life, until now I know I shall continue for as long as I am still warm. Twice I reached a point where I thought I had uncovered all of the information available and twice I finished early drafts of this biography, only for something new to turn up which shifted the emphasis completely. The last such incident was in the fall of 1969, when Doyce B. Nunis, Jr., associate professor of history at the University of Southern California, told me about running across a Kirker letter in the Public Records Office at London, where Dr. Nunis was researching another matter.

Since one Kirker letter in the archives of the British Foreign Office presaged others, I went to London to investigate. There I not only found the letter Dr. Nunis told me about, but many more, plus a batch of interesting depositions made by various American trappers in the Chihuahua area in the early 1840s.

This trip to the British Isles also gave me a chance to visit Kirker's birthplace near Belfast and to study at first hand the character of the people from which he sprang—the Scotch-Irish of Ulster. I drove completely around Lough Neagh in Northern Ireland, around which lake various Kirkers had settled and lived for centuries after coming from Scotland.

Jim Kirker was born in a tiny village called Kilcross, in Killead parish, a dozen miles northwest of Belfast. Other members of the Kirker family had moved on around Lough Neagh, settling on the eastern shore in County Tyrone, others moved to the south and set up at Armagh, while still others were living in Antrim. It is especially in this area that the Protestant and Catholic Ulstermen are still fighting the political and religious wars which began about 300 years ago. After completing the loop around the lake, I found myself driving up Falls Road from Armagh and entering Belfast. Falls Road becomes the street which divides the fighting factions of Catholics and Presbyterians in the lower part of Belfast. At every intersection British soldiers stood, guns at the ready and faces consciously blank, behind waist-high sandbag fortifications, comprising the only barrier between the Protestant and Catholic Irishmen who are apparently determined to blow each other up.

I asked Hugh Gilbert Kirker, a cousin some times removed of James Kirker, if he didn't think it odd that James, a Presbyterian, should have married a Catholic widow—and a super-devout one, too—in the United States. He replied that it was not at all unusual in Ulster, nor was it in the Kirker family, as many of them had taken Catholic mates. I asked him why, in the light of that, they were still fighting over religion. He smiled; if they weren't fighting over religion, he said, they would have found another cause by now—and, indeed, he didn't think religious differences were the real cause of the troubles.

It has occurred to me that much of the so-called American character was traceable to the large number of Scotch-Irish immigrants who came to the colonies before there was a United States and of the dominant role they played in opening the western lands and fighting Indians. President Theodore Roosevelt has dealt with this at length in his five-volume series, *The*

_Winning of the West._ "The dominant strain in their blood was that of the Presbyterian Irish—the Scotch-Irish, as they were often called," Roosevelt wrote in describing the foremost pioneers of the colonial period. "It is doubtful if we have fully realized the importance played by that stern and virile people, the Irish whose preachers taught the creed of Knox and Calvin. These Irish representatives of the Covenanters were to the West almost what the Puritans were to the Northeast, and more than what the Cavaliers were in the South . . . they . . . formed the kernel of the distinctly and intensely American stock who were the pioneers of our people in their march westward, the vanguard of the army of fighting settlers, who with axe and rifle won their way from the Alleghanies to the Rio Grande and the Pacific."

Roosevelt named as typical of these people such figures in our history as Andrew Jackson, Sam Houston, Davey Crockett, Kit Carson and Meriwether Lewis, who were backed up by a good many McGees, McCoys and McKinneys.

Jim Kirker's trail was little different from that made by those Scotch-Irish who preceded him here. He sailed from Ireland and landed in New York in 1810, and a short while later he went down the Ohio, then up the Mississippi to St. Louis, eventually across the plains and into the Rocky Mountains, to Santa Fe and Taos, to Old Mexico and finally to the Pacific Coast. He owned the Corralitos Ranch in Mexico and lived for a while in the mining village of Guadalupe y Calvo, in the State of Chihuahua, which is today virtually as primitive as when he lived there, more than a century ago.

No roads lead into or out of Guadalupe y Calvo to this day, only burro trails, and not to this day has a wheel rolled over its streets, be it on an auto, truck or cart. The village is surrounded by 11,000-foot mountains, which first must be topped on foot or aboard a burro. Then you drop down, as into a cup, some 4000 feet into the town itself, leaping from rock ledge to rock ledge for about three miles. Finally, you find yourself in a town of cobbled streets and thatched roofs, unlike any other place I know about in Mexico.

This was one of the most unusual places Kirker's trail led me, but it was a long and varied journey, and many people helped me along the way. A mention of their names here is small pay indeed, but it is all I have to offer—so I thank those who assisted me.

First is E. C. Kirker, of Miami, Florida, who made two trips to the British Isles, to North Ireland, while this book was in preparation. There he sifted genealogical evidence from dusty records and weathered tombstones in the Kilcross area, and it was he who enlisted the aid of Miss I. Embleton, secretary of the Ulster-Scot Historical Society, in determining the early Kirker family origins. While on that topic, I would like also to credit Harriet Stryker-Rodda, a professional genealogist in Brooklyn, for the important information concerning Kirker's New York City sojourn and the family he left behind there.

I wish also to thank W. Kirker Bixby, an antiquarian book dealer in Minneapolis and a descendant of Ohio's second governor, Thomas (of Tyrone) Kirker, for the letters and biographies of his branch of the family.

Anybody who studies the early fur trade seriously must ultimately end up in the Missouri Historical Society Library in the Jefferson Memorial building in St. Louis. Helping me there were the director, George R. Brooks; Librarian Mrs. Fred C. Harrington, Jr.; Archivist Mrs. Ernst A. Stadler; Orville Spreen, one-time sheriff of the St. Louis Westerners' Corral; Frederick E. Voelker, writer and historian; and also Mary E. Mewes, reference librarian at the St. Louis Mercantile Library; as well as Miss Elizabeth Tindall, St. Louis Public Library Reference Department. Mrs. Ruth K. Field, curator of the MHS Pictorial History Gallery, provided many of the photos.

Elbert L. Huber, Chief of the Navy Records Center Service, Washington, was of important aid in bringing out obscure facts concerning the privateer ship, the *Black Joke,* upon which

Jim served. Howard L. Baldwin was also instrumental in providing some historical background on this vessel.

Art Woodward, mentioned earlier, is an expert on many
things, including dirty songs, and I am indebted to him for the
information that the *Black Joke* was named after a bawdy song
of that day, as well as for his providing me with one of the very
few correct copies of Benjamin David Wilson's narrative.

Dr. Rex Strickland, formerly professor of history at the
University of Texas at El Paso, kept me straightened out on
events and the names of actors performing them in the El Paso
southwest, as did Carl D. W. Hays, now engaged in writing a
biography of mountain man David Jackson, who—until Carl's
book is published—remains even more obscure than has been
Kirker.

Dale L. Morgan, by the simple act of writing an invaluable
book called *The West of William H. Ashley,* made the work on
Kirker's biography much easier, but his personal assistance
during the several visits I made to the Bancroft Library at the
University of California at Berkeley aided even more. Thanks
also is owed to George P. Hammond, now retired, but who was
head of the Bancroft Library when he provided photostats of
the B. D. Wilson manuscript, and also to LeRoy R. Hafen, who
corrected some points in a Kirker sketch I did for him to be
included in the *Mountain Men and the Fur Trade* series.

Mrs. J. Paul Taylor, the prettiest resident of Mesilla, New
Mexico and who is working on a history of the Mesilla Valley,
provided the important information concerning Kirker's New
Mexico family, which she uncovered in the records of the
Mesilla Catholic Church. And I also owe much to Adlai
Feather, a historian from nearby Mesilla Park. He put me onto
the newspaper stories published by Sam Bean under the nom-
de-plume of *Old Timer.* Gratitude is likewise due to Myra Ellen
Jenkins, senior archivist at the New Mexico Records Center
and Archives at Santa Fe, and to her assistant, Jaqueline Hillman, for the time they spent translating Kirker material from
Spanish into English. José Cisneros, just about the only artist

who draws it like it really was in the Spanish colonial days of the Southwest, helped me by translating much of the material from the London Public Records Office.

There are so many more, such as Doyce Nunis, mentioned earlier, who is editor of *Southern California Historical Quarterly,* and Colton Storm, curator of the Newberry Library, Chicago, who provided a daguerreotype of Kirker, and Ray Brandes, who told me where it was; Harold Merklen, research librarian at the New York Public Library, who checked the sailing lists and found the arrival date of the *Nymph* at New York in 1817. Thanks, too, to Federal District Judge Payne, of Albuquerque, who told me where to find various members of the Kirker family in New Mexico.

Allan R. Ottley, California Section Librarian at the California State Library in Sacramento, provided much of the information on Kirker's residence in Contra Costa County, most especially in showing me the typescript of the 1852 special California census; and W. H. Hutchinson provided the exact date of the St. Louis newspaper containing information about Kirker's visit to Ireland in 1849.

I must also thank my friend Fred Heitfeld, who accompanied me on trips to Santa Fe and Mexico and once on a flying trip to Guadalupe y Calvo, where we chased up and down mountains while following Kirker's trail. To Fred goes the credit also of locating Kirker's grave at Somersville, California.

Kirker's personality still remains a contradiction. He was well educated for his time and place, intelligent and described by a contemporary as "gentlemanly in his deportment, and manner, a more intelligent face I have never seen on a mountain man. He would enhance any circle of society." Yet he killed for money.

I have tried to gather together all the pieces of Jim Kirker's life and put them into a pattern against the background of his environment and his time. I tell what he did, and how. Perhaps the reader can figure out why.

WILLIAM COCHRAN MCGAW

Now he adventured on a shore unknown,
Which all admire but many dread to view:
His breast was armed 'gainst fate, his wants were few;
Peril he sought not, but never shrank to meet,
The Scene Was Savage, but the scene was new;
This made the ceaseless toil of travel sweet,
Beat back keen winter's blast and welcomed summer's heat.

*Childe Harold's Pilgrimage,*
Canto The Second, Stanza XLIII,
Lord Byron

# PROLOGUE

Jim Kirker tilted a canteen over his head and a trickle of water splashed over his brow and down his face. He caught a few drops on his tongue, then took a big swig. He swallowed some of it, rolled the rest around in his mouth, then spat it out. Looking to the east, Jim watched pink streaks reach across a bright yellow horizon as a shimmering new day groped out of darkness.

It was Sunday, February 28, 1847 and Sunday mornings had a habit of finding Jim Kirker *crudo,* as they say in Spanish —hung over. Peaceful Sunday mornings emerged more often than not for Jim out of wild Saturday nights and it was true again this day, Saturday night having behaved badly once more.

Kirker shivered slightly. It was chilly that morning in Colonel Alexander Doniphan's camp, pitched on a mesa more than 4500 feet above sea level in central Chihuahua. Too, it was yet winter, even though the afternoons did heat up. Jim's stomach, already tender from too much alcohol, was eased not at all by the sound of men hacking and coughing as they awoke from a night's sleep on the cold ground.

Running his hand over his head, Jim curled his fingers just enough to form a comb and tried to work out the worst tangles

1

in his hair, still auburn at fifty-four years. He gave it up as a bad job, clamped his low-crowned sombrero over the snarls and got up. He walked toward his horse staked nearby. In the dim light the sixteen-hand purebred Kentucky horse appeared black; actually he was a dark bay. Jim pulled out a soft piece of deerskin from his saddle gear and began rubbing the animal down. After several minutes he slapped the horse away from him and off the saddle blankets underfoot. These the big man picked up, folded and placed on the horse, up near the base of the neck near the mane, then adjusted the blankets by sliding them backward so the hair would rub back the right way.

Jim then threw on the saddle, cinched the animal loosely, and put the *mochila*—a sort of large leather saddlebag—in place. He rewound the loop in his riata, then slung a pair of holstered pistols over the pommel. One of the holsters was loose, so he cut a piece of fringe from the sleeve of his hunting jacket and tied the scabbard tight to the saddle. He reached into a pouch on the *mochila* and pulled out a long flat object that looked like a rusty file, stuck one end of it in his mouth and began twisting and turning his head to bite off a chunk of the dried jerky meat.

He chewed extravagantly on this for a few minutes, swallowed hard, then extracted a small buckskin bag from his belt. He poured a fistful of yellowish meal into his cupped palm. It was piñole, made of pulverized corn, flavored with a little sugar and cinnamon. He pulled the cork from his canteen with his teeth, poured a little water into the powder, then put the cork back with a nod of his head. He stirred the mixture with his fingers until it formed a soft ball, then ate it.

Licking his fingers clean, he walked back to his mount and unfastened the cinch. He nudged his knee into the horse's ribs. They both grunted. Then Jim tightened the latigo with a heave downward. He wrapped it snug, adjusting the saddle-fender and *mochila* again. He gathered up the knives he had kept in his blankets during the night: a huge Bowie that he stuffed in his belt, a slender dirk he kept in the top of his *bota,* just below the knee, and a third—a semi-secret weapon—dangled, short bladed, on a thong around his neck and in the small of his back. He picked up his Hawken rifle and placed the butt of the stock on his knee while he peeled off the deerskin cover, which he folded and tied behind the cantle of his saddle.[1]

Jim led his horse off of the *malpais,* away from jagged, jutting volcanic rock underfoot out onto a stretch of level sand. Here he swung into the saddle, placed his rifle across the pommel, and clucked the horse into a trot. He sat erect, head straight and jaw jutted slightly. Jim had learned from the Indians how important it was to appear dignified at all times. It impressed those watching you and, even more important, it stiffened your own backbone.

Kirker was one of those rare men who become legends while they still live. He already had been privileged to read in the public prints of his own courage and peculiar virtues.[2] More stories and books were yet to be written, including one book of fiction about his scalphunting adventures.[3] Most of the men about him in Doniphan's army of Missouri volunteers were young enough to be his sons so it further behooved him to demonstrate his dignity. Only the day before the courage and integrity of the whole Kirker clan had been challenged publicly. This affront still rankled Jim, even though he knew it to be brandy talk.

A red-haired Irishman named Jim (Squire) Collins had grown nasty over a jug of "Pass Whisky" and for no apparent reason had questioned both the integrity and bravery of not only Jim but all of his relatives back in Missouri. Collins, like Kirker, was a scout and interpreter for Doniphan, having only recently joined the Missourians' ranks after breaking out of jail in Chihuahua, where he had been held as an enemy alien.

The two had joined the day before in locating a trader with a jug of *aguardiente,* or El Paso brandy, and were not long in locating one. They sat down to drink over old times and it wasn't long before Collins became abusive. Jim paid scant attention at first, knowing the drinking habits of Santa Fe trail-men. Their lives were punctuated by long periods of solitude, during which they built up resentments, real or otherwise. They gave vent to these at the first big splash of whisky.

Collins overstepped the brink of tolerance, though, when he drunkenly charged Jim with the one item that would drive him to murder: to say he was a coward. Kirker had been touchy on this point for at least twenty-five years, ever since his cousin David Kirker had been charged with cowardice for surrendering himself to a war party of Comanches and deserting ten companions. So Collins found himself looking into the muzzle of Jim's pistol in a split second after bringing up the subject.

Fortunately, Colonel Doniphan was there to step in and prevent bloodshed.[4] Doniphan's interruption, however, settled nothing between the two, only postponed the showdown until after the impending battle with the Mexicans. Jim's anger still hadn't diminished a whit but now he hid it behind a stoic countenance.

Now as the sun rose he could make out the massive forms of some 400 wagons, many with canvas tops, that were forming up in four columns. Wheels rumbled, harness chains rattled and iron-shod hoofs hammered on the lava rocks, creating a din that picked naggingly at Jim's hangover.

Captain Weightman's artillery was caught up first and was nearly all formed in the center file, between the second and third columns of wagons. Jim rode through the staging area and saw that the Second Battalion was forming between columns three and four, to the right. Jim's mount picked his way through the moving mass of men and horses to reach the two picked companies (not yet known as *troops*) of cavalry, which had been selected to ride in the van and mask the presence of mounted infantry and cannon between the wagon columns.

Jim trotted his purebred up to Colonel Doniphan, then slowed him to a walk, falling in step with the rest of the horses nodding and plodding toward Chihuahua City with their leader.

Jim was the only individual of the group who knew exactly

how much of a problem the enemy posed for he had spent three days scouting out the Mexicans' fortified position and had recommended the plan of attack Colonel Doniphan adopted. Facing the Missourians was an army of slightly more than 4000, well dug in on a sixty-foot bluff rising directly in Doniphan's path to Chihuahua City. This wedge of mountain graced an area known as Hacienda Sacramento and sloped to the west, or to Doniphan's right, just eighteen miles north of the Chihuahua capital city.

The plan Kirker suggested was to mask the troops and artillery between rows of wagons as they approached their objective. About a mile before reaching the bluff, Colonel Doniphan was to wheel his entire force of 1100 men to the right and march west, feinting as though he sought to avoid the engagement by taking shelter behind the walls of a decaying rock and adobe fort, or *torreon,* lying off in the near distance. A couple of miles to the west, Doniphan's men would reach the foot of a slope leading up the bluffs on the Mexican flank at about a twenty-degree angle. At this point Doniphan hoped to swing his small army around a full 180 degrees, launching his attack back up the slope, charging in on the west flank of the entrenched Mexicans.

Jim knew the plan had one flaw in it, that its success depended upon an important action which must be taken at the very start. Two nine-pound howitzers on the American right had to be knocked out before the bulk of Missourians came within their range.[5]

Kirker stood high in his stirrups so he could see over the heads of the other men riding in the forward ranks. His eyes searched for a black leather cap. He found it, set atop a frazzled fringe of bright red hair curling up from underneath.

That was Jim Collins.

Kirker settled back into the saddle. There must be some way to take care of his personal foe without disrupting the battle plan. ... As a sub-plan formed in his mind—a bizarre maneuver that should destroy both Collins and the howitzers

—he relaxed, smiled to himself and kept his eyes on the ground as his horse plodded toward the rendezvous at Sacramento.

With the idea of immediate revenge out of the way Jim's thoughts drifted unconsciously to the past, as is often the case with soldiers waiting out that quiet lull before a battle. Memories flooded in and all of Kirker's yesterdays began marching backward, back to Santa Fe, to St. Louis, to New York City, clear back to Belfast, Ireland, and to the little cottage at Kilcross, Killead parish. Back home.

## NOTES TO THE PROLOGUE

1. Kirker's weapons at this time are described by a contemporary and comrade-in-arms with Colonel Doniphan, Meredith T. Moore, Cedar City, Mo., quoted by William Elsey Connelley in his book, *Doniphan's Expedition* (Topeka, published by the author, 1907) p. 388, note 99. Moore, describing Jim, says, "He was dressed as a frontiersman of his day—fringed buckskin hunting-shirt and breeches, heavy broad Mexican hat and huge spurs, all embellished and ornamented with Mexican finery. He was mounted on a fine horse, which he regarded with great affection and to which he gave the most careful attention. In addition to a Hawkins [sic] rifle elegantly mounted and ornamented with silver on the stock, he was armed with a choice assortment of pistols and Mexican daggers." I have assumed the exact nature of the knives, for every frontiersman carried a large butcher, or hunting, knife (described here as a Bowie) at his belt, and those along the border invariably wore daggers at the top of their right *bota,* which they could draw with a lift of the knee, such *bota,* knife and agility having been demonstrated for me by Arthur A. Woodward, an authority on gear of the frontiersman, especially those of the Southwest. The short-bladed knife dangling on a thong at the small of the back still is used in modern military combat, according to Gordon Frost, former president of the El Paso Historical Society and a collector of this type of weapon.

2. Matthew (Matt) C. Field, writing in the New Orleans *Picayune,* March 2, 1840, had declared "Kurker [sic] himself, is brave as a lion, and a man of great enterprise as well as skill in this kind [Indian] of warfare." George Wilkins Kendall, in the *Narrative of the Texan Santa Fe Expedition* (New York, Harper & Bros., 1844), wrote in Vol. II, p. 58: "For many years Kirker led a wild border life, engaged in continual strife with hostile Indians of the prairies and of Mexico, and in all his encounters with them came off victorious."

3. Captain Mayne Reid, *The Scalp Hunters; or Romantic Adventures in Northern Mexico* (London, Charles J. Skeet, 1851, three Vols.) Another reference to Kirker was made by George Augustus Frederick Ruxton, an English adventurer and spy who roamed the Southwest and Rocky Mountains for about a year and wrote a book of his

experiences, *Adventures in Mexico and the Rocky Mountains,* (London, John Murray, 1847.) The first book, Reid's, was pure fiction, the second factual.

4. Meredith T. Moore, one-time president of the Mexican Veteran Association, described by Connelly in his *Doniphan's Expedition* as "a man of great intelligence and undoubted veracity," and who possessed a "memory that is marvelous," was a member of the company (F) and was an eye-witness to the encounter, p. 416, note 108.

5. A general notion of this plan had been in the minds of Kirker and some of his Shawnee and Delaware scouts for some time, as a Doniphan soldier, James Peacock, is quoted in Connelly's *Doniphan's Expedition,* p. 388, note 99. "James Peacock says the Delawares came with Kirker. Some of them had seen the fortifications at Sacramento and one of them in the conversation with Peacock drew in the sand with a stick a plan of all the works and a map of the locality in which they were situated. He told Peacock that the Mexicans reminded him of his first efforts to trap birds when he was a little boy; that they had constructed their fortifications on the theory that the Americans would walk into a trap set in plain view, when by deploying to the right the trap might be avoided; that the Mexicans expected the Americans would march along the road in the ravine upon which all their artillery was trained."

# CHAPTER I

Jim Kirker, mountain man and scout for Doniphan's army of Missouri Volunteers, was born in Ireland, descended from Scots.

In old Scottish, *kirker* means churchman, and this was the name of three Presbyterian brothers who fled Scotland for Northern Ireland in 1681 to escape the consequences of the Test Act, a severe loyalty oath under which they would have been forced to renounce their religion, swear allegiance to Charles II and join the Church of England.

In those days it was the custom in Scotland and some parts of Ireland to distinguish between members of a family by adding geographical tags to their names; it was thus the three brothers soon were known in Ulster as Kirker of Antrim, Kirker of Falls and Kirker of Armagh. A generation or two later one or more of the Kirkers of Armagh moved a dozen miles to the northwest and their branch became known as "Kirker of Tyrone."[1]

They all begat many children, more grandchildren, and so many more great grandchildren that it is now impossible to sort them all out properly.[2]

Certain it is, though, that James Kirker, destined to become one of the greatest Indian fighters and army scouts on

James Kirker was born in this thatched cottage near Kilcross, North Ireland, about two miles southeast of Antrim and some ten miles above Belfast. This photograph was made before major alterations, which included moving the main entrance to face the gate seen in the distant right. Built nearly three hundred years ago, the home has remained in the family without interruption, and is now occupied by Hugh Gilbert Kirker, a distant cousin of James.

the American continent, was descended from Kirker of Antrim, through the latter's son, John, who took up a farm at a place called Kilcross, only a couple of miles southeast of Antrim.

It was enough of a move for him to become known as John of Kilcross and it was there he built a thatched cottage which stands today. The home was remodeled in 1909 and the thatched roof became slate and tile. The main entrance was moved from the side to the front, facing the road, but in nearly 300 years the family occupancy remained the same—Kirkers have lived there from the day it was built until the present. The farm consisted of only twenty-five acres when the house was built, doubled in size during the next two centuries, and grew to its present ninety-nine acres when today's occupant—Hugh Gilbert Kirker—added the other forty-nine in two parcels purchased from neighbors.

It was here in Killead Parish that the future American frontiersman, James Kirker, was born on December 2, 1793, the second son of Rose and Gilbert Kirker of Carnaghlis, this being another pasture about a half mile toward Belfast, which was a good ten miles away from Jim's birthplace to the southeast. A brisk walk of an hour to the west would bring one to the shores of Lough Neagh, a lake about twelve miles long, north and south, and nearly ten miles wide.

James' mother was Rose Anderson before her marriage at St. Anne's church in Belfast. James had an older brother, Gilbert, and two sisters, Rose and Martha.

James' father, a prosperous grocer, was from a family of five children. Gilbert Kirker had two brothers, James and William, and two sisters whose names appear on the records as Martha of Carnaghlis and Elizabeth of Carnaghlis. Young James Kirker was apparently named after his uncle James who, as a young man, moved to Belfast and set up shop at 45 North Street, as a tanner and currier, purchasing the business site. This property remained in the family's possession until the 1930s, when it was sold by James B. Kirker, father of the present resident, Hugh Gilbert Kirker.

Young James Kirker had relatives galore, living all around Lough Neagh. Most were farmers; those who weren't seem to have preferred the grocery or tanning business. Some had already migrated to America. One of these, a second cousin called Thomas of Tyrone, became the second governor of Ohio.[3] Thomas was the first Kirker ever to have direct dealings with American Indians for, as governor, he presided over a treaty meeting with Tecumseh at Chillicothe, according to William Albert Galloway, historian of the Shawnees.[4]

Hugh Gilbert Kirker, who occupies the ancestral home of the Kirkers today, is posing here with one of his daughter's three Irish hunters.

Jim was born in a tumultuous period, just after America's successful rebellion against England, during the gravest days of the French Revolution, and followed by the Great Irish Rebellion of 1798. James was only four years old when he watched troops of the Ulster commander-in-chief, Henry Joy McCracken, march through Kilcross on the way to Antrim.

A few days before Jim was born, the city of Lyons, France, fell and the defending royalists were forced to flee. Among them was a mere boy, Jean Charles Fremon, who was placed aboard a ship for Santo Domingo, where it was thought by his family he would be safe. Eventually he would add a "t" to the end of his name and take to his bed a twenty-eight-year-old niece of George Washington named Anne Whiting Pryor (she was married to the seventy-five-year-old Major John Pryor) and Ann became pregnant. The chronology was kept vague, but she divorced the major, married Fremont—by now a dancing master—and had a child named John Charles Fremont, not necessarily in that order. He was later called The Pathfinder and would figure in Jim Kirker's adult life.

About this same time a family named Bean was struggling across the mountains from Maryland to Kentucky, finally settling at a town named Limestone, where Jim's cousin, Thomas of Tyrone was then living. The Beans had a boy named Phantley and he would marry Anna Gose a few years later. Their first son would be Joshua Bean, first mayor of San Diego, California and one of the first two generals of the California State Militia. Their youngest son would be Roy Bean, better known in western America and eventually in most of the world as *All the Law West of the Pecos.* The middle son, Samuel G. Bean, was destined to become sheriff of the immense Arizona Territory and Jim Kirker's son-in-law. Fortunately for future researchers Sam would also write poetry and long letters to the newspapers telling about the early settlers of the west.

These personalities, of course, were suspended in time the day Jim was born, awaiting the human catalyst who would send them into the future together.

The catalyst was that very day busy lining up cannon to blast open the port city of Toulon. He was at this time a relatively obscure artillery officer but would become increasingly fascinated with the sound of cannon, so much so he would eventually sell the 828,000 square miles of land known as the Louisiana Purchase to the United States for money to pay for powder and lead for his guns. Napoleon Bonaparte was that very day undergoing his baptism of fire, and to the world's misfortune he enjoyed it. The young captain thrilled to the leap and roar of his guns and the nerves of his stomach tingled so much he unbuttoned his military jacket and scratched his belly as Toulon fell apart.

The infant Jim Kirker could not hear the guns of Toulon but the sound of others punctuated much of the rest of his life. Seldom was he to know any real peace.

# NOTES TO CHAPTER I

1. This and subsequent genealogy was provided by E. C. Kirker, Miami, Fla., and through the assistance of Miss I. Embleton, secretary of the Ulster-Scot Historical Society, Belfast.

2. Many wills and other legal documents were destroyed in the Irish Civil War of 1922, according to the Ulster-Scot Historical Society. A large number of Presbyterian churches in Belfast have not preserved their registers for the late 18th and early 19th centuries, making genealogies previous to 1830 all but impossible.

3. Thomas of Tyrone came to the United States when he was 19, settling with his parents in Lancaster County, Pa., but in 1790 he was at Beaver, Pa., where he married Sarah Smith. He took her by flatboat the next year to Limestone, Ky., (now Maysville) and in 1794 he moved across the Ohio River to Manchester, Ohio; later he helped found the town of West Union. He was sworn in as governor of Ohio in 1807. (see J. A. Jacob Leamon, *The Atlas of Adams County, Ohio,* "Sketch of the Kirker Family," Caldwell publishers, Newark, Ohio, 1880; and Nelson W. Evans, *Pioneer History,* published by the author, 1903, "A Sketch of Governor Thomas Kirker." Both are in the possession of W. Kirker Bixby, Minneapolis.

4. William Albert Galloway, Old Chillicothe, Xenia, 1934, pp. 109, 147, 213-14.

# CHAPTER II

JAMES KIRKER came to the United States for the same reason a multitude of his fellow countrymen did: to avoid service in the British military against Napoleon. Jim was sixteen when he landed in New York on June 10, 1810.

Bonaparte's rampages across Europe and Africa forced Britain to dig deeply into her three largest bins of military and naval manpower—Ireland, Scotland and the jails. So depleted had these sources become that England was forced to board American ships and impress United States seamen.

The Kirkers were traditionally tradesmen and it is likely that Jim arrived with a fat purse from his relatively prosperous father, who would have sent him with instructions to look up certain Irish friends who had come to the new country to ply their old-country trades: the grocery and tanning businesses. The heart of New York City's tanning district stretched for three blocks along Ferry Street in those days, situated midway between today's New York City Hall and East River. When Jim first walked down Ferry Street, it ran from No. 2 to No. 51, with twenty-five business establishments interspersed along three blocks, with Ferry Street dead-ending into Gold. Ferry was intersected by three streets called Jacob, Cliff and Pearl.[1]

Ten of the twenty-five business establishments and residences were occupied by tanners and curriers, many of whom listed themselves as "morocco dressers." The largest of these companies was owned by Jacob Lorillard, president of Mechanics Bank. His brother, Pierre, operated a tobacco shop at nearby 42 Chatham.

There were five groceries in the three short blocks of Ferry Street and it was to these Jim headed after docking. He found employment with a grocer named Peter Dunigan, who had recently purchased a grocery from Thomas Wild, at 41 Ferry Street. There is no record that the Kirkers and Dunigans were acquainted in the old country, for the latter were Catholics and Jim, of course, was a Presbyterian back in Ulster. Dunigan lived on the store premises with a child bride, Catharine, who could neither read nor write but who proved later that she had a good head for business.

Jim's employment with Dunigan was brief, for it wasn't long until the war caused by the impressment of American seamen was declared by Congress—on June 19, 1812. At this time there were more Americans impressed in His Majesty's Navy—6000 of them—than there were serving in the entire United States Navy. This country didn't have a single battleship, known then as a *ship of the line,* which was a vessel of two or more armed decks with from 70 to 140 guns.[2]

The biggest ships of which we could boast were the sister frigates *United States, Constitution* and *Constellation,* outfitted with only forty-four guns each. Ocean-going steamships had not yet been built, although several steamboats were in operation on the Hudson River and there were three steamboat ferries plying the New York harbor, the finest of which was Fulton's Steamboat Ferry, made of two hulls with the wheel in between and a rudder at each end.[3]

Since we could not expect to fight the English with such a skimpy navy it was determined even before the war was declared that we would resort to legal piracy—privateering. Privateers were a happy combination of business, thievery and patriotism in the form of privately owned vessels cruising against enemy shipping. A portion of everything captured was

The *BLACK JOKE,* at right, engages a slaver in 1829, but when Jim Kirker sailed on her she was an American privateer, and her name was truly a joke within a joke. *Courtesy of New York City Public Library*

paid to the United States government, and the balance was shared variously among crew members, officers and owners. Within less than a week after hostilities became formal twenty-six privateers sailed out of New York Harbor and seventeen from Baltimore. There were already twenty-five fast schooners sailing under *letters of marque,*[4] carrying from six to ten guns each and from thirty to fifty men, besides officers.[5]

Privateering afforded Jim Kirker a triple opportunity: he would automatically become a citizen of the United States; he could serve his country in a military capacity; and he might turn a nice profit. These elements must surely have appealed to Kirker's patriotism, Irish belligerency and Scottish thrift, so it was little wonder that Jim, just eighteen, was a member of the crew of a privateer that sailed out of New York within only a few days after hostilities were declared. He sailed on a sloop named the *Black Joke,* formerly an Albany packet plying the Hudson. She was considered fast on smooth water, but slow at sea.[6] The *Black Joke* was owned by her captain, Berndt J. Brunow.[7]

Jim automatically became an American citizen when he signed articles for the voyage but this legal nicety was not recognized under British law. If captured and found out young Kirker would be shipped back to Great Britain as a traitor. At best he would rot in prison, at worst get his neck stretched.

Jim consoled himself, though, with the thought that the pay was good for in addition to regular wages and a share of the piratical profits he, like other crew members, would receive $20 every time he boarded an enemy vessel to engage in combat on the high seas.

The name of Brunow's ship, the *Black Joke,* came from a popular bawdy song of the day. It had as its refrain, "Her black joke and belly so white," the "black joke" in this tender ballad referring to the pudendum of somebody's girl friend.[8]

*Black Joke* seems to have been a rather common name for ships at about this time, probably due to the popularity of the song and the shape of the prows. Another schooner that once sailed under the name of *Liverpool Packet* during the War of 1812 took on the name of *Black Joke,* too, and has been described as "the greatest privateer of all time."[9] This same vessel is described by Charles Wye Kendall, who wrote that she was put at auction and, because of her sensually designed foreparts, "one of the wags of the town christened her the *Black Joke.*"[10]

There was still another *Black Joke,* this one originally designed for the slave trade. She was first called the *Henriquetta,* and as a slave brig earned her owners more than $40,000 by landing 3040 slaves in Brazil until captured by the *Sybille,* on September 6, 1827, at which time she went into service of the British Navy and placed on slaver patrol under the name *Black Joke.* Completely reversing her previous role, the brig virtually put a halt to the Brazilian slave traffic.[11]

Jim Kirker's *Black Joke,* even though described as slow,

must have been faster than some of the British ships she was chasing, for she made her first capture only a few days after leaving port, taking the British schooner *Mary Anne,* laden with rum and coffee, which was sent into Norfolk with a prize crew.[12] After this auspicious start, the *Black Joke* proceeded to engage in what had to be one of the silliest fiascos of the war —perhaps any war.

A deep fog had settled down over the *Black Joke* and within a few minutes the dim outline of another ship was spotted in the near distance. Quietly the *Black Joke* was edged over toward the other vessel, but got too close and they collided in the fog. Each went on the attack immediately. Guns boomed and they raked one another with shot and shell, bow to stern, for several minutes. Finally, the *Black Joke* maneuvered in close enough to board her opponent and it wasn't until the two crews were in hand-to-hand combat that the captains learned they were both flying the American flag. Adding to the awkwardness of it all, the other ship was named the *George Washington.* After the men had been disengaged and calm restored the captains agreed to sail in company, deciding that if they should separate they would rendezvous at Cartagena, where both ships planned to take on water and supplies. They agreed also to pool their prizes.[13]

Their captures were fairly numerous. The second victim of the *Black Joke* was the schooner *Sally,* out of Curacao. A prize crew was placed aboard and the *Sally* was sent to Charleston.[14] The captain of the *Sally* and most of the crew were killed during the capture, apparently wantonly, and the sight made Officer Little ill. He wrote:

"This affair very much disgusted me with privateering, especially when I saw so much loss of life, and beheld a band of ruthless desperadoes—for such I must call our crew—robbing and plundering a few defenceless beings, who were pursuing both a lawful and peaceable calling. It induced me to form a resolve that I would relinquish what, to my mind, appeared to be an unjustifiable and outrageous pursuit; for I could not then help believing that no conscientious man could be engaged in privateering, and certainly there was no honor to be gained by it."

If the rough business of privateering disgusted Jim Kirker he didn't mention it, nor did he say much of anything about this part of his career in the only biographical interview extant, probably written by Charles Keemle, an old friend who owned several St. Louis newspapers.[15] Jim described this part of his life by stating simply that he "went on board a privateer and served on the coast of Brazil until 1813." He gave no implication as to how he liked it but it probably appeared to Jim, at that age, as a profitable way to fight a war if you had to fight one. Since he was considered by the British as a subject of the king, he was in greater danger than were his comrades if taken prisoner.

He *was* captured, too, the *Black Joke* being taken by the British barque *Lion*. Jim and the rest of the crew were placed aboard a captured American ship, *William,* in tow of a British man of war, *Java.* They were being taken as prisoners to San Salvador when the U.S. Frigate *Constitution* hove into view, followed by the smaller American vessel, a brig, *Hornet.* The *Constitution* sank the *Java* and the *Hornet* captured the *William.* Jim and the other American prisoners from the *Black Joke* were exchanged without the British discovering his nationality. They were sent back to New York on the *William,* under command of Captain Davis, arriving in New York harbor during the last week of February 1813.

When Jim returned to his old place of employment, the grocery at 41 Ferry Street, he discovered that his boss, Peter Dunigan, had died meanwhile, leaving his young bride with child. This young Irish girl, Catharine, was not yet twenty years old and couldn't sign her name but was a comparatively wealthy widow. Jim married the widow Dunigan and Peter's posthumous son, Edward, was born shortly thereafter.[16]

Jim and his new wife, Catharine, prospered in the grocery business and a couple of years later they had a son of their own,

James B. Kirker. The grocery business in those days bore little similarity to that of our time. A grocery in New York City in 1813 would compare more to today's package liquor store than to any other form of current retail trade.[17]

A grocer in those days was just what the word originally implied: a grosser, or one who buys in gross, or bulk, and sells in retail quantity. Grocers dealt in such items as coffee, tea, dried fruit, tobacco, ale and whisky. Since Jim apparently catered to tanners and curriers of the neighborhood, many from Ireland, he did well. It is reasonable to believe that had he chosen to remain in New York he could have established one of the foundation families of that city, like the Lorillards across the street. The grocery did well enough over a period of years, later under the management of the illiterate Catharine, to provide a substantial fortune—enough to build a Catholic church, a book-publishing concern, a bookselling company, to purchase at least one fine residence in the fashionable brownstone section of New York City and buy other valuable pieces of property in the downtown area that would run into the hundreds of thousands, or millions, today. There was enough money left over to contribute handsomely to various Catholic charities, and still leave a substantial fortune.

Jim, however, was soon to turn his back on all of this and head west, never to return. No reason for his action is apparent; perhaps, being well educated for that day he couldn't stand living with an illiterate wife—one who was not ambitious to learn, either, for she couldn't write her name to her dying day, as demonstrated in the will she left behind some fifty years later.

## NOTES TO CHAPTER II

1. Longworth's *American Almanac, New York Register and City Directory for the thirty-fifth year of American Independence,* New York, 1810.

2. Howard I. Chapelle, *The History of American Sailing Ships,* New York, 1935, p. 52.

3.  Horatio Gates Spafford and H. C. Southwick, *Gazetteer of the State of New York,* Albany, 1813, p. 250.

4.  A *letter of marque* vessel carried cargo in regular trade and raided enemy shipping only incidentally. The privateer carried no cargo and was commissioned solely to combat enemy shipping. Both were bonded by their governments to satisfy any claims that might arise under international law for illegal capture.

5.  *Niles' Weekly Register,* Vol. 3, No. 8, Oct. 17, 1812, p. 120.

6.  George Little, *Life on the Ocean,* Boston, 1845, p. 198.

7.  Elbert L. Huber, Chief of Navy and Military Archives, Washington, writes: "Our records show that the Collector of Customs of the City of New York issued a commission number 461 to Berndt J. Brunow as owner and commander of *The Black Joke.* The ship carried five cannon and 70 crewmen."

8.  Captain Francis Grose, *A Classical Dictionary of the Vulgar Tongue,* second edition, London, 1791, reprinted, New York, 1963, p. 39.

9.  Janet E. Mullins, *Dalhousie Review,* July, 1934, pp. 193-202, calls the *Liverpool Packet* "the greatest," and told how it got the name of *Black Joke* when the "wedge-shaped schooner" was put up at auction on November 11, 1811 at Halifax.

10.  Charles Wye Kendall, *Private Men of War,* New York, 1932.

11.  Chapelle, p. 163, ff 156.

12.  *Niles' Register,* Vol. 3, No. 4 [whole No. 56,] Sept. 26, 1812, p. 60.

13.  George Little, an officer on the *George Washington,* devotes two chapters of his book, *Life on the Ocean,* to the experiences of the two vessels sailing together.

14.  *Niles' Register,* Vol. 3, No. 12 [whole No. 64,] Nov. 21, 1812, p. 192.

15.  At the time this interview appeared, July 10, 1847, Keemle owned the St. Louis *Saturday Evening Post and Temperance Recorder,* in which it was published. Keemle sold the paper the following week.

16.  Exact date of Edward's birth is not available, but the New York *Post* carried in its obituary columns for Friday, September 16, 1853: "Edward Dunigan, 40 years, brother of James B. Kirker."

17.  Horatio Spafford, writing in his New York *Gazetteer,* 1813, says on p. 13: "The vast number of inns, taverns and groceries licensed to retail strong drink, is a growing evil, felt most in the cities, but extends to some degree in every borough . . . by actual enumeration in 1811, of those in the City of New York, there were 1303 groceries and 160 taverns . . . there is hardly a street, alley or lane where a lad may not get drunk for a few cents . . . the inn is the traveler's home, and groceries are also convenient, if duly restricted in number, and well regulated."

# CHAPTER III

S UB-ZERO weather glazed the New York harbor for nearly
a week in the middle of February 1817, tying up shipping.
A thaw came in at the end of the month, bringing with it
a brig from Belfast, the *Nymph,*[1] bearing five of Jim Kirker's
relatives. Two of these were male cousins, David and Robert,
about Jim's age. Another was their younger sister, Jane, accompanied by her husband, Joseph Clegg, and their three-year-old
son, Joseph, Jr. The Kirkers and the Cleggs lost little time
finding their way to cousin Jim's dwelling behind his store at
41 Ferry Street.[2]

It is not known how long this assortment of in-laws remained as guests of the Kirkers nor how Jim's wife accepted
this situation, but it is reasonably certain she emitted a wifely
remonstrance when informed that her husband was to accompany his cousins on a trip to the western frontier—without her.
Somebody had to mind the store and raise the two infants. Jim
surely pledged a quick return from the expedition and it is likely
that neither suspected he was leaving forever.[3]

St. Louis was a comfortable haven for an Irish immigrant
in that day. More than two-thirds of the foreign-born citizens
then residing in the city were from Ireland.[4] Justices of the
peace in St. Louis then were named McGuire, Sullivan and

Walsh. The sheriff was Jeremiah Connor. The principal merchants were Brady and McKnight Company, and signs over other retail stores read Tracy, McGill, McLanahan, Murphy and McCortney. Major James McGunnegle was quartermaster at the nearby army post. The Kirkers and Cleggs must have felt at home when they arrived.

In those days the best way to get to St. Louis from New York was overland to Pittsburgh, then down the Ohio to the Mississippi, where St. Louis-bound travelers headed upstream. If they left New York when good weather set in, about May 1, the Kirkers and Cleggs would have been going down the Ohio River in June. There is no evidence they stopped over to visit cousin Thomas Kirker, who by this time was a former governor of Ohio and speaker of the Ohio State Senate. They may have stopped for a visit, though, for he lived only a dozen miles or so from the banks of the river, in a town he helped found and lay out, West Union.

The Kirkers and Cleggs must have heard a lot of talk along the river about the steamboat preparing for the first trip to St. Louis, scheduled for that summer. It was the *Zebulon M. Pike* and it docked in St. Louis on July 17, 1817, the first steamship ever to do so. The Kirkers and Cleggs even may have been on her, for this was about the time they arrived.[5]

By whatever means Jim and his relatives arrived—sail, steam or keelboat—they were sure to have been dazzled at the appearance of the little town. Approached by river, St. Louis sparkled, reflecting the sun from its whitewashed houses. Visitors were less enchanted, however, as they grew nearer and discerned that the houses gleaming like so many beads on a string along the bank of the Mississippi were made of logs, set endways into the ground, chinked with mud and caked over with many coats of lime, most of which was applied by dozens of Missouri Tom Sawyers. There were a few finer homes, constructed of limestone, and fewer yet made of brick.[6]

The steamboat *Zebulon M. Pike,* coming upriver from the confluence of the Ohio and Mississippi, remained overnight at

Herculaneum, a new town thirty-two miles south of St. Louis, promoted by a group of investors headed by Moses Austin, who was also agent for the steamboat company at Herculaneum.[7] Moses had only recently resigned as director of the Bank of Missouri to devote more time to his lead-mining business in southern Missouri. His place at the bank was filled by his son, Stephen. In mid-1817 the bank was prospering, to all outward appearances, having just paid its first dividend of eight percent on July 15. This was the last one, for the bank closed in the panic of 1819, and Moses packed his and Stephen's bags for Texas, where they hoped to recoup their fortune by setting up a whole new republic.

Money of the Bank of St. Louis looked good and green to Jim Kirker and his relatives when they arrived in the summer of 1817, even though the institution was turning out notes by the bale, from denominations of twenty-five cents to one, two, three, five, ten and twenty dollars. The five-dollar note bore an engraving of a trapped beaver, while the twenty pictured the lead smelter and buildings at Herculaneum, thus affording the mining town a little free advertising, since it was owned by Austin, Samuel Hammond and the bank's president, Elias Bates.

The ten-dollar note was engraved with a picture of St. Louis, which then stretched for about twenty blocks along the river, but extended back west from the Mississippi only three or four blocks. The population was less than 3000. Physically, the town appeared pretty much as it was laid out in 1764 by Pierre Laclede and the son of his mistress, a thirteen-year-old boy named Auguste Chouteau. The first American to settle there was a Virginian named Philip Fine, who came in 1781, followed five years later by John Coons, a carpenter. Coons, whose grandson was Benjamin Franklin Coons, a founder and first postmaster of El Paso, Texas, built one of St. Louis's first frame buildings between Third and Fourth streets. It would later serve as a blacksmith shop for James Baird, who went off with Robert McKnight to New Mexico; when the Kirkers arrived it had been turned into a theater. John H. Vos, a housepainter from South Carolina, was playing the title role in *King Richard III.* N. M. Ludlow, early theater entrepreneur of St. Louis, gave an apt estimate of Vos's talents by saying, "Vos played Richard, Macbeth, Othello and Rollo fairly well for those days, but he played poker better."

The only hotel or inn operating when Jim first came to St. Louis was Kibby's Washington Hall, situated on the southeast corner of Main and Pine. It was owned by the firm of McKnight & Brady, opened first in 1816, and run by Timothy Kibby, who hailed from St. Charles. Doubtless it was here the Kirkers and Cleggs roomed when first they came and there they would have met John McKnight, his brothers—Thomas and James—and their partners, the Brady brothers—Thomas and John. John McKnight's younger brother, Robert, was absent from St. Louis when Jim arrived, having been gone for more than six years. Robert had set out for Santa Fe with several thousand dollars' worth of merchandise and hadn't returned. Reports drifted back that he had been imprisoned there but nobody knew for sure what *had* happened to him and the dozen men in his company.

Just three months before Jim reached St. Louis a journalist-printer from Cincinnati named Sergeant Hall launched a newspaper *The Western Emigrant,* but by the time Jim came on the scene it was being taken over by another newcomer named Thomas Hart Benton, who changed the name to the St. Louis *Enquirer.* Benton came from Tennessee, where his brother Jesse had been shot in the rear end while dueling with William Carroll, seconded by Major Andrew Jackson. Somehow, Thomas Benton blamed Jackson for the duel and said so publicly. Jackson declared he would whip Benton on sight, which proved to be quite soon. They met in front of the Nashville City Hotel, where Jackson pulled out a pistol, waved a whip in his other hand, and shouted, "Defend yourself, sir." Benton backed into a passageway of the hotel and fell down a flight of steps leading to the basement. Brother Jesse came through the door behind Jackson and shot the major in the back. Jesse and Thomas then decided that the better part of valor would be to pull out of Tennessee but Thomas hadn't been in Missouri long until he became involved in the same kind of trouble.

August 4, less than a week after Jim and his cousins arrived, was election day in St. Louis, with what was known as the *junta* opposing the *anti-junta*. The former was financed by Auguste Chouteau and his brothers and consisted of Bernard Pratte, Charles Gratiot, Jules DeMun and Jean P. Cabanne of the old French families, with Governor William Clark, of Lewis and Clark expedition fame, Edward Hempstead and John Scott forming the American branch of the coalition. The *anti-junta* group was financed by Moses Austin, Samuel Hammond, William Russell and Rufus Easton, while their political champions were John B. C. Lucas, Alexander McNair, David Barton and Joseph Charless, editor of the *Missouri Gazette.* The big issue was land. The *junta* stood for liberal recognition of doubtful Spanish grants, while the *anti-junta* faction opposed recognition, mostly because its members wanted the land themselves.

Since Benton's paper was the voice of the *junta* and also because they were in possession of the land at the moment, Thomas Hart lined up with them. On election day he strode into a voting site and approached the clerks for a ballot. Charles Lucas, son of the *anti-junta* leader, J. B. C. Lucas, challenged Benton's right to vote on the grounds that he failed to produce a tax receipt.

"Out of my way," ordered Benton, "you are nothing but a puppy." Lucas demanded satisfaction and at six o'clock on the morning of August 12, 1817, just two weeks after Kirker arrived, the two men stood facing each other on Bloody Island, a dueling ground in the Mississippi River. Both men fired on signal. Benton received only a bruise as the bullet brushed his knee, but Lucas was struck in the neck, the ball severing a large blood vessel. Dr. Garrit P. Quarles refused to allow another fire because blood was gushing from Lucas' wound and he was unable to continue. This cooled Lucas' ardor for combat but not Benton's. He blustered, "I am not satisfied," and refused to leave the ground until Lucas pledged to return to fight again when his wound was healed. The next meeting was on September 27, at which time they shot at each other on the same dueling ground and again both guns sounded at once.

Lucas fell, shot in the heart. He struggled to say something.

"What does he say?" asked Benton. "I trust he forgives me."

Lucas, speaking from the ground, charged, "Colonel Benton, you have persecuted and murdered me. I can't forgive you."

Benton dropped his pistol and ran to the young man. He bent over and reached for the fallen youth's hand, murmuring something too low to be understood by witnesses.

"I forgive you," Lucas said just before he died.

That was far more than other partisans did. The next day in front of the Washington Hall Hotel, William Smith met William Tharp and they argued over the duel. Smith called it murder and slapped Tharp's face. The latter shot the former, with Smith dying instantly, face down in the gutter. This hotel was the center of things in St. Louis and probably where Jim was domiciled, so he may have witnessed the murder.[8]

That was the St. Louis that Jim Kirker found, a city full of tinsel honor and foolish pride, sensitive to the slightest insult but courageous to the final gasp. No doubt Jim had learned by this time that he was living in a cruel and bloody town, where violence was easily come by and death was rather casual.

## NOTES TO CHAPTER III

1. The *Shipping and Commercial List* for March 7, 1817, has the *Nymph* clearing for the West Indies on March 5, indicating it arrived about February 25, as it would take approximately 10 days to two weeks to turn a ship around in New York.

2. E. C. Kirker, in correspondence to author, June 23, 1964, quotes from the Belfast *Newsletter* that the Kirkers and Cleggs "on arrival in New York went to the home of James Kirker."

3. Longworth's *New York Directory* continued to list James Kirker as a grocer at 41 Ferry Street from 1823/24 until 1827/28. Later editions placed the store at 25 Ferry Street, where Catharine moved it. The retention of his name in the listing indicated Catharine expected Jim to return—at least until issuance of the directory for 1828/29, when the entry appears as *Catharine* Kirker, grocer, 25 Ferry Street. The directory of 1831/32 indicates she had given up all hope when her situation was given as *Catharine widow of James,* although there is no record she had him declared legally dead. It shows, too, that Jim wrote no letters, sent no word.

4. Thomas J. Scharf, *History of St. Louis City and County,* Philadelphia, 1883, 2 vols., p. 198.

5. Frederic J. Billon, *Annals of St. Louis in its Early Days,* St. Louis, 1888, p. 73, reports July 27 as the arrival date, while Scharf's *History* erroneously gives the date as August 2, 1817.

6. The first two brick dwellings in St. Louis were built in 1812, one for Bartholomew Berthold and the other for William Smith. Both were combination homes and stores and both were to become fur-trade headquarters. The former would house the Western Department of Astor's American Fur Company, and the latter would be occupied by the firm of Sublette & Campbell.

7. *Missouri Gazette,* September 2, 1817.

8. There are many accounts of the Benton-Lucas duel. The account followed here is from the *Missouri Gazette,* October 4, 1817, and from William N. Chambers' narrative, "Pistols and Politics," MHS *Bulletin,* St. Louis, October 1948, pp. 5-17.

# CHAPTER IV

THE McKnight and Brady families dominated the economic life of St. Louis when the Kirkers arrived and it was only a matter of days before Jim, David and Robert Kirker were drawn into the McKnight and Brady scheme of things. This affiliation lasted until the whole combine fell apart six or seven years later, when most of the principals either died, left St. Louis or became inactive.

One story has it that the McKnights and Bradys were known as "the Irish crowd," and that the whole "gang came to St. Louis together, rowing their own boat down from Pittsburgh, reaching St. Louis in 1809,"[1] but this isn't quite the way it happened. According to an authoritative biographical sketch of Thomas McKnight,[2] he was born in Augusta County, Virginia, on March 10, 1787 and at sixteen began to sell drygoods from house to house. His parents were Timothy and Eleanor Griffin, who came to this country from Ireland in 1774, moving to Augusta County shortly after George Washington's Fort Defiance made things safe for settlers.

About 1805 Thomas accumulated enough money to follow his older brother John to Nashville, where they entered the mercantile business. Early in 1809 they left Nashville for St. Louis, arriving there in April, and formed a company with the

Brady brothers soon after. They purchased sixty feet of frontage
on Main Street, at the corner of Pine, and there erected their
first headquarters, a combined store and business office. They
soon established branches in St. Genevieve and St. Charles,
described then as "the most important localities in Missouri."

When the firm of Brady & McKnight was organized, with
Thomas McKnight and Joseph Brady as principals, there were
two firms operating in St. Louis with almost the same names:
McKnight & Brady, and Brady & McKnight, with brothers of
both families involved in each. It soon became difficult to sort
out which McKnights were with which Bradys, but perhaps it
didn't matter much, for throughout John McKnight was leader
of his family group and Thomas Brady was the important one
on the Brady side.[3]

The McKnights and Bradys possessed the happy faculty of
staying on both sides of all issues, whether political or economic. When the *anti-junta* Bank of St. Louis was chartered
and began operating in 1816 Thomas Brady was one of the bank
commissioners; when the *pro-junta* Bank of Missouri was incorporated in December, 1816 John McKnight was a commis-
sioner.

They straddled not only issues but also the Mississippi. In
October, 1817, the firm of McKnight & Brady founded what is
substantially now lower East St. Louis, naming it Illinois Town.
They platted it, sold it and established retail and wholesale
houses to supply the needs of the new community.

Even the waters of the Mississippi were brought under
their control, too, according to James Haley White, who arrived in St. Louis in 1819. In an article, "Early Days in St.
Louis,"[4] White declared that McKnight & Brady owned the
largest shipping house in St. Louis and were sole owners of the
keelboat lines, with the exception of a handful of boats owned
by Halderman and Lindell, who shipped only their own trade.

McKnight & Brady also built the first two structures especially designed as hotels in St. Louis. The first was Washington
Hall, followed by the magnificent three-story Missouri Hotel,

Thomas McKnight, one of the original McKnight brothers who, in partnership with the Bradys, controlled much of the early St. Louis economic life. In the 1820's following the death of his wife and daughters in an epidemic, he moved to Galina, Illinois, where he went into the lead mining business. Later he moved to Iowa, where he died shortly after the Civil War. *Courtesy of the Missouri Historical Society*

recognized for years by its distinguished "Sign of the Bison" swinging over the door.

With so many avenues of endeavor controlled or influenced by the ubiquitous McKnight & Brady outfit the Kirkers must have been happy to join them, although as newcomers they were only on the periphery of the organization. Robert Kirker had soon worked his way up to Thomas McKnight's trusted assistant.[5] Jim went back into the grocery business, with his cousin David as a very junior partner, or perhaps even an employee. They rented their building from M. D. Bates and Paul Anderson.[6] It was a frame warehouse on Water Street, above Cherry, and it was described in the *St. Louis Directory* as "under the bluffs." Joseph and Jane Clegg also opened a grocery, according to the *Directory,* on Sixth Street, above Chestnut.

The grocery business in St. Louis was not at all as limited as it was in New York, it being conducted much more like today's general store. Most groceries in frontier cities handled drygoods as well as foodstuffs and a few even carried hardware. Jim Kirker sold both groceries and drygoods; there exists a receipt, dated July 17, 1822, for a pair of pantaloons he sold for five dollars to Major Thomas Forsyth, one of his regular customers. The Major, agent for a number of years to the Sac and Fox Indians, also bought his liquor from Jim.[7]

Transactions were not always for money. Jim, like all other St. Louis grocers, accepted furs and peltry as cash. They were a form of recognized currency, with one dollar in specie equal to $1.25 in peltry. There was not sufficient coin in the whole Louisiana Territory to take care of the retail business. What there was consisted mostly of silver coins minted in Mexico and Central and South America by the Spanish Colonials. From this situation, the term "bit" entered our language, as an expression for the value of one *real.* Two bits equaled one-quarter of a dollar in U.S. money. This came from the practice of cutting a Spanish "piece of eight" into pie-shaped segments worth one *real,* or 12½ cents each. Often the coin-cutting was done by sharpies who could get nine "bits" to the dollar, or "piece of eight."[8]

Bernard Pratte, another prominent St. Louis merchant and an acquaintance of Jim's, once advertised he would take in lieu of hard currency such substitutes as "furs, hides, whiskey, country-made sugar and beeswax."[9] Lead, tobacco and deer-skins also served as currency. Deerskins ranged in value from one to two *livres,* according to quality. A *livre* was valued at five to a U.S. dollar.

Customers didn't want to be inconvenienced by carrying around quantities of furs, peltries, skins, lead and tobacco to pay their bills, so traders soon developed the device of storing furs, skins and other items in warehouses and using the receipts for money. Bread, too, became a basis for currency, as were duebills for drinks of whisky; a man named Vickers was one of the biggest whisky bankers until he closed up his saloon and left with plenty of his script still floating around.[10]

The Kirkers didn't handle fresh meats or produce, as do grocers today. Fresh butchered meats were obtained at the St. Louis town market; game, like turkeys at twenty-five cents each, was supplied by Shawnee hunters. A quarter of a dollar would also buy a quarter of venison from the Indians. One contemporary wrote that "bear in the forest surrounding St. Louis was very large and very fat, and furnished more delicious hams than did hogs."[11]

Jim and David also traded in buffalo robes, which found a good market in St. Louis, from where they were shipped to slave states farther south to make inexpensive beds for Negro slaves.[12]

The location of Jim's grocery was enhanced in value by an event which took place in the spring of 1820, when a horse-team ferry was installed across the Mississippi river by Samuel Wiggins.[13] Those bound east across the river had to wait in front of Jim's store until the ferry returned, while travelers headed west were deposited on his doorstep. This pause in traffic at his entrance must have been important for it was mentioned as a part of the advertising in the listings of the 1821 *St. Louis Directory,* which explained that Jim was a "grocer," located on "north Water, above Team Boat Ferry."

That was in the northern part of town, absolutely the

toughest part of St. Louis in that day. Here keelboatmen loafed between trips, playing noisily, fighting and fornicating, where the likes of Mike Fink and William Carpenter, two of the best rifle shots on the frontier, drank and cavorted in company with Ed Rose, a very tough mulatto who had been a Crow Indian chief and a pirate with Jean LaFitte.

These were the men surrounding Jim at his north St. Louis establishment and, a traditional gathering place, it must have resounded hour after hour with tales of wanton violence, loose women, gelt and gore, but there is no indication they held out any lure for Jim. He had reached maturity over a tough road and had long since given up all visions of quick riches and romantic swashbuckling. His business built steadily, even though a depression plagued St. Louis for two or three years beginning in 1819, for in the spring of 1821 he expanded his operation significantly, undertaking the construction of a new stone building to house his store and home. On May 23, 1821 he secured the exclusive right to the use of the land lying between his new structure and the Mississippi by leasing this property from John McKnight for twenty years, indicating he planned a long future at that location.[14]

Meanwhile, Jim's younger and less experienced cousin David became fascinated by the tales of high adventure to be found in the west and in the Rockies. David apparently longed to accompany one of the parties headed in that direction and his opportunity came finally in January 1821, when three bedraggled and exhausted men limped back to St. Louis after an absence of nine years. They were Sam Chambers, Peter Baum and Benjamin Shreve, who had accompanied Robert McKnight on the trading expedition to New Mexico that had left St. Louis in April 1812.

## NOTES TO CHAPTER IV

1. Billon's *Annals, Territorial Days,* p. 232.

2. Missouri Historical Society archives, Item 40612, St. Louis.

3. Howard L. Conard, *Encylopedic History of Missouri,* St. Louis, Haldeman, Conard & Co., 1901, Vol. 4, pp. 271-3.

4. *Glimpses of the Past,* MHS publication, Vol. VI, Nos. 1-3, January–March, 1939, p. 7.

5. The degree of responsibility entrusted to Robert Kirker by McKnight is demonstrated in the following advertisement which appeared in the St. Louis *Enquirer,* Saturday, October 29, 1820: "Notice. Will be sold at a reduced price for ready money, sugar or coffee, a lot of ground, about ninety feet above warehouse of Messrs. John and Thomas Brady, Jr. Thirty French feet, fronting on the Mississippi, running back 200 feet. Indisputable title will be given. Enquire of Robert Kirker, at the warehouse of Thomas McKnight."

6. Scharf's *History,* Vol. I, p. 154.

7. Major Forsyth bought a half gallon of cider at the same time he bought a pair of pants, according to receipts found among the Forsyth papers at the MHS. In the same spring, he bought whisky from Jim for "one bit," or 12½ cents, a quart, but receipts show that by the next fall the price had gone up, or the Major was drinking better whisky, for the cost was 18¾ cents a quart. Other items purchased regularly by Forsyth were tobacco and lard, the latter selling for five cents a pound.

8. *Ibid.,* p. 73.

9. *Missouri Gazette,* January 11, 1809.

10. James H. White, *Glimpses of the Past,* Vol. VI, Nos. 1-3, January–March, 1939, p. 13.

11. "Life in Colonial St. Louis," *Glimpses of the Past,* Vol. I, No. 10, September, 1934, p. 87.

12. Henry Marie Brackenridge, *Views of Louisiana,* Pittsburgh, 1814; reprint, Chicago, 1962, p. 94.

13. Billon's *Annals,* p. 322.

14. A record of this lease, under the date of May 23, 1821, is in the office of the Record of Deeds, City and County of St. Louis, Book L, pp. 75-78, containing both a legal description of the lease property, and also a description of the building Jim had under construction adjacent to it. This lease was witnessed by Otis Reynolds and Patrick Shearman, not otherwise identified (nor are they listed in the 1821 *St. Louis Directory.*) Their identity would be of little importance had they not gone before Justice of the Peace Thomas McGuire on the next April 8, 1822, to swear under oath that they "deposeth and sayeth that James Kirker the subscriber to the above instrument of writing is the person and only person recognized in the above instrument and the only owner of the property therein contained," indicating that some person or group was attempting to claim Jim's property, apparently in his absence and in the absence of John McKnight, who was at that moment in New Mexico searching for his younger brother, Robert.

# CHAPTER V

J OHN McKNIGHT called to his office the three returning members of his younger brother's ill-fated expedition to Santa Fe. There he asked them to tell the story of the nine years, including the reason why Robert had not returned to St. Louis with them.

The three men—Chambers, Baum and Shreve—explained that their trip was relatively uneventful until they reached Taos. There they learned the Mexican Revolution had failed and that they were suspected of being spies in the service of the United States. New Mexico Governor José Manrique placed them all under arrest, confiscated their trade goods and hauled them to Santa Fe in chains. Later they were marched to Chihuahua City, and were subsequently dispersed into various towns, where they were held under loose detention.

Robert McKnight went to northern Chihuahua, near the ancient town of Casas Grandes, with another member of the party, Alfred Allen. Robert began mining at nearby Galeana and opened a mercantile business.

James Baird, the blacksmith, was leased out as a bond servant in the city of Durango to Don Francisco Valasquez, who put Baird to work making silver spoons, knives and forks.

Michael McDonough joined the Order of Friars Minor at Zacatecas, in the College of the Propagation of the Faith.

William Mines and Thomas Cook went to Mexico City, where Cook died. No one knew what happened to the expedition's interpreter, Carlos Myette Cuado.[1]

After they had been in the country nine years, Ferdinand VII, King of Spain, suspecting that Mexico was going to obtain its independence anyway, thought he would make himself a nice fellow while he still had the power and issued orders liberating all foreigners imprisoned in Mexico. The three men now in John McKnight's office didn't know why Robert McKnight and Baird had not returned to Missouri with them; they all had been staying in different areas and communication had been difficult.

After mulling over their story for several days, John McKnight determined to clear up the mystery by leading an expedition to Santa Fe himself. Always the businessman, he thought he might as well turn a profit on the trip and decided to take along a substantial amount of goods to sell. He enlisted the help of Thomas James, who had on hand about $10,000 worth of merchandise he had brought from Pittsburgh and for which he could find no market in St. Louis.

Next to join the enterprise was David Kirker, who had little to dispose of, unless it was an excess of energy. He may have been advanced a small amount of goods by his cousin Jim.

Others in the company were John James, brother of Thomas, William Shearer, Alexander Howard, Benjamin Potter, John Ivy, Frederick Hextor and James Wilson, who didn't join the party until after it had left St. Louis. The day of departure was May 10, 1821.

The leaders had been led to believe from information supplied by the returning members of the Robert McKnight expedition that it was possible to reach Santa Fe entirely by water, so McKnight and James planned to go down the Mississippi to the Arkansas River, then up it to their destination. When they encountered another group also headed for Sante Fe—led by Hugh Glenn, a Cincinnatian—they were informed that they couldn't go all the way to Santa Fe by boat. McKnight and James then switched their crew to horses, buying twenty-three mounts from the Osages.

Traveling overland, they proceeded to a place called Shining Mountain, south of Cimarron in what is now Major County, Oklahoma, where they killed and dried some buffalo meat. A large Comanche war party spotted buzzards circling the buffalo carcasses, and at dawn the next morning the McKnight camp was awakened by what sounded like loud applause, a wild clapping of hundreds of hands—red-skinned hands, as it turned out, for the Comanches were spooking their horses.

Thomas James was first on his feet. He grabbed an American flag and charged the Indians as he waved it in their faces. Diverted, the redmen backed off and watched his antics for a short while. They then started a slow advance into the camp, more curious than hostile.

James explained as well as he could what the flag was all about, that it represented his nation, which was powerful and could kill a lot of Indians, but at the same time to show his friendliness and that of his government James began handing out presents. It wasn't long until he had given away $3000 worth of their trade goods. While conversing with one of the Comanche chiefs, Big Star, he learned that the Indians were disturbed primarily because James' men were on horses with Osage markings and that Osages were the traditional and bitter enemy of the Comanches. James told the chief how they had acquired the horses and assured him they were in no way aligned with the Osages.

Big Star, apparently accepting the explanation, volunteered the advice that James, McKnight and the men should not go farther up the Arkansas River because if they did they would encounter a mean Comanche war chief with only one eye who was sure to ambush them. Consequently, the Missourians went two days without water across a dry stretch to reach the Colorado River, which they then followed.

In about a week, when almost across the staked plains of Texas, they saw, according to James's account, "a great number of mounted Indians coming over a rising ground in our front." James soon recognized their leader to be his old acquaintance, Big Star, who embraced James Indian-fashion and invited the group to go with him to his village, which was two miles away and turned out to be a large settlement. According to James it numbered "a thousand lodges, situated . . . near the base of a large mound."

When they reached the Indian settlement it became apparent that the Comanches had grown insatiable in their desire for gifts.

"The Indians then demanded presents and about a thousand chiefs and warriors surrounded us. I laid out for them tobacco, powder, lead, vermillion, calico and other articles, amounting to about $1000 in value. This did not satisfy them, and they began to break open my bales of cloth and divide my finest woolens designed for the Spanish market, among them. After losing about $1000 more in this way, I induced them to desist from further robbery."[2]

The next day the one-eyed chief about whom James had been warned rode into the settlement. One-eye brought about 100 warriors with him and they too demanded presents, which they received.

Meanwhile, in an attempt to placate the individual James considered to be the most powerful among the chiefs, the Missourian presented Big Star with a finely jeweled sword with the request that the chief withdraw his braves and allow the Americans to continue on their way. When One-eye heard about this he lined up his braves—armed with guns, bows, arrows and lances, with their faces painted black—across one entire side of the village. James then offered to give these Indians an additional 500 yards of cloth provided they too would agree to let his men pass. The Indians refused.

Desperate, James was driven to the ultimate decision, the one he hated to make. He instructed his comrades to load up the goods on their horses and prepare to leave the next morning regardless, even if they had to fight their way out.

At sunup a large number of Indian boys began a bombardment from the top of the nearby mound, hurling down rocks and boulders into their camp. During the ensuing melee six of the Missourians' horses were stolen.

It was then that their "friend" Big Star rode into their camp, showing what appeared to be exaggerated concern for their safety.

"Do not," Big Star warned, "try to get back the horses, and keep together, or you will all be killed."

McKnight, the James brothers, David Kirker and the others formed a circle around what remained of their trade goods. Everybody had a gun, except Jimmy Wilson, who had armed himself with an ax.

"Thus we stood," said James, "eleven against two thousand, with death staring us in the face. The suspense was awful. I stood between John McKnight and my brother, and noticed their countenances. McKnight's face was white, and his chin and lips were quivering . . . not a man but seemed bent to die in arms and fighting, and none were overcome by fear."[3]

At length one of the chiefs, White Bear, wearing a whole bearskin with the claws dangling over his hands, rode swiftly toward the Missourians, lance upraised, as though to annihilate them all at once, but brought his horse up sharply about five paces away, glaring at the men as he took out his pistol and reprimed it. He saw that James had him covered with a rifle, however, and he kept the pistol at his side, muzzle down.

"Let us commence, James," pleaded McKnight, "you'll be the first one killed—this suspense is worse than death; the black chief is my mark."[4]

James said no, that it would be folly to begin a battle against such odds, but added that as soon as a single gun was fired, they were to rush in and sell their lives as dearly as possible.

Sweat dripped down David Kirker's brows, smarting eyes already glazed with the loss of three nights' sleep. Suddenly the futility of their situation swept over him and he raised his gun high over his head. Walking out toward the Indians like a man in his sleep, he handed over his musket to the mounted warrior, White Bear.

A cry of *"Tabbaho! Tabbaho!"* (White man! White man!) swelled up from hundreds of Indian throats as David disappeared into their midst, leaving his ten erstwhile companions to face the 2000 Comanches.

The remaining men, stunned and almost automatically closing ranks to fill up the gap left by Kirker's departure, interpreted the cry to be one of exultation resulting from David Kirker's defection, until they spied six uniformed horsemen racing across the prairie toward them. The small circle of men heard these riders shout, *"Salvenlos, salvenlos!"* (Save them, save them!) The mass of Indians parted before the oncoming lead horseman, who galloped up to the beleaguered men and dismounted at a run.

"Thank God!" he exclaimed in Spanish. "We are in time. You are safe and unhurt."[5]

The Spanish officer assured the distraught men they were safe, then turned and spoke sharply to the Indian leaders in Spanish, demanding to know why these men were to be killed.

"To keep our word to your governor," one replied. The chief explained they were employed by the Santa Fe governor to intercept all Americans. James' group of obstinate Americans seemed determined to pass, so, the Indians explained, they had no choice but to kill them.

The Spaniard replied that such instructions were no longer valid, Mexico having won its independence from Spain.

David Kirker is not mentioned during the balance of James' narrative. It is almost certain he was sent home a few days later with another Missouri trader, William Becknell, who departed from the same area to return to Missouri. Becknell passed through the village of San Miguel, near today's Las Vegas, New Mexico, and there, according to Becknell's "Journal," he picked up two men and returned with them to Boonville. Becknell's caravan departed San Miguel on December 13, 1821, and arrived back home about February 1, 1822. Becknell's "Journal" entry is tantalizingly brief:

" . . . we left that village [San Miguel] December 13, on our return home in company with two other men who had arrived there a few days before, by a different route."

Since there is no record of any other party traveling then in that area, it is assumed one of these was David Kirker. The other may have been William Shearer, a member of the James party in poor health who died some time after returning home.

Meanwhile, McKnight and James, with the balance of their party proceeded to Santa Fe, where James was disappointed to realize no more than $2000 for what was left of the goods he had paid $10,000 for in Pittsburgh. Of this amount he advanced $200 to John McKnight so the latter could go in search of his younger brother, Robert, in Mexico. When he reached Casas Grandes, Chihuahua, and the village of Galeana, the reason for Robert's remaining in Mexico was evident. Robert had married a young Mexican woman named Brigida Trigeros about a year before his release from confinement and when Baum, Chambers and Shreve were starting back to St. Louis the youngest McKnight brother elected to remain in Chihuahua, because his bride was confined and expected a child any day. Robert was present at the birth of his first child, a daughter, whom they named Refugio.[6]

Some members of the John McKnight party busied themselves trapping beaver on nearby streams. James meanwhile was honored by being invited to take charge of the huge celebration of the first Independence Day for Mexico, on January 6, 1822.

John McKnight persuaded his brother Robert to accompany him back to Missouri and they both showed up in Santa Fe ready to begin their return journey by late spring. Members of the McKnight party joined with Hugh Glenn's people, who had also been in Taos and Santa Fe, for the trek back to Missouri, leaving on the first day of June.

## NOTES TO CHAPTER V

1. Frank B. Golley, "James Baird, Early Santa Fe trader," MHS *Bulletin,* Vol. XV, No. 3, 1959, pp. 178-9. Golley is a descendant of Baird.

2. General Thomas James, *Three Years Among the Indians and Mexicans* (Waterloo, Ill., printed in the office of the "War Eagle," 1846; reprinted St. Louis, MHS, 1916, notes by Judge Walter B. Douglas, and Chicago, Rio Grande Press, 1962) p. 119. Events and direct quotations used here are taken directly from James' book, which was dictated to Colonel Nathaniel Niles at Bellville, Ill. It was suppressed shortly after publication by Niles because of James' statements concerning the Missouri Fur Company and especially the Chouteaus, Manuel Lisa, Sylvestre Labadie, and others, which Judge Douglas terms "ill-advised . . . even if they had been true" because these men were "of high character, ranking among the best citizens of St. Louis."

3. *Ibid.,* p. 123.

4. *Ibid.*

5. *Ibid.* p. 124.

6. Robert McKnight's marriage and birth of his daughter were uncovered in 1969 by Mary Taylor while researching the Juarez Catholic Church records for her forthcoming history of Mesilla Valley, N. M. These baptismal records, dated October 30, 1838, show that Roberto Flotte, son of Luis Flotte and Refugio McKnight, daughter of Robert McKnight and Brigida Trigeros [or possibly *Frigeros,* as the handwriting is difficult to decipher] was baptized by Father Ramon Ortiz, later to gain notoriety during the 1841 Texan invasion of New Mexico and again in 1846 when the territory was invaded by the Missouri Legion. As was the custom, the paternal grandparents also were given—Louis Flotte, Sr., and Henriqueta Walker, Baltimore—and the godparents, Hugo Stephenson, the first American settler at what is now El Paso, Texas, and his wife, Dona Juana Stephenson, whose family held the land grant to much of the property comprising the modern city. There are still living in the southwest many Flottes and Stephensons. Refugio's age is given as 16, indicating she was born just about the time McKnight was expected to return to St. Louis.

# CHAPTER VI

THE cowardice exhibited by his cousin David no doubt gave Jim Kirker a sense of deep shame. Cowardice on the frontier was a graver fault than it is now, the safety of all being endangered by a "man who in perilous emergency thinks with his legs." Embarrassment over the family disgrace may have played a part in Jim's decision to join a trading and trapping expedition to the Upper Missouri organized in 1822 by General William H. Ashley, or he may have been motivated only by the desire to make money: beaver had jumped from $2.50 to $3.50 a pound as a result of the burgeoning beaver-hat fad in England.

Thomas Hart Benton, writing in his St. Louis *Enquirer,* predicted that the Upper Missouri "contains a wealth of furs, not surpassed by the mines of Peru," and Henry M. Brackenridge had predicted ten years earlier an "immense profit from the Indian trade of the Mississippi and Missouri."[1]

Boredom and a desire for adventure could have played a strong part in his decision, for few things satisfy the vanity of man so much as membership in an elite group of adventurers who wear an outward symbol of their nobility. Crusader knights displayed their ladies' kerchiefs flying from their armor, buccaneers wore their kerchiefs around their heads and tattoos on their arms, and chap-legged cowboys jingled spurs as trademarks of their special caste. Likewise, the trapper proudly wore his distinctive badges: his fur cap, fringed jacket, moccasins and Hawken rifle. People understood even then that the trappers were showing off with their exaggerated dress and behavior; it was the subject of an 1838 newspaper story.[2]

The fur trade has been largely ignored in histories of this country. For example, only two sentences are given to it in a recent work.[3] It is, then, in order to present a brief resume of this trade as it functioned in St. Louis.

Under French and Spanish rule, the Indian trade was conducted through monopolies granted to certain favored families—such as the Chouteaus, who held exclusive rights to the Osage business. These were terminated when the United States took over in 1804, following the Louisiana Purchase. After members of the Lewis and Clark expedition returned with exciting stories of rich beaver lands to the north, visions of quick fur profits were soon kindled. Manuel Lisa mounted three expeditions to the Upper Missouri with mixed success. In command of one of Lisa's parties was Andrew Henry, a minor partner who withdrew from the Lisa enterprise to become a major in the Washington County regiment in the War of 1812. Commanding Henry's regiment was Lieutenant Colonel William H. Ashley, who had known Henry for a number of years and had been a witness at his wedding in 1805. Both men were born in about 1775, Henry in York County, Pennsylvania, and Ashley, about whose antecedents not much is known for sure, in Virginia.[4]

Ashley was in the gunpowder business in Missouri's Mine à Burton mining district, where Henry had a lead mine. Ashley's partner was Lionel Brown, a nephew of Aaron Burr, and the two moved their headquarters to St. Louis in 1819, but in September of that year Brown was killed in a duel with Colonel John T. Smith, an old friend of Ashley's. Meanwhile, Ashley had come across what he considered to be some promising real estate while surveying for the United States government in 1816 and 1817 and as a result of this knowledge he acquired another partner, William Stokes. Stokes was an Englishman who came to St. Louis in 1819 with $100,000 and a pretty sister. He entrusted $60,000 to Ashley for real-estate investments and handed over his sister in marriage to John O'Fallon, a nephew of General William Clark, Superintendent of Indian Affairs. Within three years, Stokes had died broke, helped along, according to St. Louis gossip, by a divorce.[5] He certainly could not have been helped by his involvement with Ashley, either, as their combined partnership assets were given as only $3000 in the 1821 St. Louis tax lists.[6] All of this, combined with the depression of 1819, set the enterprisers of St. Louis casting about for a financial solution.

First public notice of the Ashley & Henry undertaking was made in an advertisement in the St. Louis *Missouri Gazette,* which appeared several times, beginning on February 13, 1822. "The subscriber wishes to engage ONE HUNDRED MEN, to ascend the river Missouri to its source, there to be employed for one, two and three years.—For particulars enquire of Major Andrew Henry, near the lead mines, in the county of Washington, (who will ascend with, and command the party) or the subscriber at St. Louis, Wm. H. Ashley."

Jim implied in an interview that he was a member of the party commanded by Henry[7] and if he was one of those who "enquired for particulars," he would have been offered an unusual proposal, one that was destined to alter the future of the western fur trade, in an arrangement never before tried.

The Ashley and Henry company agreed to provide shot and gunpowder to the hunters and trappers enlisting with them. The latter, however, were expected to provide their own subsistence *aux aliments du pays,* as the natives of St. Louis would have put it, which meant the employees must live off the land by hunting for their food. The men would receive no wages; they would keep half of all the furs they trapped, with the other half going to the company. The hunters would also be obliged to pole or row the company boats filled with trade merchandise upstream, for which labor they would receive no direct compensation from the company. This arrangement would relieve Ashley and Henry of meeting a payroll which might become relentless, but if the expedition were successful they would be surrendering some of the profits. There was a slight hitch to this deal, too, but apparently few paid any attention to it then, or since. That was the fact that Ashley and Henry did not have a license to *trap* on Indian lands, only to *trade*. This amounted to the company's part of the deal being completely legal, while that involving the hunters and trappers was just as definitely clandestine, and furthermore involving an activity that was sure to infuriate the Indians. Benjamin O'Fallon, Indian Agent for the Upper Missouri and another nephew of General Clark, who was also his guardian, wrote to Secretary of War John C. Calhoun, complaining of the action and predicting trouble with the Indians. In doing so O'Fallon bypassed his immediate superior —his uncle, General Clark, who was Superintendent of Indian Affairs—and went over his head to Washington with his complaint.

After assuring Calhoun that the Indians in his district had been friendly O'Fallon then warned: "I understand that license has been granted Messrs. Ashley & Henry to trade, trap and hunt on the Missouri. . . . I am in hopes that limits have been prescribed to their hunting and trapping on Indian lands, as nothing is better calculated to alarm and disturb the harmony so happily existing between us and the Indians in the vicinity of Council Bluffs."[8]

Secretary Calhoun dispatched a letter to Clark, dated July 1, 1822, reminding the Superintendent of Indian Affairs that "the license which has been granted by this Department by order of the President to General Ashley and Major Henry confers the privilege of trading with the Indians *only* [itals. added], as the laws regulating trade and intercourse with the Indian tribes do not contain any authority to issue licenses for any other purpose."[9]

By this time, however, the men were gone, and the United

States government at that time had no means of enforcing any of its laws or directives in the wilderness. Ashley had successfully cut this corner while General Clark was looking the other way. Where and how he obtained his financing is not clear. He could not have had too much cash on hand for his most recent enterprises had not proved profitable. He was named Lieutenant Governor of the State of Missouri in 1821, however, and this should have recommended him as a man of trust and substance. It was no easy job in those depression days of St. Louis, however, to find enough money to float such a venture.

The keelboats, for example, cost $3500 each and Ashley bought two of them at the outset. Each cargo tucked away in their holds was worth about $10,000. The keelboats were sixty-five feet long, fifteen feet in the beam and about four feet deep in the hold. A cargo box extended from the deck upward about five feet. The housing was about forty-five feet long, leaving some ten feet clear at the bow and stern. A twenty-foot-high mast rose a little forward of center, equipped with a ten-foot-square sail, which provided one of the many modes of propulsion. A hawser extended down from the mast and through the ring in the bow. Often the men trudged along the bank pulling this rope and moving the vessel slowly up stream. This was called cordelling. To pole the boat, each man grasped a long pole with a nob at one end padded with leather. This fitted into the hollow of the shoulder. The men planted the other end of the pole in the river bed and pushed steadily while walking along the running boards toward the stern. When water was too deep for poling oars were broken out.

When the first long keelboat of the Ashley-Henry enterprise swung out into the river and headed upstream the west bank of the Mississippi was lined solid with spectators that day, April 3, 1822. There were about a hundred men aboard and another fifty going overland on horseback. There is no way of knowing for sure if Jim was among either group, but it is certain that Mike Fink was aboard the keelboat, and where Mike was there too would be his friend, Carpenter.

Almost from the beginning the men went hungry. There was little or no game to be shot near the shores of the river and the men began deserting, falling away in two's and three's. Finally nine left at once.[10]

Undermanned and straggling up the river without rations, Major Henry's company suffered a serious blow when he was bamboozled out of some fifty of his horses by the Assiniboin Indians. Unable to make it all the way to the Three Forks of the Missouri, Henry decided to build a fort on the Yellowstone and he sent word down to St. Louis for Ashley to bring another supply of horses up the river.

Meanwhile Ashley was having his own troubles. The second boat to leave was out only about a week before striking a snag in the river and sinking. No hands were lost, but the entire cargo, valued at $10,000 was, as well as the $3500 keelboat. Within two weeks, though, Ashley had outfitted another and was again on the way upriver, this time in charge of the boat himself. After arriving at Fort Henry, Ashley turned and went back downriver in a pirogue within only a few days, as he wanted to get back at work outfitting more keelboats to head up in the spring.

It was during this winter that Mike Fink became disgruntled with a short whisky ration, so he and Carpenter withdrew from Fort Henry and lived in a cave, where they soon quarreled over the affections of a common girl friend known as Pittsburgh Blue. During a drinking and shooting bout Mike missed a can of whisky on his friends's head and shot Carpenter between the eyes. Following this, Levi Talbott, a gunsmith, unloaded two pistols in Mike's vest and that was the end of him. Talbott didn't live long, either, but was drowned trying to swim the Teton (Bad) River a few months later.[11]

Ashley meanwhile was encountering trouble in the form of St. Louis businessmen who were beginning to have their doubts that the fur business would rival the wealth of Peruvian mines, for the general had sunk some $50,000 into the venture without getting back so much as a "bit." Ashley, however, was courageous enough, gambler enough, to know that this was no time to withdraw from the game. He was in too deep, and the lure of success in the big gamble on the frontier remained strong. It speaks well of his reputation that he was able to borrow still more capital, to attract still more investors.

## NOTES TO CHAPTER VI

1. Brackenridge, *Views of Louisiana,* p. 94.

2. *Missouri Gazette,* April 4, 1838, carried an article describing the dress and actions of Ashley mountain men as they appeared in 1822: "Armed and equipped for desperate encounters with red men . . . or grizzlie bear, these men paraded the streets. . . . Like a reckless crew of a man-of-war about to cruise against the enemy's squadron, they indulged deeply in the luxuries that they might never again realize."

3. Charles A., Mary, and William Beard, *The Beards' New History of the United States* (Garden City, Doubleday & Co., 1968) p. 52.

4. Dale L. Morgan, *The West of William H. Ashley* (Denver, Old West Publishing Co., 1964) p. xv.

5. Scharf's *History,* pp. 197, 351.

6. *Ibid.,* p. 360.

7. St. Louis *Post,* July 10, 1847, reprinted in *The Santa Fe Republican,* November 20, 1847, in which Jim is quoted as saying he joined Ashley in "the spring of 1821," which was a whole year before *any* Ashley boats left and indicating he must have departed early. The interview continues with the statement that "The company of Ashley and Henry were ordered to form a junction with Gen. Leavenworth at the Arickera village. Mr. Kirker, with others, accordingly *descended* [italics mine] the Missouri to that place." To *descend* to the Arickera village, could mean only that they were above it, which would place Kirker with Major Henry, for at this time Ashley and his boats were *below* the Arickara villages.

8. National Archives, War Department Records, Letters Received by Secretary, 0-5 (16) 1822, also reprinted in Morgan's *West of Ashley,* p. 6.

9. National Archives, Records of the War Department, Office of the Secretary, Letters sent, Indian Affairs Record Group No. 75, Vol. E, p. 295.

10. Daniel T. Potts, one of the nine who deserted, tells of his ordeal in a letter to his friend, Thomas Cochlen, which was copied by Potts's sister of Cheltenham, Pa., and is now in the Yellowstone National Park Museum. Morgan, in *West of Ashley,* reproduces the letter on page 7.

11. There are many versions of the Fink-Carpenter-Talbott shooting, but perhaps the most reliable is the one which appeared in the St. Louis *Reveille,* October 21, 1844. This was written by Joseph M. Field, a partner in the publication with Charles Keemle.

# CHAPTER VII

J IM KIRKER once told a reporter from a St. Louis newspaper that he lived in St. Louis "until the spring of 1821, when he joined the mountain company of General Ashley and Major Henry, and departed for the upper Missouri region."[1] He made this statement some twenty-five years after the event and must have made a mistake of one year in his recollection, for it was the spring of 1822, not 1821, that Ashley sent his boats up the Missouri.

Evidence that Kirker may have remained in St. Louis that summer is afforded by a couple of receipts found in the papers of Indian Agent Thomas Forsyth, but on closer examination it is evident they really have little to do with establishing exactly when Kirker left St. Louis. One of the receipts is dated July 17, 1822 and bears the name of "Jas. Kirker," signed in St. Louis, but it is in the same handwriting as the name below it, "David Kirker," who apparently was acting as James' agent in collecting accounts. Another receipt in the Forsyth file bears the name of "J. Kirker," but below it also is "By P. Shearman," and this bears the date of April 7, 1821; this apparently is the date of the account and not the date when the bill was receipted. None of these men were partners, for the same Shearman and one

51

Acknowledgment of payment of his bill was received by Thomas Forsyth in an account with James Kirker's store. Payment was apparently made on April 7, shortly after Jim left on the Ashley expedition for the Upper Missouri, and is receipted for James Kirker "by P. Shearman." The latter, on April 8, appeared before Justice of the Peace Thomas McGuire to swear that "James Kirker is the only owner" of the store, indicating that some other person was claiming part ownership or partnership. *Courtesy of the Missouri Historical Society*

Otis Reynolds swore before a justice of the peace on April 8, 1822 at St. Louis that Jim was the sole owner of his grocery.[2]

The evidence therefore indicates that Jim probably spent the first winter on the upper Missouri, as he said he did to the St. Louis interviewer.

Major Henry took eleven men on a spring trapping expedition up the Missouri and to the mouth of Smith's River, but he brought back only seven, the other having been killed in a battle with the Blackfeet. The men lost 30 traps and were forced to cache 172 more so they could escape the Indians. It was then decided to remain within the walls of Fort Henry until Ashley's arrival with more men and horses. To expedite this, Jedediah Smith was sent downriver to inform Ashley of their needs.

The general meanwhile was gathering equipment and recruiting men for his second expedition. Ashley employed James Clyman, an itinerant surveyor, to enlist the additional men, most of whom came from "grog shops and other sinks of degredation," Clyman later wrote, adding that "Falstaff's Battalion was genteel in comparison." They couldn't all have been people of a lower order, though, for among those going up the second year were William Sublette, Tom Fitzpatrick, Hugh Glass, Edward Rose and Clyman himself.

General Ashley led the second expedition personally, setting out from St. Louis on March 10, 1823 in two boats, the *Yellowstone* and the *Rocky Mountains,* but while Ashley's

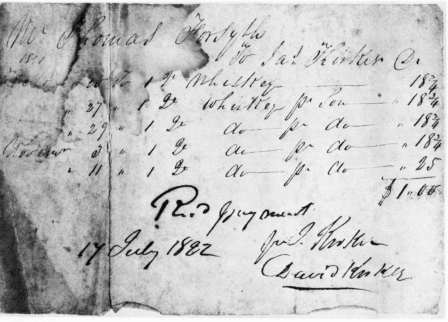

David Kirker probably was the party claiming part ownership of the Kirker store, for it is his name which appears under the name of James Kirker as agent for James in collecting this bill from Thomas Forsyth, dated July 17, 1822. A handwriting expert has declared both of the above signatures as the same handwriting, obviously that of David Kirker. James at this time was still with the Ashley men in the wilderness. *Courtesy of the Missouri Historical Society*

men were headed upstream, more than a hundred Arickaras were coming down, bent on mischief. They robbed a party of whites, then attacked a trading house belonging to the Missouri Fur Company. Many of the Indians were wounded and two were killed, one of them the son of a famous Arickara chief, Grey Eyes.[3] This skirmish was to have sad repercussions on Ashley's party, for the general hoped to obtain horses from the Arickaras by trade, as Wilson P. Hunt had done some years before. Ashley knew the Arickaras always had plenty of horses but he didn't know they were sulking over the injuries and deaths they had suffered at the hands of Joshua Pilcher's Missouri Fur Company men. Of course Ashley was a competitor of Pilcher but the Indians did not see the difference—they considered *all* white men guilty of the actions of *any* white men.

Ashley arrived before the two Arickara villages on May 30, anchoring his two keelboats well out in the middle of the river, while he took two men with him ashore in a skiff. He found the principal chiefs of the tribe not only willing to trade but apparently friendly, and Ashley gave them gifts, explaining to them that the trouble they had suffered at the hands of Pilcher and the Missouri Company was in no way the work of Ashley and his men. The Indians replied in good humor, declaring they understood and that they considered Ashley and those with him as their friends,[4] according to Chittenden's account.

Clyman, however, wrote a version some years after the event and since he was on the spot it is probably more correct in detail. According to Clyman, the Arickaras demanded that Ashley pay for the damages the Indians had suffered at the hands of the Missouri Fur Company people and that Ashley refused, saying he was not responsible for the actions of people employed by Pilcher but that he would make the Arickaras presents.[5] The Indians then agreed to open trade "on the sand bar in front of the village but the onley [sic] article of Trade they wanted was ammunition . . . we obtained twenty horses in three d[a]ys trading, but in doing this we gave them a fine supply of Powder and ball which on the fourth day [June 2] wee found out to [our] sorrow."[6]

While Ashley was trading ammunition for horses some of his men were trading with the Arickara women for another type of commodity. Ten years before, Henry Brackenridge had visited the Arickara villages and noted that "Chastity appeared to be unknown as a virtue" among them. "Their females had become mere articles of traffic: I have seen fathers bring their daughters, brothers their sisters, and husbands their wives, to be disposed of for a short time, to the highest bidder."[7] There were apparently plenty of bidders every time a group of white trappers stopped at the villages; Brackenridge told of seeing an Arickara chief, who in a thoughtful mood asked if there were any white women as well as white men where the trappers came from. Brackenridge assured him there were.

"Then," asked the old chief, "why is it that your people are so fond of *our* women, one might suppose they had never seen any before?"[8]

Ashley's men acted no different than those who had come before them. Several of the men visited the village after the trading and began negotiating on their own. Among them was the black interpreter, Edward Rose; another was a trapper named Aaron Stephens. Stephens was stabbed to death in the midst of a sex episode and Rose came running into the Ashley camp with news of the murder. Forty of the Ashley men were on a sand bar near the river bank with the horses and when hearing that the Indians were aroused they started swimming the animals toward the keelboat anchored in midstream, but they didn't have time to make it.

The men were cornered on a bare strip of sand, completely unprotected, and the Arickaras were behind wooden pickets surrounding the Ree villages.

"You will easily see," explained Clyman, "that we had little else to do than Stand on a bear sand barr and be shot at, at long range. Their being seven or Eight hundred guns in village and we having only the day previously furnished them with an abundance of Powder and Ball [There were] many calls for the boats to come ashore and take us on board but no prayers or threats had the [slightest effect] the boats men being completely Parylized Several men being wounded a skiff was brought ashore all rushed for the Skiff and came near sinking it but it went to the boat full of men and water the shot still coming thicker and the aim better we making a breastwork of our horses (most) they nerly all being killed."[9]

Finally some of the men made their escape in the brush along the bank and others got back to the boats, one way or another. There were fifteen dead and nine wounded, two of the wounded dying later.

The attack was so concentrated and well directed that the whole encounter took no more than fifteen minutes. One anchor was raised and another cut loose, so that the two boats drifted downriver and out of range of the Arickara guns. They finally came to a halt behind a clump of timber on an island located near the site of today's Pierre, South Dakota.

Here Ashley devised a plan and called his men together to explain it. He said he thought they could cut sufficient timber to build a thick wall, which they would place on the keelboats to protect them from the Arickara marksmen and then try to make another run past the villages. The men bluntly refused to do so, saying they would rather drop farther down the river and await reinforcements.[10]

Ashley transferred most of the goods to the keelboat *Yellowstone* and prepared to send the other boat, *Rocky Mountains,* back downriver with the wounded. He then asked for volunteers to remain with him on the island where they pulled the *Yellowstone* ashore. Thirty men elected to remain with Ashley, of whom only five were boatmen, and the rest headed downstream with the wounded. Ashley then dispatched Jed Smith back upriver to tell Major Henry of the debacle and advise him that instead of receiving reinforcements, Henry's men *were* the reinforcements needed urgently to help extricate Ashley from his predicament.

Smith arrived back at Fort Henry about June 15, and as soon as he had related his woeful story Henry called for volunteers to go to Ashley's aid, while the rest of the men were to remain in the fort to protect the stockade while they were gone. At least one expert (Dale L. Morgan) disagrees, but it is my opinion that Kirker was among those who volunteered to go to Ashley's assistance, primarily because he said so. The St. Louis interview that appeared in the *Post* July 10, 1847 says that the company was ordered "to form a junction with General Leavenworth at the Arickera village. Mr. Kirker with others, accordingly descended the Missouri to that place."[11]

In considering that volunteers were called for it must be remembered that these men were *not being paid* by Ashley and Henry, that the only way they could earn any money was by trapping. They would be paid nothing for fighting Indians—and might lose their lives. Regardless, all but twenty men left to guard Fort Henry immediately began their descent of the Missouri to help Ashley, who meanwhile had written a letter to Major O'Fallon in which he pleaded for the government also to come to his aid.

This letter was sent by carrier on the keelboat *Yellowstone,* which reached Fort Atkinson on June 18, with forty-three men, some of them wounded, the others low in spirit. Major O'Fallon immediately consulted with Colonel Henry Leavenworth, commander both of the Sixth Infantry and the fort, about the contents of Ashley's letter. Leavenworth decided to act boldly and at once, without waiting to check with his superiors at St. Louis. He asked O'Fallon to prepare the *Yellowstone* for a return trip upriver and to implore as many keelboatmen as he could convince to reconsider and accompany Leavenworth back up the Missouri with troops to punish the Arickaras. Twenty of the forty-three men agreed to return and Leavenworth began organizing his own forces into a punitive expedition.

Meanwhile Ashley arrived at Fort Kiowa, still searching for horses, and there he received word by letter from O'Fallon that the government was readying an expedition of six companies of soldiers and enough artillery to teach the Arickaras a lesson. Elated, Ashley turned around and returned to his temporary camp, where he had left his own volunteers, by this time augmented by the reinforcements brought by Major Henry. Word had also come down that Pilcher, who had suffered from both the Blackfeet and the Arickaras, was sending all of his men; he had also sent runners out to enlist the aid of as many mounted Sioux warriors as they could. The Sioux were traditional enemies of the Arickaras.

Leavenworth had headed upriver with three boats, two his own and the third the *Yellowstone,* loaded with extra muskets to be used by volunteers. On July 3 one of the army boats overturned and sank. Six privates and one sergeant were drowned and seventy government muskets were lost. This disaster somewhat cooled Leavenworth's ardor for his mission; it was going to be difficult to explain the loss of seven men and seventy muskets before he had even engaged the enemy.

The colonel's troubles were further compounded five nights later when a storm drove the *Yellowstone* onto a sand bar; the mast was lost and only by the most energetic efforts was another disaster avoided.[12] Colonel Leavenworth reached Fort Recovery on July 19, where he halted for three days to recruit and reorganize his command, then headed upstream again on July 23, reaching Ashley's camp a week later.[13] Here, on July 30, Colonel Leavenworth put together the combined forces of the army, Ashley, Pilcher and about 500 Sioux horsemen who showed up to assist in the campaign.

General Ashley's men numbered approximately eighty men and those under Pilcher forty. Leavenworth, whose command initially comprised some 230 officers and men of the Sixth Regiment, now had less than 225 due to losses incurred when the keelboat sank.

Pilcher, head of the Missouri Fur Company forces, was given the rank of major. William Henry Vanderburgh, a West Pointer, was made captain, with Angus McDonald captain of the Indian command. Moses Carson, an older brother of Kit, was made first lieutenant and William Gordon second lieutenant.

The Ashley men were divided into two companies of about forty each, commanded by Brigadier General Ashley, with Major Henry as his aide. Ashley nominated his officers, confirmed in orders, as follows: Jedediah Smith, captain; Hiram Scott, captain; Hiram Allen and George C. Jackson, lieutenants; Charles Cunningham and Edward Rose, ensigns; a Dr. Fleming, surgeon; Thomas Fitzpatrick, quartermaster, and William Sublett, sergeant major.

Jim Kirker is not mentioned by name in any of the official reports, nor in newspaper accounts or private diaries. The only hint as to how he participated is contained in the St. Louis *Post* interview, probably written by Charles Keemle, who was in the Arickara campaign himself as one of the Pilcher men. Keemle, although he had been in charge of a brigade under attack by the Blackfeet, was not made an officer in the Leavenworth forces, either. "Owing to some disagreement which took place between Mr. K. and the leaders of his party," says the *Post* interview, "he left the company and joined the force under General Leavenworth."

The total force was about 800 men, counting the 500 Sioux horsemen, all of whom wore white headbands so they could be distinguished from the Arickaras once the battle started. Most of this Indian force was sent out ahead, in the hopes that the Arickaras would think they had only the Sioux to fight and wouldn't run off and hide. This was on August 9, 1823, after Leavenworth and his men reached Grand River, about six or seven miles below the villages.[14]

Next came the riflemen under Captain Bennet Reilly, later to become famous for his exploits along the Santa Fe trail and in California, where he was the first military governor. This contingent was followed by Ashley and his mountaineers, while four companies of the regular infantry were next in line. A half-hundred Sioux rode the flanks and formed the rear guard. Another special detachment of regulars under Major Abram R. Wooley brought the boats up, loaded with additional supplies.

The Sioux warriors became impatient and galloped ahead, reaching the Ree villages nearly an hour ahead of the main body, and as soon as they were discovered the Arickaras sent out a force of braves to engage them. The Indians were locked in battle about a half mile below the towns, swirling and clashing in hundreds of small encounters before the Leavenworth forces came on the scene.[15]

Clyman wrote that "as soon as we came in sight the Rees retreated to their village. The boats came up and landed a short half mile below the village but little effort was made that afternoon except to surround the Rees and keep them from leaveing the Sioux coming around one side and the whites around the other. Quite a number of dead Indians streaud [sic] over the plain."[16]

As dusk began to settle on the two villages, the Americans and their Sioux allies could hear the wailing and screaming of the Arickaras lamenting the deaths of fallen husbands, fathers and comrades, the pandemonium augmented by the yapping of dogs and the firing of guns. As dusk turned to night the Sioux retired to an Arickara field of corn and began gathering roasting ears, which they shucked and ate for a late supper.

Shortly after dawn Leavenworth's artillery, which had been moved in under the cover of darkness, opened up with a six-pound howitzer barking from the heights on each side of the villages. The elevation was too high at first but soon the balls were landing in the villages, bouncing around and blasting open the moundlike, round-top huts the Indians called their lodges. After the battle was over it was learned that one of the balls scored a direct hit on Chief Grey Eyes, apparently the only Indian who lost his life as a result of the bombardment.

This cannonading from a distance bored the Sioux; to them this was a poor substitute for real fighting. After they had their fill of Arickara corn they began riding away from the battlefield, leaving behind only one of their number to talk with a representative of the Arickaras. Leavenworth, fearing the Sioux might be planning to switch sides, sent Ed Rose out to learn what the two were talking about. Rose returned to inform the Colonel that the Rees had taken enough punishment and wanted to talk peace. Rose also informed Leavenworth of the death of Grey Eyes, who had been—according to the other chiefs—responsible for the trouble in the first place. A parley was therefore arranged for the next day.

At the meeting Leavenworth told the Arickara chiefs that they must return all of the property stolen from Ashley, promise never to attack Missouri trappers again and deliver up five good-faith hostages who would be taken back to Fort Atkinson with Leavenworth. The Indians agreed to the terms and a treaty was finally concluded, but only over the loud objections of Major Pilcher, who thought the Indians should be taught a harder lesson.

Three days later the Indians had returned only one spavined horse, eighteen buffalo robes and one gun. The Rees claimed the Sioux had killed all of Ashley's horses during the battle and that the rifle and handful of robes were all that remained of their loot.

At this development, the Missouri Legion officers met with Leavenworth and decided to renew the attack the next morning. The Indians apparently got wind of this decision, for they moved out during the night. This was exactly what Ed Rose had predicted would happen, so Leavenworth sent Rose to search out the Arickara leaders and ask that they not abandon the villages, declaring that the portion of the peace treaty demanding the return of property would be deleted.

The villages were empty of people the next morning, except for a few old women, one of whom was Chief Grey Eyes' mother.

Pilcher, whose Missouri Fur Company was nearly finished anyway, was appalled at this tender treatment of the Arickaras and demanded that they be punished further or, he predicted, there would be even greater uprisings in the future. Ashley must have felt much the same way but he was not so openly opposed to Leavenworth because he still had a lot of property up the river, with more coming, and men strung all up and down the waterway. What Ashley wanted most was to move unmolested, either by persuading the Indians or filling them with fear.

Colonel Leavenworth ordered his men back down stream and they hadn't been on the water an hour before flames were seen shooting up from the Arickara towns from fires set by Angus McDonald and William Gordon, of the Missouri Fur Company. Apparently the two were acting without Pilcher's knowledge. Leavenworth, furious, wrote to Pilcher: "The Colonel commanding is extremely mortified to say, that he has reason to believe, that the Ricarra towns have been set fire by your company, contrary to the most positive orders, and in violation of their word of honor to obey orders; with such men he will have no further intercourse."[17]

Pilcher replied, in part, to this: "You came to restore peace and tranquility to the country & leave an impression which would insure its continuance, your operations have been such as to produce the contrary effect, and to impress the different Indian tribes with the greatest possible contempt for the American character."[18]

This exchange of letters between the two men did not end the public airing of their differences, which continued for several months in the press. Each one was sure that he was right; and each perhaps was, in the light of the differences in their interests and objectives.

Jim Kirker had just witnessed some classical demonstrations of inept leadership and what seemed a comic-opera method of dealing with Indians. His immediate reaction was to return to St. Louis, which he did, as he said in the *Post* interview, accompanying General Leavenworth downstream. By fall of 1823 he no doubt was once more behind the counter of his grocery store "near the Team Boat Ferry."

This couldn't last long, though, for Kirker had caught the most deadly disease of the time, one rapidly becoming epidemic. It was known as "mountain fever." Once you had it you simply could never feel at home on the prairie again. There was only one treatment: a huge dose of mountain trails.

## NOTES TO CHAPTER VII

1. The St. Louis *Post,* July 10, 1847.

2. Somebody, perhaps his cousin David, apparently was claiming an interest in Jim's business during his absence, for Patrick Shearman and Otis Reynolds appeared before St. Louis Justice of the Peace Thomas McGuire on April 8, 1822—just five days after the departure of the first Ashley boat—and swore that Jim Kirker was sole owner. In the office of Recorder of Deeds, City of St. Louis, Missouri, Book L, page 77, is a lengthly deposition of the two men, probably clerk employees of Jim's, who "did deposeth and sayeth that James Kirker . . . is the only owner of the property therein contained." Shearman and Reynolds do not appear in the St. Louis Directory for 1821 and the author can discover no more of their identity.

3. Hiram Martin Chittenden, *The American Fur Trade of the Far West,* Vol. I, (Stanford, Academic Reprints, 1954), pp. 264-265.

4. *Ibid.* 267.

5. James Clyman, *Frontiersman, The Adventures of a Trapper and Covered-Wagon Emigrant, as told in his Experiences and Diaries,* Charles L. Camp, ed. (Portland, Ore., Champoeg Press, 1960) pp. 8-9.

6. *Ibid.* p. 9.

7. Brackenridge, *Views of Louisiana,* p. 257.

8. *Ibid.* p. 258.

9. Clyman's *Frontiersman,* p. 9.

10. Letter, dated June 4, 1823, from Ashley to Benjamin O'Fallon, National Archives, Records of the War Department, Office of the Secretary, Letters received, C-77 (17) 1823, as published, Morgan's *Ashley's West,* pp. 27-28, with omissions supplied from another copy from Adjutant General's Office G-94/1823 incl.

11. Unfortunately there is no list of those who were with Major Henry over that winter and no record in the National Archives: the War Department explains that no

record at all was kept of the men who served with Leavenworth, that they were handed discharges but none was retained by the government.

12. Morgan's *West of Ashley* p. 52, paraphrasing Leavenworth's official report.

13. *Ibid.*

14. *Ibid.* p. 53.

15. Clyman, *Frontiersman,* p. 13.

16. *Ibid.* All subsequent details of the Arickara campaign are taken from Clyman's account, or Leavenworth's report, as the latter appears in Morgan's *West of Ashley,* pp. 52-57.

17. Dale L. Morgan, *Jedediah Smith,* (Indianapolis, Bobbs-Merrill, 1953) p. 77.

18. Morgan's *West of Ashley,* p. 57

# CHAPTER VIII

S T. LOUIS was emerging from a financial lethargy inherited
from several years of economic stagnation when Jim
Kirker came back from the mountains to take up his business again. He would find most of the merchants optimistic,
mainly because many of them had become energetic entre-
preneurs, gambling money both in the fur trade and in commerce with Santa Fe.

There was really little reason for cheer, however, for Ashley's fur enterprise had done nothing but sink him more deeply
in debt (as much as $100,000, according to Thomas Forsyth's
calculations)[1] and the Santa Fe trade so far had not been all that
profitable. Captain Becknell had thus far enjoyed only mild
good fortune although he made things much more promising
when he located the Cimarron Cut-off, shortening the trip to
Santa Fe by 100 miles and proving the route suitable for wagons
by driving three of them over what was then just becoming
known as the Santa Fe Trail.

Hard facts were obviously not responsible for the traders'
soaring hopes but they did sniff prosperity in the offing. Most
of the St. Louis business leaders felt it would be only a matter
of time until Ashley was successful and they backed up their

opinion with money. They loaned Ashley enough to keep him floating in the face of adversity.

On the positive side, too, there were good signs: the price of beaver was still climbing and transportation to New Mexico was easier, opening a door to the most profitable market on the American continent. This everyone had known since the publication of *The Expeditions of Zebulon Pike* in 1810. Pike wrote:[2]

> The following articles sell in this province, as stated, which will show the cheapness of provisions and extreme dearness of imported goods: Flour sells per hundred, at $2; salt, per mule load, $5; sheep, each $1; beeves, each $5; wine del Passo, per barrel, $15; horses each, $11; mules each, $30; superfine cloths, per yard, $25; fine cloths, per yard $20; linen per yard, $4, and all other dry goods in proportion.

Pike further informed his readers that the Spaniards and Mexicans were not inclined to manufacture, "as the Spaniards think it more honorable to be agriculturists than mechanics." This disinclination to manufacture had forced New Mexicans to purchase 112,000 pesos' worth of goods each year from the south of Mexico while selling only 60,000 worth of agricultural products, at depressed prices, in return. This left an imbalance of more than 50,000 pesos each year, a staggering sum for that time and place.

New Mexico was being drained of its hard money, mostly high-grade silver coin. Consequently, New Mexicans would be happy to buy manufactured goods from the United States because the prices would be lower and the products better, with a greater selection. Additionally, import tariffs—when collected and kept out of the collectors' pockets—increased the provincial treasury.[3]

When St. Louis merchants learned that yard goods were selling for as much as $20 and $25 a yard, with all other prices comparable and paid for in silver, they knew they had a very good thing lying across the prairies, better—in the long run—than fur trapping.

Jim Kirker must have become aware of this circumstance shortly after his return. Cousin David had been running the store in his absence, acting apparently, from such receipts as those given to Thomas Forsyth, with power of attorney. David's single trip to the wilderness had quenched any desire he might previously have felt for adventure, and he was now planning to settle down and marry a pretty neighbor, Mariah Robinson.[4]

Being in the retail business, Jim was all too well aware that hard currency had become almost non-existent and when he heard that some eighty merchants were planning to take some $35,000 worth of goods in a caravan to New Mexico, it is a good bet he threw in with them. Jim had celebrated his thirtieth birthday on December 2, 1823 and he surely realized that he was getting too old to play the waiting game at the home end of the trail, where profits were counted in dribs, drabs and pennies. He also felt his health would improve on such a trip.[5]

The proposed trade caravan was organized by Captain Becknell, in partnership with Meredith Miles Marmaduke and Augustus Storrs. Marmaduke, a native of Virginia, has been a colonel in the militia during the War of 1812, and came to Missouri only the year before, settling at Old Franklin. Storrs was a native of New Hampshire. Of the more than 100 men making the trip, nineteen were going as employees, while the other eighty or so were proprietors. Jim was probably one of the latter.[6]

The wagon train, made up at Franklin, consisted of two wagons, twenty dearborns, two carts and one small cannon, all of which were pulled by 200 horses and mules. The expedition was under the command of Alexander LaGrand, the elected caravanbachi, as he was called by Alphonso Wetmore, in a letter to Congressman Scott.[7]

The caravan left Franklin on May 16 and exactly four months and ten days later, it was back in Missouri with a gross return of more than $180,000 in precious metals, plus another $10,000 in furs and hides. They added up to an average net profit of about $15,000 for each merchant, on an investment of only $3500.

It is possible that Jim remained behind in New Mexico trapping over the fall and winter or he may have come back with the rest. There is no doubt at all that the expedition was sensationally profitable for the Missourians who participated in it. The smell of money wafted all the way to Washington, where Senator Benton sent out letters to the proprietors asking them to answer twenty-two questions, covering all phases of the trip. He wanted this information to help launch a federal survey for a road to run between St. Louis and Santa Fe.

Augustus Storrs' succinct and detailed reply was so comprehensive that it was published by the Senate and comprises a cornerstone in the body of information and literature we have on the opening of the Santa Fe Trail.[8]

Meanwhile, General Ashley continued to slip more heavily in debt with each passing day and in the summer of 1824 he decided to run for the office of governor of Missouri against Frederick Bates. This move, according to at least one expert on early St. Louis history,[9] was probably to keep Ashley's creditors' minds off of his deplorable financial condition. Ashley lost the election and at about the same time Major Henry withdrew from the partnership, giving the whole thing up as a bad job and leaving Ashley with all of the debts and responsibilities.

Henry's judgment proved to be as bad in this instance as it had been in the past, for Ashley left St. Louis once more, vowing to himself and those close to him he would never come back except as a rich man and that turned out to be exactly what he did. Bad luck finally quit dogging Ashley and he returned with enough furs to pay his debts and leave a substantial fortune.

The misfortune, however, that lifted from Ashley's shoulders seemed to descend on those of the McKnight family. This

John McKnight, the adopted son and nephew of John McKnight who was killed by the Kiowas in 1824, returned to St. Louis a wealthy man in 1844, following several years he spent as a trader in Santa Fe. *Courtesy of the Missouri Historical Society*

once powerful clan had begun to disintegrate. Young Robert joined his older brother John and Thomas James in an Indian-trading venture, for which they built a fort about seventy miles north of today's Oklahoma City, in Blaine County. The Comanches, again led by old Chief One Eye—the same who had given David Kirker's expedition so much trouble—wouldn't leave them alone. Finally One-Eye was successful in getting John McKnight murdered in an Indian village, at which point Robert decided he had had enough of the American frontier. He and James started beating their way back to St. Louis but by the time they had made it into Arkansas, they were so starved and emaciated they were barely able to stumble into the home of John Rogers, an ancestor of comedian Will Rogers. The head of an advance Cherokee settlement in that area, Rogers nursed them back to health, mainly through proper diet.

They continued on, but more gloom was added to Robert's life when he arrived in St. Louis to learn that his sister-in-law had just died of cholera and her husband, Robert's older brother, Thomas, was pulling stakes for Galena, Illinois, where he planned to go into the lead business.[10]

With all of the members of his family either dead or removed from St. Louis and a wife and child awaiting him in northern Chihuahua, Robert McKnight decided to return to Mexico. He was still bitter at the United States government for not helping him obtain redress for the money he lost when the New Mexico authorities confiscated his trade goods during his trip some ten years earlier. Robert was traveling under a proper United States passport and he felt it was the responsibility of his government to protect him and his property under such circumstances. Washington didn't see it that way, however, and now Robert was almost broke and terribly bitter.

"There is better chance for obtaining justice from the Mexicans, scoundrels as they are," he said, "than from my own government. I will go and recover as a citizen of Mexico what I lost as a citizen of the United States. My own government refuses to do me justice, and I will renounce it forever. I would not raise a straw in its defense."[11]

Meanwhile, Missouri Senator Benton got Augustus Storrs appointed United States Consul at Santa Fe and the latter set about organizing the greatest trade expedition ever to head west. As long as he had to go all the way out there anyway to assume his duties he might as well make the trip profitable. This caravan, said Storrs, he would lead himself and he enlisted the participation of ninety merchants, who collected $65,000 worth of trade goods to take with them in thirty-four wagons and by pack mule. This caravan left Franklin on May 16, 1825, the same day of the same month as had the train the year before.

In this company were men destined to shape the early history of the Southwest, including Kirker, Robert McKnight, Elisha Stanley, Ira Emmons, Hugh Stevenson, Lewis Dutton, Henry Corlew, Lucas Doan, Joshua Sledd and Stephen Courcier, or Estevan Cushie, as he was called by the Mexicans.[12]

Kirker had been busy earlier in the year with the affairs of William Shearer, who had been on the McKnight and James expedition with David Kirker. Shearer died in February, 1825 and Jim, along with James Lansdell, was named as surety on the administration bond, dated February 26, 1825, in the St. Louis probate court.[13]

It is not clear whether Jim turned the operation of the grocery over to Cousin David at this time or sold the business. There are no St. Louis directories during this period to give any hint, and only the skimpiest of other records. Jim's property, in Block 17 next to the river, was listed as delinquent in taxes to the sum of $7.50 on December 31, 1823 and again on January 10, 1825, but apparently the first of these small sums was paid and probably the second, indicating that Jim probably was absent previous to these dates, unavailable to pay taxes.[14]

Whatever Jim did concerning the business, it is clearly evident he did not dispose of the property nor give up the lease he held with John McKnight until March 2, 1832, on which date it was bought in at a sheriff's sale by George W. Scott, an in-law of Thomas McKnight, for the sum of $50.[15] By this time Jim was long gone from St. Louis and obviously had abandoned the property, probably never giving the grocery business another thought. He was completely absorbed in trading with the Indians and trapping in New Mexico.

Governor Antonio Narbona showed his cooperative attitude toward Americans by granting more than a hundred of these strangers arriving with the caravans from the United States special permits to "trade" for furs, which really meant to "trap." These men, including Kirker, were scarcely out of sight of the presidios before they uncovered hidden traps and strung them along New Mexico's streams, especially the Gila River.

Shortly after arriving in Santa Fe in July both Kirker and McKnight had applied for Mexican citizenship, probably to assist them in obtaining trapping and mining privileges.[16] Afterward the two journeyed a couple of hundred miles south, to Galeana in northern Chihuahua, where Robert had been "imprisoned" in Mexico while operating mines, running a store and raising a family. Prospects in this region must have appeared favorable still, for Robert settled back into his various businesses and the bosom of his Mexican family, while Jim apparently set out for St. Louis once more, intent upon settling whatever of his business interests remained there and cutting final ties with his life in Missouri.

This trip back was probably made in the company of Ewing Young, Thomas Boggs, James Dempsey, Paul Baillo and some members of the road-survey crew Senator Benton had been successful in creating. The group left New Mexico in mid-February 1826, and Jim had completed all the business he was able to negotiate by August of that summer (apparently he was unable to sell his store property on East Mississippi Street in Block 17). At this time a fairly large train was making up at Fort Osage, preparing to depart for Santa Fe. Jim was probably made wagonmaster of this caravan and there is evidence it was he who gave Kit Carson the job which afforded Kit an opportunity to come west in the fall of that year, 1826.[17]

This caravan, a considerable part of which was owned by Stephen Turley, reached Santa Fe in midfall and Jim took up trading and trapping along the Gila that winter, stopping over at the Santa Rita copper mines and making this his base of operations. Nearly a century and a half later there still would be Kirkers—dozens of them—working in and around the Santa Rita mines, which could easily mark the longest uninterrupted family occupation at a single business site in this country's history.

## NOTES TO CHAPTER VIII

1. Extract of a letter from Thomas Forsyth to Secretary of War Lewis Cass, dated October 24, 1831, U.S. Senate, Executive Documents, 22d Congress I session II, No. 90, p. 70, a copy of which is in longhand, National Archives, S. 22A-E7.

2. Pike's narrative has been reprinted numerous times. The one followed here is edited by Elliott Coues, *The Expeditions of Zebulon Montgomery Pike,* 3 Vols., New York, 1895, p. 740.

3. Max L. Moorhead, *New Mexico's Royal Road,* (Norman, U. of Okla., 1958) p. 65.

4. W. B. Douglas, editor of Thomas James's *Three Years Among the Indians and Mexicans,* p. 98, fn 8, says in this 1916 edition that the couple was married on March 2, 1826. David is described as "a farmer of the McKnight district." A daughter was born to them on November 28, 1828, and was named Anne Jane. David died less than two years later, and his widow married John Z. Mackay, son of James Mackay, an early settler in the region.

5. Exactly what was wrong with Kirker in 1824 is not known but in his 1847 interview with the St. Louis *Post* he says the trip helped him in his "recovery of an impaired state of health." He also calls it a "trapping trip," which is what many of the men did upon reaching Santa Fe, although it was illegal.

6. M. M. Marmaduke's "Journal," Missouri Historical Review, October, 1911, lists few of the proprietors, but Jim himself said he went to New Mexico first in 1824, and this was the major expedition of that year, with the odds in favor of his having accompanied it.

7. This letter from Franklin, Mo., dated August 19, 1824, was published February 14, 1825, as Senate Document 79, Second Session, 18th Congress, and a reprint is found

in *Santa Fe Trail, First Reports: 1825,* (Stagecoach Press, formerly of Houston, now of Albuquerque, 1960).

8. Senate Document 7, serial 108, Second Session, Eighteenth Congress, and also reprinted in Stage Coach Press' *Santa Fe Trail.*

9. Fred Voelker, author of numerous fur-trade articles.

10. Thomas McKnight Biography, MHS archives, item 40612, (BM218). Thomas was later to marry Cornelia Hempstead, daughter of Stephen, and settle in Peru, Iowa, a part of today's Dubuque. Robert Kirker was Thomas McKnight's chief assistant and it is assumed he accompanied his employer to these places.

11. James, *Three Years Among the Indians,* p. 155.

12. McKnight, Stanley and Emmons are named as members of the caravan by George C. Yount in his *Chronicles of the West,* edited by Charles L. Camp, Denver, 1966, while the last six, and McKnight, are listed as the men who accompanied Kirker, McKnight, et al, to New Mexico by Jim Kirker's son-in-law, writing under the name of "Old Timer" in the *Rio Grande Republican,* October 26, 1889, although Bean has his dates wrong.

13. Douglas note in James, *Three Years Among the Indians,* p. 98.

14. Missouri *Republican,* Dec. 31, 1823; January 10, 1825.

15. Office of Recorder, City and County of St. Louis, Book R, pp. 692-3.

16. Father Stanley, *Giant In Lilliput, The Story of Donaciano Vigil,* (Pampa, Texas, 1963), p. 29.

17. It has long been a matter of speculation as to who was the wagonmaster that signed Kit on for the latter's first Santa Fe expedition. Kit, in his dictated autobiography, fails to name him, but Kirker is declared to be that man in an introduction to a biographical sketch of Carson appearing in the St. Louis *Saturday Evening Post,* July 17, 1847, no doubt written by its owner, the veteran trapper Charles Keemle. Keemle wrote: [It was our desire to present the readers of the POST with a likeness of the celebrated Kit Carson, one of the most daring of the mountaineers, but his recent visit to this city was so short in duration that in this we failed. Below, however, we give a brief sketch of his life and exploits, which compare favorably with those of the man with whom he made his first trip to the Mexican country—our friend Kirker, whose daring feats we gave a bird's eye view last week.]

# CHAPTER IX

THE Santa Rita mines afforded Jim an excellent location in which to cache his furs and illegal traps. He figured he could work at the mines in the summer and during the winter he could trap and hunt for furs. By this time the copper mines at Santa Rita had been in operation about a quarter of a century. They were first discovered by the Spaniards about 1799 but they had been known to exist for years before this by the Apaches, especially the Mimbrenos, whose tribal home was in that part of southern New Mexico.

Lieutenant Colonel José Manuel Carrasco is officially credited with discovering the copper there, having been directed to the deposits by an Apache he had befriended.[1] The Indian told Carrasco that his people had been coming there for as long as the oldest tribal member could recall to obtain metal which they hammered into useful articles as well as jewelry. A huge ornament suspended by a thong around the neck, a sort of chest-plate made of copper, was reported to have been worn by a Kiowa chief as far east as Kansas and the metal from which it was made no doubt came from from the Santa Rita mines.

Carrasco filed a claim under Spanish law but he didn't possess the necessary capital to start mining operations and so enlisted the aid of Don Francisco Manuel Elguea, a wealthy Chihuahua merchant and a native of Spain, or a *Gachupin,* as the Mexicans called such people. The mining concession was named the Santa Rita del Cobre grant.[2] Operations were begun a short time later and when all the surface metal was removed, shafts were dug extending down at about seventy degrees to reach the deeper deposits.[3] From here, ore was borne to the surface on the backs of men carrying huge leather *seronis,* or containers, which weighed, loaded, eight *arrobas,* or 200 pounds, apiece. Many of these workers were Indian slaves, others convicts from Chihuahua, and they had to climb in and out of deep, dank holes sometimes as much as 100 feet by means of notched poles, or "chicken ladders," called *muescas* in Spanish. In 1804, Elguea built a triangular fort on the site, with a martello tower of adobe at each corner, and purchased Carrasco's remaining interest. A short time later, Elguea made a contract to supply the government with copper for coinage, the common copper coin being the *tlaco,* an eighth of a *real,* itself being an eighth of a *peso.*[4]

Workers and soldiers protecting the installation from Indian attack were housed within the fort, which was supplied by regular pack train from Chihuahua City by way of the ancient village of Janos.[5] Ore was packed by mule over the same route. According to Zebulon Pike, who visited there in 1806, 22,000 mule loads, weighing 300 pounds each, were hauled out annually, which would mean that a 100-mule train was leaving every day and a half. This indicates a yield of ten tons of ore every day.

Elguea died in 1809, at which time his widow leased the property to Juan Oñis or Oniz, who was operating the mine, according to James Ohio Pattie, when he and his father, Silvester, came there in 1825 or '26. They acted as guards for a short time, then arranged to lease the mines for $1000 a year, or until it was confiscated by the Mexican government under an 1826 statute making it impossible for a native Spaniard, or *Gachupin,* to own property in Mexico.[6] From 1826 to 1834 the property was in the possession of Robert McKnight and his friend Steven Courcier, according to a report submitted by Rossiter W. Raymond, Commissioner of Mining Statistics, for 1870.[7]

Under the Patties, the Santa Rita mines became the headquarters for American trappers, primarily because abandoned mine shafts made excellent hiding places for illegal furs and traps. Trapper bands, returning from the Gila, could cache their beaver packs in the mines and remove only a small number at a time to sell in Santa Fe, so it wouldn't attract attention. This ruse probably didn't fool very many people but it added a nicety to the operation and kept from embarrassing Governor Narbona, who had issued numerous permits to "trade" in the area.

James Baird, a member of the McKnight expedition of 1812, had also returned to Mexico and he too became a citizen of Chihuahua. He knew of this subterfuge, and opened a letter-writing campaign to keep his former colleagues from the United States from trapping in Mexican territory. Baird wrote to Alejandro Ramirez, prefect of the District Bravo (of the general region of El Paso del Norte):[8]

I have learned that with scandal and contempt for the Mexican nation a hundred-odd Anglo-Americans have introduced themselves in a body to hunt beaver in the possessions of this state and that of Sonora to which the Rio Grande belongs, and with such arrogance and hautiness that they have openly said in spite of the Mexicans, they will hunt beaver wherever they please . . . I beg that your excellency may make such provisions as you may deem proper, to the end that the national laws may be respected and that foreigners may be confined to the limits which the same laws permit them, and that we Mexicans may peacefully profit by the goods with which the merciful God has been pleased to enrich our soil.

Baird's complaint didn't stop or reduce the illegal trapping by Americans, but it brought pressure on Governor Narbona to enforce the law. Not long after that Narbona instituted a policy of confiscating contraband beaver, which made the Santa Rita copper mines a more popular hangout for American trappers than they had been before.

Exactly who owned and operated the Santa Rita mines during this time is somewhat obscure. James Ohio Pattie claims he and his father came there in April 1825 and took the mines over, but Dale L. Morgan and others contend the Patties didn't arrive in New Mexico until late in 1825, which makes it impossible for them to have operated the mine at all that year. R. W. Raymond, in his widely accepted mining statistics, claims McKnight and Courcier (see note 7, this chapter) took over Santa Rita in 1826, which would leave the Patties hardly any time at all to operate the concession. Testimony of those in the area at the time has Kirker himself active in its operation when the Patties were supposed to be there. One of these was Jonathan Trumbull Warner, who later changed his name to Juan José Warner and became a famous California pioneer, who said in a written reminiscence:

"In the fall of 1827, Nathaniel Pryor, an American, who with James Kirker, had been working the Santa Rita Copper Mine in the then northern part of Chihuahua, associated himself with Jesse Furgerson, Richard Loughlin, George Yount, Slover, Pattie and son, J. O. Pattie, and William Pope started out from the copper mines which were near the southeast course of the Gila river and trapped that river . . ." Warner here names Pryor and Kirker as working the mines but doesn't mention the Patties as engaged in this occupation.[9]

Stephen C. Foster, an early mayor of Los Angeles and New Mexico trapper, says much the same thing except he implies that Pryor, Kirker and the Patties all owned the mine: "In 1827 . . . the Patys [sic] Richard Laughlin, James Kirker . . . and others . . . were ousted from possession by Robert McKnight . . ."[10]

Foster indicates here that Kirker and others were operating the mine until they "denounced" it, with the Patties being only two of many who were in on the operation. Foster also said in the same article that Robert McKnight took possession of the mining property when the others left and it would seem logical that Jim Kirker interested McKnight and Courcier, who were by this time Mexican citizens, to take over the operation.

The trapping expedition referred to by Warner and Foster is described in considerable detail by its leader, Yount, who subsequently published *Chronicles of the West,* relating many of the incidents that occurred during the excursion.[11] After the Patties and others split off from Yount and Kirker's second trapping expedition the elder Pattie died in California, while his son returned to Cincinnati to relate his adventures to Timothy Flint, a writer and former resident of St. Louis.

The band of trappers under Yount's leadership had a brush with Apaches and their camp was attacked by a rabid wolf which bit two of their dogs. A few days later, just as the men were entering a Pima village, the two dogs showed signs of the disease and were destroyed.

Initially the Pimas were friendly but later attempted to restrict the movements of the trappers. Kirker and the others learned that the Pimas had murdered a party of sixteen Missourians under Michel Robidoux the year previous and were afraid the trappers would uncover evidence of the massacre and seek revenge. The trappers did find the bodies of their murdered compatriots and gave them Christian burial. Certain now that they faced punitive retribution, the Pimas attacked immediately.

The thirty-two trappers got behind trees and beat back the attack without any injury to themselves but the Pimas suffered heavy losses, their primitive weapons being no match for the rifles in the hands of experts. They retreated in disorder and returned the next day begging for peace. The trappers then proceeded up the Gila, the first time Kirker ever had been in the area destined to be his hunting and trapping grounds for the next decade. Here they found black beaver, the highest quality and most valuable of that kind of fur, in abundance. After trapping most of the available beaver they hollowed out cotton-wood logs and ascended the Colorado River to the Mohave villages.

The "Mohavies," as Yount called them, were so fascinated with the trappers's clothing that the men were able to trade strips of material ripped from their garments to the nude Indians for vegetables.

These Indians, too, decided they would attack the trappers in force but the Missourians got wind of it and gathered around the campfire for a council of war. The men, seated on logs, determined that at the first arrow shot at them they would pick the Indians off with their rifles.

Soon enough an arrow zipped into a log one of the trappers was sitting on, grazing his testicles and drawing blood. The injured man leaped into the air, clutching his crotch with both hands, and screamed:

"Fellows! The foe, the foe! I have his arrow sheathed below!"

(At least that is what Clark said Yount said the poor man said.) Everyone took to a tree and added to the shouting of the almost-unmanned trapper, a maneuver that confounded the Indians.

"Had we kept quiet," explained Yount, "they would have been upon us in a moment, and probably few of us would have survived an hour. But our replying cheerily [to the Indians' war-whoop] inflicted on them the very feeling their own yell was intended to inflict on us." Ten of the Indians were downed and the rest of them fled. The trappers then headed for home.

An incident occurred a short time after this which may be the origin of the story of the Lost Peg-leg Mine. Thomas Long Smith, who the following year had a leg amputated and acquired the name of Peg-leg, was with the Yount and Kirker party. On the way back, about one and a half days' march from the head of the Colorado, the trappers ran onto a ravine full of a heavy substance they thought might be gold.

"One of the party," said Yount, "gathered several pounds and brought it into camp. All deemed it a species of copper."

The story has been told around a thousand campfires in the century or so since the event. Later, Peg-leg Smith credited the find to "Dutch George," presumably Yount.

Food interested the party more than gold, however. They were close to starving and stayed alive only by eating their pack animals. They finally were received hospitably by the Zuni Indians, who "shewed them no little kindness, nursing both them and their animals."

Finally Yount and his men beat their way back to Taos, only to have their furs confiscated, or rather, according to Yount, "appropriated by his Excellency to his own private benefit." Kirker of course lost his beaver, too.

Yount and some of his men operated an illicit still near Taos until they got another small stake together, then began organizing another trapping party. This time they planned to hide their catch before reaching Taos, or Santa Fe.

Much the same group of men, including Kirker, got their traps together and went hunting beaver again. Once more they started from the Santa Rita mines and it wasn't long until they were in the land of the Pimas and the Maricopas. This time the Indians treated them with more respect, but when the Indians grew peaceful, the trappers started fighting among themselves. The Patties and six others in the party became what Yount described as "insubordinate" and left. The catch was divided up and the Pattie contingent took off with theirs for California, where they thought they could get higher prices. These eight were the two Patties, Nathaniel Pryor, Richard Laughlin, Jesse Ferguson, Issac Slover, William Pope and Edmund Russell.[12] Jim Kirker elected to remain with Yount and the others, probably because his friends—McKnight, Courcier and others—had established themselves in New Mexico and Kirker wished to be near them.

The Mohave Indians, defeated by the trappers the year before, had decided to use guile in place of frontal attack. As the white men approached Mohave territory, they were met by

Gabriel Allen, an old Mountain Man and Indian-fighter with Jim Kirker's small army. Gabe, as he was called, also served in Doniphan's army with Kirker.

a chief of this band, one they had never seen before. He called himself Cargas Muchachas. *Cargas* means in Spanish a great plenty, an abundance, and *muchachas* means girls, so the chief's alleged name would translate into An Abundance of Girls, or perhaps A Bunch of Broads. It should have tipped off the men that all was not kosher but nobody seemed to question his strange appellation.

Cargas Muchachas told them a story about a beautiful squaw his tribe had captured from a party of white trappers, said to have been the mistress of William Sublette. Cargas Muchachas described her as so beautiful that any man who set eyes on her would immediately be consumed with passion and carnal desire. What was more important, the old chief slyly confided, the squaw really liked it. She didn't disappoint. She was a red-skinned nymphomaniac who delivered the goods with a fury; ordinary Indian bucks were not capable of cooling her ardor. He urged the trappers to come and try to quench the demonic fires that raged within her.

This sort of call for help seldom goes ignored, especially if those called have spent the last several months along lonely streams trapping for beaver. Even George Yount confessed that he got so worked up at the proposal that he resigned the leadership of the expedition because he simply couldn't trust himself to make sane and proper decisions under such erotic circumstances. He suggested that the men elect a new leader with the stipulation that they would follow his orders without question. Gabe Allen, somewhat older than the rest, was chosen. His decision was a compromise: they should go to the chief's village and have a look at this frontier sexpot but at the same time provide themselves with additional armament in the event something went wrong. They all cut and made themselves lances from saplings; they also carved clubs from heavier timber. Yount explained that they went forward in all speed:[13]

> Passion strove to blind the trappers to the threatening danger—the captive squaw, now almost in their embrace, possessed charms almost paramount to every consideration . . . These men of the Wilderness were not singular. We have all need of a Helen and a Cleopatra.

A few miles farther, though, an event took place which forced Kirker and the others to harbor some doubts about the old chief's story and about his true design. Jim, as well as most of the other men, had been over the territory the year before and they all knew there was a fine lake nearby. They suggested to Cargas Muchachas that their canteens were getting low and that it might be a good idea to fill them with water. The wily old chief replied that there was no water near. He didn't realize they knew better, that they had spent two days the year before on the shore of a lake "within a mile or two of the place where they were." Yount said they all remembered the lake "was of the purest water, abounding with trout."[14] The chief confidently assured them that the closest water was at his village, then he rode ahead, telling them he was going to prepare for their reception. By this time they didn't doubt that in the slightest, although there was some question as to what sort of reception it would be. They went to the lake, filled their canteens and held another council of war.

"My orders are," said Gabe, "that we begin the march for home. We've got plenty of beaver. Let's leave these equivocal Mahuvies at once. The feast they propose is likely to cost us more than it can possibly be worth to us, even though they act in good faith. And as for the prisoner, the squaw they talk of, it is quite doubtful to my mind whether they have now, or ever had one. Should it prove they entertain evil against us, we may be an overmatch for them, but at least we will be subjected to much inconvenience, lose some of our beaver, and perhaps our animals also, and we shall gain absolutely nothing. We shall, therefore, at an early hour tomorrow morning, resume our march, not for the Mahuvies, but for Taos, in New Mexico."[15]

Jim noticed that there were still a few who would be willing to gamble their beaver, and their lives, for a go at the red-hot squaw, but "all repacked at dawn and pressed on their way."

They were on the trail only a short time when they were overtaken by Chief "Heap of Girls" on his spotted pony.

*"Hombres!"* yelled the disappointed chief, *"que paso?"* "Men, what are you doing?"

Julian Workman raised his rifle, cocked it and was ready to shoot the chief out of the saddle, when Yount deflected Workman's gun upward. Yount said he would go down the trail and have a talk with the chief, that shooting him would accomplish nothing but bring on more trouble for all of them.

Yount rode to the chief and explained to him the reason

they were heading home, that it was because the chief had turned out to be a liar.

"Go home," said Yount, "and take care of that captive squaw yourself." He then whirled his horse and trotted back to the rest of the men. He said he was shaking "like an aspen leaf" as he realized the "captive squaw would have doomed them all."[16]

The trappers came upon a Hopi village a few days later where they were treated hospitably and with great kindness.

"Our animals were led off to pasture," said Yount, "and the families vied with each other in bringing into our apartment food and luxuries. We were feasted daily." After a few days of rest and recuperation, the men moved on.

Recalling how their furs were confiscated by Governor Narbona when they returned the year before, most of the men cached their furs near the Jemez River, but Jim took his on down south to the mine shafts. He brought them out only a few at a time, so as not to arouse suspicion.[17]

As it turned out, the furs cached on the Jemez River were discovered by Narbona's agents and confiscated anyway.

## NOTES TO CHAPTER IX

1. T. A. Rickard, "The Chino Enterprise, History of the Region and the Beginning of Mining at Santa Rita," *Engineering and Mining Journal-Press*, Vol. 116, No. 18, Nov. 3, 1923.

2. Santa Rita is the patron saint of stray lambs, or humans, and *cobre* is Spanish for copper.

3. *Ibid.*, p. 758.

4. *Ibid.*, p. 754.

5. Parts of the old fort were intact until a few years ago, when Chino Mines Division of Kennecott Copper Corporation, had it torn down. Many of the old adobes and some of the old equipment is stored near the site.

6. *Ibid.*, p. 756.

7. *Ibid.*, p. 756, citing "Statistics of Mines and Mining in the States and Territories West of the Rocky Mountains," p. 403.

8. Archivo de Gobernacio, Mexico City, Comercio, Expediente 44, cited by Thomas M. Marshall, "St. Vrain's Expedition to the Gila in 1826," *Southwest Historical* Quarterly, XIX (Jan. 1916).

9. J. J. Warner, "Reminiscences of Early California," *Annual Publication,* Historical Society of Southern California, 1907–8, p. 183.

10. Stephen C. Foster, "A Sketch of the Earliest Kentucky Pioneers of Los Angeles," *Annual,* Historical Society of Southern California, Vol. 1, part 3, 1887, p. 30.

11. The best account of Yount's adventures in a single volume is in *George C. Yount and His Chronicles of the West,* comprising extracts from his "memoirs" and the Rev. Orange Clark "Narrative," edited by Charles L. Camp, Old West, Denver, 1966.

12. *Yount's Narrative,* Editor Camp's note 11, p. 253.

13. Yount's *Chronicles,* p. 52.

14. *Ibid.*

15. *Ibid.,* pp. 52-53.

16. *Ibid.,* p. 54.

17. Rafael Kirker, Jim's grandson, living still near the Santa Rita mine, at Fort Bayard, N.M., described this method used by Kirker not only to hide furs, but gold and jewelry, in an interview with the author in 1962.

# CHAPTER X

WITH little to show for two years of trapping, Jim Kirker decided to combine fur-hunting expeditions and employment at the Santa Rita mines with his old friends Robert McKnight and Stephen Courcier. They may have given him a minor interest in the mining enterprise, for he made the Santa Rita his business headquarters from 1828 to 1836, the eight years during which it was under production for McKnight and Courcier. During this period Courcier alone is reported to have "cleared from it in seven years about a half million dollars."[1] Jim made nothing approaching this amount, of course, but his association must have been lucrative: there is evidence that he had resources of several thousand dollars with which to pay his trappers. During one period of a few months, Jim paid eighteen men working for him over $5000 for "catching beaver," according to a sworn statement by Kirker.[2]

In about 1832 Jim established his residence at Janos, an ancient village and presidio in northern Chihuahua. During the summer he supervised the guarding of mines and mule trains of ore from Santa Rita to the smelters at Corralitos, Barranca and Chihuahua City. The path along which these trains passed became known as the Copper Trail, and led southwest from Santa Rita, following the waterholes, down the east side of a

Old mission church at Janos. Bells at right were brought from Spain, and are more than six hundred years old.

small range of mountains known as the Burros, then passed between two of the tallest peaks in that part of the southwest, the Big Hatchet and the Animas, both of which jut into the sky at least a mile and a half above sea level. The trail continued south to Janos, a decaying town even in those days (Janos is more than 100 years older than Chihuahua City, and is said to have been established by Coronado). Located midway between Chihuahua City and the Santa Rita mines, Janos had an abundance of water and pack trains usually stopped off there to recruit both men and animals.

From Janos the trail led to Corralitos, where Robert McKnight had constructed several smelter furnaces, the remains of which may be seen today. Charcoal was manufactured for the furnaces at Barrancas, a village built on the Casas Grandes river by McKnight to exploit an abundant grove of cottonwoods from which the charcoal was made. The next stop was Casas Grandes, which was adjacent to elaborate ruins, a

Remnants of the smelter on the Hacienda Corralitos, a few miles north of Casas Grandes, Chihuahua.

Corralitos Hacienda appears not much different today than in the days when Jim Kirker and his family lived there. Once the home of some fifteen hundred residents during the halcyon mining days, the Hacienda is now owned by Bill Wallace, who lives there with his family and about a dozen ranch hands.

Center Street in the Hacienda Corralitos, one-time home of James Kirker and his family, later owned by J. P. Morgan interests, and now the headquarters for Bill Wallace's ranch.

one-time home of the pre-Columbian tribe of Paquime Indians, who lived in three- and four-story apartment houses, equipped with running water and air-conditioning, surpassing even the fabulous Seven Cities of Cibola. After passing through Galeana, where McKnight had lived during most of his ten years' imprisonment in Mexico, the Copper Trail then wandered on into San Buenaventura, where Captain Mariano Ponce, the commandant, was a close friend of Kirker's. From this tiny town, the trail angled south through Encinillas to Hacienda Sacramento and finally to Chihuahua City. This trail "was plainly to be seen as late as 1885."[3]

This trail cut like a jagged scar through the very heart of Apache country and it was over this run that Kirker was responsible for protecting ore trains from Apache attack. Protecting anything from Apache attack in that part of the country was a feat nobody had ever before accomplished.

The Apaches originated in Canada, where they were known as Inne, and were of the Athapascan linguistic family. They came down from the north, venturing as far east as western Kansas, into Oklahoma and the Texas Panhandle, but were pushed back south and west by the Comanches and Kiowas in the late seventeenth century. Thereafter they remained in southern Colorado, New Mexico, eastern Arizona, and Sonora and Chihuahua. One small band, the Lipanes, roamed the border between Piedras Negras and Eagle Pass, Texas.

The word Apache is said to come from *Apachu,* Zuni for enemy, and apparently the Apaches had no other name for their whole tribal group, although the Navajo, related to the Apaches, referred to themselves as *Dineh,* meaning The People.[4] Warfare was the Apaches' trade, forming the basis of the economy of these hardy Indians, which makes it of considerable curious interest that the Pimas and Maricopas consistently defeated the Apaches in combat. Against the white man, however, the Apaches were supreme. They were successful in battle because they rarely fought frontal engagements or took on well armed or superior forces. They invariably ascertained the enemy's strength and condition through a system of lookouts maintained in the heights.[5]

The Apaches were superb at the art of camouflage, melting in and out of the desert scene like so many mirages, and they were highly mobile. The young were taught to recognize every hill or mountain from every angle and at all hours of the day or night. If an Apache was on his way some place and didn't cover fifty miles a day he was loafing; he could consistently make seventy and had hardly any problem with logistics. Apaches carried a concentrated food, called in Spanish *piñole,* in a pouch at their waist. Made of ground and flavored corn, it provided a nourishing meal on the run when mixed with a little water in the palm of the hand.

In addition to speed, the Apaches possessed another quality which was of supreme value in combat. When a war party was defeated its members would disperse in all directions, like quail, and would reassemble, like quail, when the danger was past.

Their tactics in raids were brilliant. An attack force would travel together until within a mile or two of an objective, when they would split up into small bands, having previously agreed on a site at which to rendezvous when the engagement was completed. They would then stage a series of lightning stabs, striking here and there, robbing when the opportunity offered. Stolen stock they shuttled immediately into a holding corral, somewhere in the rear.

Beleaguered defenders were never offered an opportunity to strike at the main body nor to venture too far in any direction. When the Apaches had accomplished their mission, they would split into still smaller parties and flee in all directions at once. They might proceed for miles in one direction away from their final destination and then when they were sure there wasn't anybody on their trail they would swing about and head for the rendezvous point. There they would divide up the loot, dance and carry on a feast lasting several days, which could become very lively if liquor happened to be in the booty.

The Apaches actually *harvested* the Mexican pueblas in northern Mexico, rather than making helter-skelter raids.[6] They took much of the food and material possessions of a village but always left enough so that the residents would not become completely discouraged and abandon their homes. In this way they kept the towns producing crops of wealth so that future raids would be profitable.

By 1770, Apaches had made things so miserable for the Mexicans on the frontier that the Marques de Rubi developed a plan for organizing a series of fifteen presidios, stretching from the Gulf of Mexico to the western part of Sonora. Each was assigned a captain, a lieutenant, a chaplain, a sergeant, two corporals and forty men, with ten Indian scouts.

These presidios were spaced about 100 miles apart and a Spanish soldier, General Don Hugo Oconor, was named to carry out the plan. For five years General Oconor worked at building the presidios and finally, in the summer of 1775, gathered an army of some 2500 volunteers and regular soldiers to sweep the states of Sonora and Chihuahua free of Apaches.

Oconor met and defeated the Apaches in fifteen battles, killing 104 and recapturing about 2000 head of stolen stock. He again took up operations in 1776, but could locate only enough Apaches for five battles, in which he killed twenty-seven Indians and captured eighteen. After two seasons of grueling combat Oconor was so exhausted that he was relieved of his command by Don Teodoro de Croix. Not so able, de Croix still managed to surprise a large band of Apaches during a raid on Janos October 12, 1777 and defeated them. He offered terms of peace based on their giving up their warlike existence, laying down their arms and moving into Janos with their families. It was like asking Pentagon brass to start farming. It didn't work.

At about this time Don Juan Bautista de Anza was beginning a two-year term as governor of New Mexico. At de Croix's suggestion they joined in a plan aimed at the total destruction of the Apache tribes, based largely upon building roads through the Apache heartland. De Ansa began his road-building expedition in November, 1780, but when he got near Apache country, his nerve failed him and he only skirted the edge, giving the Apaches a chance to laugh and relax. There was nothing for them to laugh at a half-dozen years later, though, when in April and May of 1786 Felipe de Neve drove them back into the wilderness, killing sixty-eight and capturing eleven in a single battle.

The Apaches lurked in the fastness for as long as de Anza was governor because he had made an effective agreement with the Navajos to help keep their Athapascan brothers, the Apaches, away from civilized areas and confined to the wilderness. When de Anza resigned the governorship, though, the whole fabric of containment fell apart and the Apaches returned. After that nobody had been able to do a thing with them. The Mexicans and the ruling Spanish were engaged in the long struggle that resulted in Mexican independence. The situation was not lost on the Indians. As military resistance to them crumbled on the frontier, they grew bolder. They were able to plunder Sonora and Chihuahua almost at will from 1813 until Kirker arrived.

The Spanish used the generic term *Apache* to designate at least eleven different bands of Indians (Tontos, Chiricahuas, Gilenos, Mimbrenos, Taracones, Mescaleros, Llaneros, Lipanes, Navajos, Jicarillos and Coyoteros). Geographically they were divided in four main branches:

The *Jicarillos* held southern Colorado and any area in northern New Mexico not occupied by Mescaleros.

The *Mescaleros* spread over the northeastern part of New Mexico, as far east as Hondo, north of Santa Fe, west to the Rio Grande, and as far south as the Texas Panhandle.

The *Western Apaches,* which included the Coyoteros, Tontos, Cibeque and San Carlos bands, roamed over all of what is now the San Carlos and White Mountain reservations, and as far west in Arizona as they could without having to fight the Pimas and Maricopas.

The *Chiricahuas,* closely allied with the Mimbrenos and Gilenos, were bounded on the east by the Rio Grande, on the north by the City in the Sky, called Acoma, on the west by today's eastern boundaries of the San Carlos and White Mountain reservations, and including Sonora and Chihuahua.[7]

Kirker recognized early that if he were to defend the Santa Rita operation in its entirety it would not be by force but by guile. He led trapping parties each winter back into the Apache strongholds and he became acquainted with important Apache leaders, including one known as Juan José Compa, who had been educated in Spanish Mission schools and could read and write. Kirker and Juan José were close friends and worked together to their mutual benefit.[8] Jim understood human nature enough in general and Indian nature in particular to know that the more he could help the Apaches the more they would be inclined to help him, so he began brokering their goods and livestock stolen by the Apaches from the Mexican settlements in Sonora and Chihuahua, arranging to drive mules and horses across Texas to Louisiana markets for sale.[9]

Kirker was known throughout the southwest within a short time as Don Santiago Querque. Santiago is the Spanish equivalent of James and the patron saint of Spain; Jim's last name was so spelled because there is no "k" in the Spanish alphabet.

Jim usually spent the late spring and summer guarding the copper mines and trail, but this gave him enough time for periodic visits to El Paso del Norte (today's Juarez) for brief respites and entertainment. For Jim this consisted mostly of gambling and drinking the excellent brandy and wine produced in that valley. It was during one of these short vacations that he met one of the most beautiful women in Chihuahua, Rita Garcia. They were soon married. Ben Wilson, Kirker's onetime employee who was to become the grandfather of World War II General George S. Patton, Jr., wrote that Jim "was married to a Mexican lady in El Paso, Chihuahua. She was handsome and a fine woman, whom I saw many times."[10]

No church records of Kirker's wedding to Rita Garcia have been found but it probably took place in the Church of Guadalupe in El Paso del Norte (Juarez) in about 1831, which made it bigamous as far as Jim was concerned. That same year, however, his wife Catharine listed herself as *widow* in the New York City Directory.

The year 1831 was marked also by a fresh and violent outbreak of Apaches, as well as by a revolt among the Opatas, Yaquis and Seris. On May 5, 1831, José Joaquin Calvo, a native of Cuba and a colonel in the Mexican army since the days of Iturbide, was made governor general of the state of Chihuahua and the territory of New Mexico, with special orders from the Secretary of War to bring the Apaches to heel. Calvo was successful only in making a shaky peace treaty, dictated by the Apaches.

The torreon, or fort, at the corner of the old wall surrounding Janos, Chihuahua, where Jim kept his family at first while he was out chasing Apaches.

It was probably in the first year of his marriage that Jim established his home in Janos, the village located about midway along the Copper Trail which allowed him to spend more time with his family, as well as placing him in a more central location to combat the Apache menace. There, on August 22, 1833, his bride bore him their first child, a daughter, whom they named Petra.[11]

Meanwhile, Santiago Querque had become an influential figure among the Apaches. They had made him a war chief, an honor, no doubt, but one which was to bring him more trouble than advantage.[12]

At this moment, however, his problem was recruiting trappers and helpers, so in the fall of 1833, after the birth of Petra, Jim went to Santa Fe on a trip designed to lure young men to work with him. One of those agreeing to throw in with him was Benjamin David Wilson, a native of Nashville, Tennessee, who had only just arrived in New Mexico, completely broke and looking for an opportunity. It was probably at this time, too, that another Tennessean, a half-breed Cherokee named Pauline Weaver, joined forces with Jim.[13]

Another hunter and frontiersman with Jim was from one of the first families of St. Louis, Francisco Ortiz, as the Mexican legal secretaries spelled his name; in St. Louis it was usually spelled "Hortiz," for a reason now obscure. Frank Ortiz, or Hortiz, was the second son of Joseph Alvarez Hortiz, born in Lienira, Estramadura, Spain, in 1753, who came to St. Louis as a young Army officer with the first Spaniards. One of the best educated people in St. Louis, the elder Hortiz was secretary to both governors Trudeau and Delassus, uncle of Ceran St. Vrain.[14] Francisco was somewhat older than Jim; little more is known about him than that.

Colonel Calvo, meanwhile, having been appointed governor of Chihuahua and commandant general for the territory of New Mexico, began shoring up his defenses against the Apaches. He dispatched Captain Cayetano Justiniani to the Santa Rita mines to reconstruct the triangular fort, strengthening the towers, or torreons, at two points of the triangle. The captain, under the nominal command of Ponce at San Buenaventura, was given a small garrison of troops and it was hoped their presence would deter the Apaches.

When Jim returned from a successful trapping trip of approximately eighteen months in the late spring of 1835, he re-examined his guard for the Santa Rita mine and mule trains, working with these defenses for the balance of the summer. On October 17, 1835 he was granted a permit by Governor Albino Perez to hunt and trap in Apache country. The permit, written in Spanish read:[15]

> By these presents I [Governor Perez] grant ample license to the naturalized Irishman in the Republic of Mexico, Don Santiago Kirke [sic] can practice the catching of beaver with the company of five Mexican servants with him.

The same Kirke is responsible to make faithful use of this
license for the term of six months without the benefit and
profit of no other foreigners who might take advantage of
a privilege reserved only for our nationals. The said Kirke
is responsible for any infidelity concerning this permit.
Signed Sante Fe, October 17, 1835.

There was an accompanying instruction, also signed by
Governor Perez, allowing Jim to take with him a total of eighteen "servants," Mexican and naturalized, and for the entire
group Governor Perez specified safe conduct in a letter addressed to whom it might concern:[16]

> . . . to give free and safe passport with his servants to any
> points of the nation, convenient to his own business and
> commerce, so that he may not be molested by either civil
> or military authorities in the territory under my command
> and I beg and ask all others to give him the necessary help,
> as long as he pays a just price for such help. Signed by
> Governor Perez at Santa Fe, October 17, 1835.

With a permit and letter of safe conduct Jim was finally
operating under a proper license to trade and trap among the
Apaches, or any other Indians within the command of Don
Albino Perez, and was—probably for the first time—conduct-
ing this business legally. The situation must have given him an
additional sense of obligation to the government. During the
winter trapping expedition Jim sat in on a war council of
Coyotero Apaches, Utes and Navajos and heard them plan a
mammoth attack against Sonora—most specifically the presidio at Bavispe—in June, 1836 with a force of 1400 Indians. This
marked the first time any tribes had planned mass warfare
against the Mexican army and the dimensions of the threat
moved Jim to relay this intelligence to Captain Justiniani on or
just before March 20, 1836, thus giving the army some three
months' warning and time to send messengers and assistance to
the sister state of Sonora to ward off the invasion.

After getting the details of the Indians' plan from Kirker Justiniani dispatched a letter to Governor Calvo, outlining the plot against Sonora. Meanwhile Jim went back to his trapping headquarters in what is now northern Arizona and New Mexico. Calvo's reaction was surprising. Instead of thanking Kirker for the information he blamed Jim for the threat and seemed to suspect him of cooking up the whole affair. Calvo's reply to Justiniani stated:[17]

> Your official note, No. 27, of March 20 past, has informed me that Don Santiago Kerker, naturalized Irishman in this Republic, at his beaver hunting headquarters, has stated that the Coyotero Indians, Navajos and Utes were preparing a campaign of 1,400 warriors in order to attack the presidio of Bavispe and other points in the Department of Sonora next June. It is very possible that all or part of the said campaign is also directed against this department [Chihuahua] so the information is interesting in that there may be preparations to resist it; but it is very well known that Don Santiago Kerker, without previous license of this government, has been engaged in the beaver trade contrary to the laws, and also that he has been treating with the enemy, when it may be necessary, so that they do not cause him damage, that he win them over with presents of gunpowder and other articles of war. For all of this danger, you will carry out a confidential investigation of which you will send me an account, and if it would result that the said Kerker is guilty, you will send him as a prisoner to this [Chihuahua Commandancia] so that he may be judged as proper. God and liberty. Chihuahua, April 19, 1836.
>
> Jose Joaquin Calvo,
> Senior Commandant,
> Western Frontier

The penalty for the crime of which Jim was accused was death, under a code newly passed by the Chihuahua legislature at the behest of Calvo, one part of which read: " . . . *prohibio baja pena de muerte el trafico comercial entre los inhabitantes del Estada y los Apaches sublevados.*" [Commercial traffic between citizens of Chihuahua and the rebelling Apaches is prohibited under punishment of death.]

After receiving this surprising reply from Calvo, Captain Justiniani must have conferred with Captain Ponce at San Buenaventura, Justiniani's immediate superior in chain of command. Ponce, who had seen the permit and letter of safe conduct before Jim and his trapping party departed, knew that his expedition was legal in every respect and because of his long friendship with Kirker he somehow got himself placed in command of the "investigation" and pursuit of Kirker. There is no evidence that any report was ever made as a result. Interestingly, Jim's license was issued by Governor Perez, nominally a cavalry officer of the regular Mexican Army appointed governor of New Mexico Territory, which had been so gerrymandered as to not include Santa Rita. Perez was also in trouble elsewhere because of reforms he instituted in education and taxation. The result was that ultimately, at Calvo's instigation, Perez had Jim declared an outlaw, with a price of $800 on his head.[18]

Jim meanwhile, knowing nothing of this intrigue against him, continued with his men, trapping in the wilderness until his license to do so had expired, then loaded some fifteen packs of beaver skins, containing seventy pelts each, making a total of 1050, which Jim estimated at a value of $10 apiece.[19] The skins and equipment were loaded on 176 mules accompanying the party and, with eight breeding burros, they began their trek out of the wilderness, bearing a small fortune.

"With this produce of my expedition," Jim later wrote,[20] "I was about proceeding to the United States to dispose of it when upon entering the settlements of New Mexico between Zuna [sic] and Laguna [a few miles south of today's Grants, N.M.] the Navahoe and Zuna Indians robbed me of 176 [mules] and 8 burros and on applying to the authorities for assistance to recover them, I was informed much to my astonishment and consternation that the Governor of New Mexico, Colonel Albino Perez, had declared me an Outlaw under the pretext that I was trading with the Indians notwithstanding that he himself had given me the permission to do so and the limits of which permission I did not exceed either in hunting or trading."

It was probably fortunate that Jim's friend, Ponce, was in charge of the detachment of Mexican cavalry to whom he applied for succor. Ponce did not place him under arrest but allowed him to make a run for it to Bent's Fort, in Colorado, which was then considered a part of the United States.

"In consequence of this intelligence and knowing from good authority that troops were in pursuit of me with orders from the governor to shoot me wheresoever they might take me, I was forced to abandon my property and make my escape alone in a state of utter destitution . . . "[21]

Apparently, however, he was not completely alone. Pauline Weaver, in a sworn statement forwarded to the Consul Mackintosh later, said, "It is true that he [Weaver] was in the Department of New Mexico with Don Santiago Kirker and that he accompanied him to the U.S. when he [Kirker] became a fugitive of the Government of New Mexico."[22]

Piecing all of this together, Jim lost 176 mules, eight burros and 1050 beaver skins to a party of Zuñi and Navajo Indians, who no doubt slipped in by night and stole off with them, as there is no mention of a fight. When Jim rode to the nearest point for military assistance he encountered Ponce, who informed him there was a price on his head and that he had better clear out of New Mexico. Meanwhile, Ponce and perhaps other Mexican army units took up the pursuit of the Indians and apparently recaptured much of the stolen furs and mules while Jim and Weaver were fleeing into Colorado.

Jim, when he found out about this later, was of the opinion that his whole trouble was caused by Perez' desire to take for himself the skins, mules and burros, valued at $32,900:[23]

> Though feeling the greatest reluctance to assert any thing
> so degrading to the character of so high a public function-

ary as the governor of New Mexico, yet I am bound to state
that it is my firm conviction that the only motive for the
persecutions with which he was pleased to visit me latterly
was the hope of obtaining for himself the whole or part of
the produce of my expedition with the value of which he
was well acquainted, and that part of it did fall into his
hands and was disposed of by him I well know.

Jim produced sworn statements from Mariano Maciera, a
Scotchman named James Glenday, Tomas Valencia (a hat
maker by trade), Jose Maria Melendres (a wool weaver), Jose
Dolores Madrid, and even Captain Mariano Ponce, that Perez
finally obtained Kirker's goods and used them for his personal
profit. Glenday further swore that he saw Kirker's beaver pelts
"being sold in the U.S. with the mark of Kirker without his
authorization or having received any pay for them."[24]

Jim must have reached Bent's Fort around the first of
August, about the time that Nathaniel C. Wyeth, who had also
suffered some bad luck in a trading and trapping expedition to
the Columbia River, was visiting there. Wyeth was being feted
and consoled by the Bent proprietors while they discouraged
him from getting into the freighting business. After all, that was
the Bents' main business and they didn't want any more compe-
tition.[25]

After Wyeth left, Jim stayed on at the Fort with Pauline
Weaver, nursing a tremendous grudge against Indians generally
and Governor Perez specifically, a grudge which grew into a
hate and certainly bode no good for either. It was also during
these long winter months that Kirker met a new friend, a
Shawnee Indian named Spybuck, who was to serve Jim well as
a tool in the task of wreaking vengeance on his enemies.

## NOTES TO CHAPTER X

    1. Dr. Frederick Adolphus Wislizenus, M.D., *American Journal of Science,* 1848,
cited in Rickard's "The Chino Enterprise," *Engineering and Mining Journal-Press,*
Nov. 3, 1923, p. 755.

2. This statement is contained in papers in the Public Record Office, London, Foreign Office papers FO 204/79/1 105, one of which is a deposition made before a Chihuahua City judge, dated August 18, 1842, purporting to support a claim Kirker was then advancing against the Mexican government for damages incurred by him some six years earlier. He swore he had paid 18 men the sum of one peso, or one dollar (both then worth approximately the same) per day and that up until the time the loss occurred, he had given them a total sum of $5,022. Since Kirker was attempting to enlist the aid of the British Government to help him collect the claim, this deposition reached London by way of Mexico City, where it was sent by Kirker to Consul Ewen C. Mackintosh, a brother of one of Kirker's friends in the Guadalupe y Calvo area.

3. Rickard, "Chino Enterprise," *Engineering and Mining Journal-Press,* p. 758 (quoting Edward Moulton, a famous resident of the district).

4. Gordon C. Baldwin, *The Warrior Apaches* (Tucson, Dale Stuart King, 1965) p. 21.

5. Frank C. Lockwood, *The Apache Indians* (New York, Macmillan, 1938), provides the basis for much given here on the nature and charactor of the Apaches, with certain other references taken from Alvin M. Josephy, Jr., *The Indian Heritage of America,* (New York, Knopf, 1968).

6. Apaches planned their raids carefully and selected targets with some discrimination at more-or-less permanent rendezvous points. One major Apache meeting ground for such planning was atop a small mountain west of Janos, called Carcaj, Spanish for quiver, or container for arrows, according to Bill Wallace, a Mexican national of Scotch descent who owns the Corralitos Hacienda today. Bill relates stories his grandmother told him of the days when she was a girl at the Corralitos. She told him how the Apaches would gather at Carcaj, powwow for several days, plan new raids and break camp. Their next stop would be Corralitos, where, since the days of Kirker, a certain number of cattle were always set aside for the Apaches to slaughter and eat, holding another two- or three-day dancing feast. By this thoughtfulness, the Corralitos was protected from Apache raids, as the Indians wanted to preserve it as a future haven for feasts and dancing, knowing there would always be meat and drink for them if they didn't destroy it or molest it too much.

7. Lockwood, *The Apache Indians,* pp. 7-56.

8. Benjamin David Wilson, "Observations on Early Days in California and New Mexico," *Annual Publication* of the Historical Society of Southern California, Los Angeles, 1934, pp. 74-126, David Wilson writes on pp. 77-78 that he was with a Kirker party trapping in 1833–'35 and during the time "that I was in that country, Juan Jose was frequently in our camp and had mails brought to him to read, which had been captured by his men. We thus became informed of the military movements contemplated by the Mexican government. That government would not give permission for Americans to trade or trap in their territory, we were there as interlopers, and smugglers, and would have fared badly had we fallen into the hands of their forces. Juan Jose's friendship was in every way valuable to us."

9. Kirker's involvement in fencing stolen property for the Apaches is related in a letter written by Bernardo Revilla, while the latter was acting governor of Chihuahua, to Governor and Military Commandant José Joaquin Calvo, who was in the field for a period from July 3–16, 1838. Letter dated July 11, 1838. Item #5500, Mexican archives, N.M. State Records Center, Santa Fe.

10. Wilson, "Observations," p. 77. Rita Garcia's name, never mentioned by Wilson, was turned up by Mrs. J. Paul Taylor in the Catholic Church baptismal records at Mesilla, N.M., showing that at the baptism of Maria Virginia, daughter of Sam Bean and Petra Kirker, dated July 7, 1854, the listed *abuelos paternos* (paternal grandparents) were Phantley Bean and Ana Gose, while the maternal grandparents were named as Santiago Kirker and Rita Garcia. The godparents were Santiago Lucas and Francisco Samaniego, one of the leading land-grant families of that part of the southwest.

11. Petra's birthdate is given in the second of a series of articles written by Katherine D. Stoes on the Bean family, as Kirker's daughter later became Mrs. Sam Bean. This also is the date given on her death certificate. Mrs. Stoes's articles appeared in the Las Cruces *Citizen,* February 17, 1955.

12. Captain James Hobbs, *Wild Life in the Far West,* Hartford, 1875, p. 88.

13. In a sworn statement before a Chihuahua City judge, dated August 18, 1842, Pauline Weaver, or as the Spanish wrote it, Don Pablo Guiber declared he was an American citizen who had been with Kirker for the previous six or eight years and specifically was with him in 1835 and thereafter on hunting and trapping expeditions in Apache country. This statement is contained in a 10-page deposition sent by Kirker to the British Consul in Mexico City, who forwarded it to the Foreign Office in London and is today in the archives of the Public Record Office, London, reference # FO 204/79/1 105. Weaver was born in White County, Tenn., early in 1800. His father was an Englishman, Henry Weaver, and his mother a Cherokee. He was employed by Hudson's Bay Company in 1820 and migrated to the southwest in 1830. He later became noted as able to speak several Apache dialects, no doubt learning them while with Kirker, and he is also credited with aiding early settlers of Arizona and western New Mexico by keeping the Apaches peaceful. He was for many years a guide for the U.S. Army and was a guide for Philip St. George Cooke in his march to California with the Mormon Battalion. Weaver died at Fort Lincoln, Arizona, about October 1, 1867.

14. Billion, *Annals of St. Louis,* p. 446.

15. FO 204/79/1 105, Public Records Office, London.

16. *Ibid.*

17. Calvo letter to Justiniani, #4676, Mexican Archives of New Mexico, State Records Center and Archives.

18. Kirker interview, St. Louis *Post,* July 10, 1847.

19. Letter, Kirker to British Consul Ewen Macintosh, written Guadalupe y Calvo, August 20, 1842, to Mexico City, Foreign Office records, Public Record Office, London, FO 204/19/1 105, p. 205.

20. *Ibid.*

21. *Ibid.*

22. *Ibid.*, p. 214.

23. *Ibid.*, p. 206.

24. *Ibid.*, p. 213.

25. David Lavender, *Bent's Fort* (New York, Doubleday, 1954) p. 183.

# CHAPTER XI

SPYBUCK, like most Shawnees of that day, was widely traveled. He was a member of the *Thawegila,* or Missouri, band of Shawnees[1] and had been brought as a child from Ohio to Cape Girardeau, Missouri, by his father, *Sob-be-willia,* or Growing Antlers. Spybuck was tall, powerful, light-skinned and handsome, an Indian of the type the Shawnees called *spi-to-tha,* or *hair-faced* Indian, a term applied idiomatically to halfbreeds. Spybuck was part French.[2]

James Hobbs, as a boy, crossed the plains with Spybuck, later hunted and trapped with him, and left an intimate picture of the Shawnee brave: "Spiebuck [Hobbs' spelling; the family used Spybuck] was a noble looking Indian, full six feet high, had a high forehead, Roman nose, malicious looking black eye, and was rather lighter colored than most of the Shawnees . . . He was the best shot with a rifle, at long range, I ever saw."[3]

Rufus Sage is another mountain man who encountered Spybuck and was equally impressed. Sage first met him a decade after Hobbs and he calls him "Old Spybuck, the famous Shawnee war-chief . . . covered with scars, which gave indubitable evidence of the place he occupied in the hour of danger."[4]

Spybuck, as striking as he was, however, was by no means the only unusual character working out of Bent's Fort at the time Kirker was in exile. Among the regular guests was Jim's old companion Tom (Peg-leg) Smith, who got his nickname in the fall of 1827, shortly after leaving the Yount expedition with Kirker. Smith was shot above the ankle by an Indian, the bullet shattering both bones. When he couldn't get anybody in his party to amputate his lower leg and foot he did it himself, using a butcher knife and tying off the blood vessels with buckskin thongs. By the following spring he was well enough to wear a wooden leg and carved himself one out of oak.

Jim also renewed his acquaintance with Gabe Allen, the stalwart who led Yount's men away from the Indian siren, and John W. Spencer, a native of Indiana. Spencer came from a town of the same name and was descended from an officer who served with General George Rogers Clark. Spencer was destined to join Jim in his Indian fighting, and he would later leave to help establish a fort at Presidio, Texas, where Spencer has numerous descendants today, all of whom think of themselves as Mexicans.

Jim hunted and trapped with this band over the winter of 1836–37, and meanwhile two of the bloodiest murders in the history of New Mexico were perpetrated, the results of which profoundly altered Kirker's future; indeed, he may have had a hand in one of them, for one of the killings freed Jim of his exile. The other gave him a reason to go back to New Mexico.

The death which allowed Jim to return was the assassination and beheading of Governor Perez by a mob at Sante Fe, revolting against his authority generally but specifically against his tax reforms. Perez' foes, of whom Jim Kirker certainly was one, had spread the rumor that the governor planned not only to tax the people poor but was also contemplating a stiff tariff on sexual intercourse, which of course stirred up considerable opposition.

Fanning the anti-Perez sentiment was Manuel Armijo, an ambitious politician who aspired to succeed Perez; Armijo is even thought to have directed the assassination. Many Mexicans believed that much of the Perez opposition was inspired by Kirker. At any rate Perez' execution on August 9, 1837 left the door to the governorship open to Armijo and it may be significant that one of his first acts as governor was publicly to invite Kirker to return to New Mexico.

The other murder, which had taken place four months earlier, gave Jim a good reason to do so. This was the massacre of Apache chief Juan José Compa, a close friend of Jim's and of other Americans. A sad song, a wailing ballad of poor Juan José's end, may still be heard in the outlands of Mexico, where an account of the deed is preserved orally and chanted to the sound of guitars, telling of the treachery of Juan, or John James, Johnson.[5]

The song provides a fairly accurate account of how Juan José Compa was murdered; translated almost literally, it tells this story:


> He went to the famous mountains
> Of Animas, which he approached
> One day, he who killed Juan José
> And the others in his company.
>
> He was an infidel by birth
> He became a Catholic of faith
> This false Judas and Tyrant;
> He said he was an American
> Where will his fate take him?
>
> Don Juan pretended
> He did not know where he was going
> When he found himself
> Already in the village.
>
> And Juan José, annoyed with
> His arrival, asked him
> What are you doing here,
> For there is no road?

Don Johnson told him
Thou art not a citizen
I am going to my homeland
For I am not wanted in this country

Juan José invited him to a meeting
At an appropriate place.
Americans, friends,
Do you bring powder to sell?

Don Johnson told him
I am going to my own place
I am carrying very little
And the road is long

Juan José with treachery
Offered to give him protection.
Why do thou want to go so far?
Stay thou and live with me.

Juan José Johnson told him
If you want the powder,
Give me the captive girl
You carried away from Oposura.

As Juan José wanted to trade
He gave his word quickly
To bring on an exchange
Since he didn't know what was going to happen.

Don Johnson with trickery
Said to the brave Juan José
Command the help of your people
To select the sack.

Juan Diego, his younger brother,
Not knowing to wait,
Was cut to pieces by
The stout chain from the cannon.[6]

Many different versions of the killing of Juan José have been told. A rather full report has been made available recently when a letter from Johnson to Chihuahua Governor Calvo, dated April 24, 1837, was discovered by Dr. Strickland in the *Papeles de Chihuahua.*

Janos, Chi., April 24, 1837, J. J. Johnson to Excellent Commandant General Governor of the Department of Chihuahua:

Excellent sir: On the 3d day of the present month I left Villa de Moctezuma in company with sixteen Americans and five mozos who served as drivers of the pack mules loaded with provisions to follow the enemy under permit obtained from the government of the Department of Sonora: on the 12th I left Fronteras with the persons indicated along the cattle trail which led from that place, and I wish to have the honor to show to your excellency the detail of events that took place, from the beginning to the end of the undertaking: after having searched some mountains and waterholes where we found neither Indians or herds, I followed a trail that led toward the point of the Animas Mountains and there I found four chieftains, Juan Jose Compa, his brother, Juan Diego, Marcello and Antonio Vivora, with eighty armed renegades; As I recognized the superior numbers, I delayed my attack from the 20th to 10 o'clock on the morning of the 22nd, not feeling it possible to delay for a longer time due to the acts of distrust and treason that I observed from their preparations and the failure of intelligence, I was goaded to the attack to meet face to face and overcome whatever dangers and difficulties that could be met. And as a result there were left on the field of battle twenty dead Indian renegades, including the three chiefs Marcello, Juan Jose and Juan Diego, whose scalps I have presented to the commandants of this presidio (Janos) with additionally fifteen or twenty wounded persons, according to a statement of a female captive and five Indian boys whom I left shot, not thinking it possible to carry them, since because of the liveliness of the fight which lasted more than two hours to the projection of the mountains, a fact that kept me from making a third reconnaissance exact of the field, since a third of my pack train had been lost with clothing, and the expense money for my party. At this time I take the opportunity to extend to your excellency the appreciation which I feel for the chance to render a service to the country in which I live and am a resident in company with my countrymen the proof of whose fidelity is not made today, but is repeated for all time. Juan Johnson, Benjamin Leaton, Francois Brazeau, Baptiste Mareum, Andrew Anderson, Jonas Beidles, John Wolfshead [John Reid Wolfskill], Jorge [Julian or William] Pope, Benjamin Prigmore, Laurent Mazurl, Augustine Martin, Charles Woolsey, Charles Ames, Itenzecos Anderson, William Knight, William Day, Peter McKenzie, George Ryerson.

According to Johnson's account, he and seventeen other mountain men came upon Juan José Compa and about 100 of his followers near the dry lake, or Las Playas (near today's Cloverdale, N. M., in southern Hidalgo County) and were confronted by Juan José and his people. There followed a pitched battle and Johnson overcame the enemy, killing three of the chiefs and a couple of dozen of their followers.

This is a noble face put upon a massacre—at least two other versions of the fight call it that, not counting the popular ballad of folk literature. B. D. Wilson, who claims to have been only thirty miles away when it happened, and Philip St. George Cooke, who passed the site with the Mormon Battalion about ten years after the event and heard the whole story from witnesses, both wrote their versions and they agree in all particulars of importance.[7] They tell a far different story from that reported by Johnson to the governor. They say Juan José was tricked by Johnson, who invited him and his people to enjoy a bag of *piñole*. Johnson opened a bag of the food in a clearing and when the Indians gathered around it, he fired a small cannon hidden under a stack of saddles, blankets and *aparejos*.

The shot, consisting mostly of chain, struck in the midst of the unsuspecting Indians, killing many and maiming more. Meanwhile Leaton and Johnson personally murdered Juan José some distance from the general massacre, where they had enticed him on the pretext of showing Juan José an exceptionally fine mule. The story has since become distorted, especially as to the location. Rickard said the massacre happened at Santa Rita, but this is not correct and probably was started by John C. Cremony, an interpreter with John R. Bartlett, who camped at Santa Rita during his survey of the U.S.-Mexico boundary in 1850–51. Cremony's lurid version had Johnson ordering a *fiesta* and inviting "between 900 and 1,000" Apaches; "a six-pounder gun, loaded to the muzzle with slugs, musket balls, nails and pieces of glass" was hidden under a pile of "pack saddles" while Johnson "stood ready with a lighted cigar to give the parting salute, and while all were eating . . . the terrible storm of death was spread into their ranks, killing, wounding and maiming several hundred."[9]

The Juan José massacre has been placed in various southwest locations and a few versions say the Indians were killed by poisoned pinole, rather than a hidden blunderbuss. Regardless of such details the incident led to a running fight all the way back to Oposura and within a day or two the whole Apache nation rose up and began murdering American hunters, trappers, settlers and miners.

McKnight and Courcier were forced to close the Santa Rita mines, which had been netting as much as $2000 a day, because the Apaches shut off their supply line. "The copper mines of Santa Rita were furnished by supplies from the City of Chihuahua," wrote Rickard, quoting from Herbert E. Bolton's *The Spanish Borderland,* "by guarded wagon-trains (*conductas*) that brought in provisions and hauled back ore. The time for the arrival of the train came and passed, but no train appeared. Days slipped away, provisions were almost exhausted. The supply of ammunition was nearly gone. Some of the miners climbed to the top of Ben Moore [later Cooke's

Peak], which rises back of the mines, but from its lofty summit no sign of an approaching *conducta* was visible. Starvation was imminent. The only hope of escape for the miners and their families was in making their way across the desert expanse that lies between the mines and the settlements. They started, but the Apaches, who had destroyed the train, hung about them and attacked them so persistently that only four or five succeeded in reaching their destination [Janos]."

McKnight and Courcier knew that if the Apaches were to be quieted and the mines put back in operation there was only one man who could do it—and that was Jim Kirker, in exile at Bent's Fort. A runner was sent to appeal to Jim to come to their assistance.

McKnight's messenger reached the fort about the same time as the notice of Armijo's amnesty for Kirker so Jim collected a total of twenty-two men and Spybuck, consisting mostly of Delaware and Shawnee Indians, but with a few French, English and perhaps a Hawaiian or two, plus a giant Negro named Andy. They were a tough collection of hombres.

Jim knew that no amount of wile would work this time. He couldn't even get near enough to the Apaches in authority to talk to them. With the few men he had, Jim threw a loop of warriors around an Apache village in southern New Mexico and at dawn struck so furiously as to kill fifty-five Apache braves out of a total population of about 250, while taking nine female prisoners. He captured about 400 head of stock and destroyed the village, sending one of the captives as messenger to inform the Apaches this was only a taste of what they could expect unless they stopped bothering McKnight's and Courcier's *conductas* as well as the men working the mines.

Only one of Kirker's men was killed and eight were injured. The remaining able-bodied frontiersmen drove the livestock ahead and assisted the wounded across the Black Range and into the little village of Socorro, New Mexico, about midway between El Paso and Albuquerque.

There the little army was given a wild reception to cele-

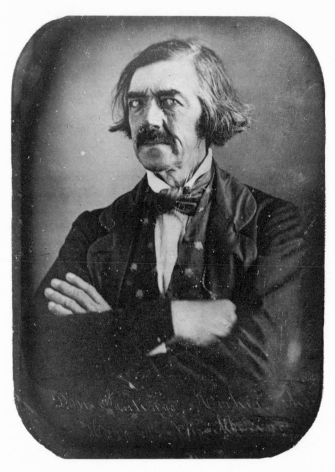

Jim Kirker, from a daguerreotype taken by T. M. Easterly at St. Louis in early July, 1847, after Jim had returned there with Doniphan's army. Scratched in the plate at the bottom, apparently by the photographer, is the inscription: "Don Santiago Kirker, the 'King of New Mexico.'" *Courtesy of the Missouri Historical Society*

brate their victory and Kirker's fame soon began to spread. From that time on he was known throughout the region as the scourge of the Apaches and was even called "The King of New Mexico" by some of the more exuberant. This title was scratched in the plate of the only daguerreotype ever made of

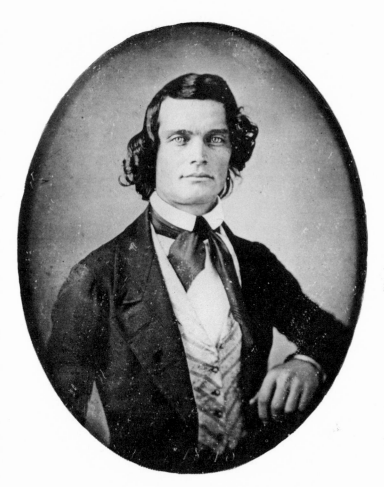

T. M. Easterly, the daguerreotypist who made Kirker's portrait, also had this likeness of himself made at about the same time. Easterly later wrote *An Emigrant's Guide to California,* which became a best-seller among those bound for the gold fields. *Courtesy of the Missouri Historical Society*

him. (Adulation, however, provided no funds and Jim's family was growing at the rate of about one child every two years. Petra was followed by James, then Rafael, Roberto and another daughter, Polinaria.)[10]

Kirker's burgeoning reputation as the only successful protector of people and property from Apache attack was embarrassing to military and civil authorities of Chihuahua, especially to Bernado Revilla, a legislator and one-time governor who owned mines at Jesus Maria, called Ocampo today. Revilla was envious, too, of the protection enjoyed by McKnight and Courcier, who were operating full blast at Santa Rita, while his own mines were shut down for fear of Indian depredations.

Revilla was acting governor of Chihuahua during Calvo's absences in the field with troops and he took advantage of one such opportunity while filling in at the governor's office to send a letter to Manuel Armijo, governor of New Mexico:[11]

> This government is certain that the Anglo-American Santiago Querque, the 14th of May last, passed Socorro (settlement of this department) for the United States with a large quantity of horses and mules together with his fellow countrymen. This individual has encouraged the Apaches in their murders and robbing and they have devastated the settlements in this department and not many days ago under his direction they attacked a convoy of carts carrying provisions to the copper mines, taking these provisions and mules that pulled them.
>
> For conduct so criminal and pernicious to the settlement, he merits a severe and exemplary punishment, and the authorities of both departments have the obligation of pursuing and apprehending this perverse man in order that he be judged accordingly to all the rigors which they provide, a penalty he justly deserves for such atrocious crimes.
>
> In this way and considering that your excellency is interested as I in obtaining the object of this communication, I hope you will be pleased to carry out the most active and opportune measure for apprehension of the said Santiago, and send him to the capital with all the securities corresponding to the ends I have indicated.
>
> With this motive, I repeat to your excellency the assurance of my highest consideration and regard. God and liberty. Chihuahua, July 11, 1838, Bernard Revilla.

At the time the letter reached Armijo, he and Kirker were already embroiled in a disagreement over the way in which the murderers of Andrew W. Daley were brought to justice. Daley had first come to Sante Fe as a freighter in 1834 but had turned to prospecting for gold, with some minor success. His body was found during the winter of 1836–37 at a small diggings near Santa Fe, murdered solely for plunder, according to Josiah Gregg, another freighter and trader. The two assassins were arrested shortly thereafter, confessing guilt.[12] However, the pair escaped punishment and within a couple of days were again running at large, looking for new victims, according to Gregg, "in violation of every principle of justice or humanity."

A group of Americans, including William Dryden, Julian (or William) Workman, William Gordon, John and Thomas Rowland, William Knight and B. D. Wilson inquired of Kirker if there wasn't something he could do to bring the culprits to justice. Kirker met with Armijo and asked the governor why the confessed killers remained at large. Armijo replied that he couldn't catch them with the scanty forces at his disposal. Kirker then formed a posse of his American friends, plus some of his Indian-fighting brigade, and in a matter of hours he had the murderers in hand and turned them over to Armijo.

·Kirker directed a memorial to Armijo, pointing out that immediate prosecution was expected and the missive was so strongly worded that the governor chose to look upon it as a "conspiracy" against him. He called out his militia, a raga-muffin lot, and formed them in the public plaza. He then pulled out the condemning letter from Revilla and acted as though he were going to place Kirker, and perhaps his companions, under arrest instead of the murderers.

Kirker replied by deploying his men as skirmishers about the plaza. They cocked rifles and advanced upon the governor's militia in front of the palace. The militia ran inside when they saw this band approaching, and in short order the governor and his troops were bottled up within. Armijo sent out a note of apology to Santiago Querque and his men, saying he was sorry they misconstrued his meaning and promised "to duly execute the law" against the murderers.

Kirker disbanded his men but it would be inaccurate to conclude that justice had been done. According to Gregg, *"the governor's due execution of the laws* [Gregg's italics] consisted of retaining [the two murderers] a year or two in nominal imprisonment, then they were set a liberty."

## NOTES TO CHAPTER XI

1. This Shawnee clan is better known today as the *Absentee* band of Shawnees, so named because the Kansas Shawnees sold land belonging to the Missouri Shawnees without either the latter's permission or knowledge.

2. Spybuck's origin and early history is supplied in an unpublished interview with Henry Spybuck by Jesse Chisholm, a field worker for the Indian-Pioneer History project, which papers are in the library of the University of Oklahoma, Phillips Collection, Vol. 17, pp. 444-46. The Shawnee clan history is from *Old Chillicothe, Shawnee and Pioneer History,* by William Albert Galloway (Xenia, Ohio, Buckeye Press, 1934).

3. Captain James Hobbs, *Wild Life in the Far West,* (St. Louis, Hartford, Wiley Waterman & Eaton, 1875) p. 19.

4. Rufus B. Sage, *His Letters and Papers, 1836–47,* LeRoy R. and Ann W. Hafen, editors, (Glendale, Clark, 1961) p. 296.

5. Johnson is variously called John James and Juan. In one letter, he signed his name officially as J. J. Johnson, and is referred to by B. D. Wilson in his memoirs as "James." It is probable the Kentuckian was named John James Johnson. He came to Moctezuma, or San Miguel de Oposura, as it was called before 1828, and married Delfina Gutierrez in 1835. He was a dealer in mules and silver. Dr. Rex Strickland, of the U. of Texas at El Paso history department, has done considerable research on him and delivered a paper on Johnson before the Arizona Pioneers Society in the spring of 1967. Johnson had several children, among them Manuel, who died a hero's death at the Battle of Culiacan, between March 26 and May 6, 1872. Among Johnson's many descendants living in Sonora during the last half of the 20th century was the governor of the State, elected in 1966.

6. Dr. Strickland, who writes that "it yields rather awkwardly to translation," says one clarification might be added and that the "powder" mentioned by Juan José in the sixth stanza might not be "gunpowder" but powdered corn, sweetened and flavored with herbs, called *pinole,* a food highly valued by the Apaches.

8. Philip St. George Cooke, *The Conquest of New Mexico and California in 1846–1848* (reprint, Chicago, Rio Grande Press, 1964) pp. 132-134; Benjamin David Wilson, "Observations," *Annual Publication,* Historical Society of Southern California, Los Angeles, 1934, pp. 78-82.

9. John C. Cremony, *Life Among the Apaches* (San Francisco, Roman & Co., 1868, reprinted Glorieta, N. M., Rio Grande Press, 1969) p. 31. The Fort Leaton site version is contained in a book by Leavitt Corning, Jr., *Baronial Forts of the Big Bend* (Austin, Trinity U. Press, 1967) pp. 25-26, in which Ben Leaton, who was with Johnson, is credited with the terrible deed alone but is supposed to have pulled it off at the fort he established near Presidio, Texas which is named after him. This version, credited to Victor Leaton Ochoa, has Leaton inviting "all the Indians" to Fort Leaton and "when they were all gathered around the banquet board in one of the largest rooms, Leaton excused himself for a moment . . . went out [and] a cannon concealed behind a false wall was fired . . . ending in a complete massacre of the Red men . . ." Leaton was actually an accomplice and in the repetition of the story from generation to generation the place simply got changed.

10. Living descendants are not clear as to exactly how many children were born to Kirker and Rita Garcia, and there is some contradiction in names, as James is sometimes referred to as José, or perhaps they are different children. There is a confusing entry in the Mesilla Catholic Church records, dated August 29, 1859, in the *Libro de Entierros,* or burial book which, translated one way, seems to read: "Polinario, infant son of Santiago Querque and Rita Garcia, was buried." It is likely that the "o" at the end of two important words was read as "a." The Spanish *hija* (daughter) was confused with *hijo* (son) and the same was true with the ending of Polinaria, because Sam Bean writes of the death of a daughter, buried in Mesilla, and the Spanish word *infante* generally means a child under eight, not necessarily a baby.

11. The original of this letter is #5500, Mexican Archives of New Mexico, State Records Center and Archives, Santa Fe, translation by Jacquelyn Hillman, archivist.

12. Josiah Gregg, *Commerce of the Prairies,* (Norman, U. of Oklahoma, reprint, edited by Max Moorhead, 1958) p. 262.

13. Gregg, in *Commerce of the Prairies,* describes the action but names none of the principals. In Bustamente's account, however, cited in Bancroft's *History of Arizona and New Mexico,* (San Francisco, 1889) p. 321, fn., Kirker is named as commander of the disgruntled Americans.

# CHAPTER XII

W HEN all of the parades were over, lances lowered and speeches finished, the fact remained that neither Spain, nor Mexico, nor the states of Chihuahua and Sonora could protect the people from the Apache menace.

After Governor Calvo instigated Johnson's massacre of Juan José and his followers by the promise of reward, the rest of the Apaches were so outraged and emboldened that they murdered residents in bright daylight in the streets of Chihuahua City. Farms were abandoned, freighting in and out of the frontier lands stopped and mines were shut, except those owned by Courcier and McKnight, protected by Santiago Querque.[1]

Governor Calvo died in office in 1838 and there followed the three brief interim administrations of Baer, Revilla and Orcasitas. José Maria de Irigoyen then became governor and he was determined seriously to find a solution to the Apache problem.[2] It was obvious to Governor Irigoyen and to the many mine owners living in Chihuahua City that Kirker was the only one who could provide protection from the Apaches, no matter how distasteful this might be to Mexican pride.

Courcier (whose name in Chihuahua was spelled Curcier) had meanwhile become one of the wealthiest men in the state, due to profits from his mining ventures with Robert McKnight and others. His influence grew apace with his wealth, for Estevan—as he now called himself—was located at the seat of power, Chihuahua City. Robert McKnight remained most of the time in solitude at the primitive community of Hacienda Corralitos.

Courcier suggested to the governor that they organize a private society to raise a war fund with which to combat the Indians; he thought the citizenry was sufficiently aroused to subscribe liberally to such a fund and that they could strike effectively at the Apaches through a private company headed by Kirker. It would take professional fighting men to do the job, he said, not politically led militia.

Governor Irigoyen responded by requesting Courcier to organize just such a society, obtain the services of Kirker and oversee the quasi-military company's actions. Courcier then called a meeting on April 9, 1839, at which he was elected president. Officials named to assist him in the undertaking were Vincente Palacios and Juan Vivar Balderama.[3]

The society's objective was to raise a fund of 100,000 pesos, slightly more than $100,000, to outfit a band of Indian fighters and to have Kirker train local militia to combat Apaches. This was no doubt the origin of a rumor prevalent at the time that Kirker had signed a contract to eradicate every Apache from the face of the earth for $100,000. Out of the total sum Kirker had to pay his private army, as well as sustain them in the field; he himself received the pay of a colonel.[4] The idea was to keep the whole project out of the hands of the Mexican army and the debilitating control of politics and pelf. Courcier sent a broadside to all municipal authorities in the affected area. The proclamation opened with a recapitulation of their dilemma:

> There is scarcely a citizen of Chihuahua without reason to mourn some calamity resulting from Indian ferocity; nearly every family has lost a member, or a friend, to their depravity, and all who love their fellow creatures must burn in the passion of just hatred against an enemy so

bloody. Every single citizen wants to protect the lives and interests of himself and his family, but he doesn't know what to do. "How can it be done?" he asks. "How can we put an end to this evil?" The only answer is that we must pull ourselves out of this lethargy caused by our fear.

The leaflet then called for the organization of chapters in each locality plagued by the red menace into a general organization named the *Sociedad de Guerra Contra Los Barbaros,* Society for War Against Hostile Indians. Local members were urged to solicit money by subscriptions to maintain the army of Indian fighters. The fund was quickly subscribed.

Jim chose Spybuck as his first assistant, and they gathered an initial force of about fifty men, most of whom were recruited from Bent's Fort, but some from various parts of Mexico. There is no roster of these men, but Pauline (sometimes called Paulino, as in the 1860 census) Weaver was one and others were Jim Hobbs, Gabe Allen, John Spencer, James Glenday, Francis Ortiz (or Hortiz), the giant Negro named Andy, Tomas Valencia, Jose Maria Melendres and Jose D. Madrid. Since Spencer was with Jim, it is a good bet that Ben Leaton was, too, for Spencer and Leaton became partners a short time afterward.

Jim had his small army in the field by September 1, 1839 and on September 5 they fought their first engagement. Kirker remembered how he had his 176 mules and eight brood mare burros stolen a short time before, so he put another remuda out as bait to entice another attack. It worked and this encounter was reported by Matt Field, who went across the prairies for his health in 1839 and after his return wrote a series of articles for the New Orleans *Picayune.* Matt's stories on Kirker's battles with the Apaches were carried in the New Orleans paper on February 28 and March 2, 1840.[5] His account of the fight follows.

The people of that part of Mexico known as the Department of Santa Fe, have for many years been harassed and annoyed by the depredations of the Apachus Indians. An American by the name of Kurker at that time of our visit, had just entered into a contract with the government to whip the Indians and bring them to a permanent treaty, for the sum of one hundred thousand dollars, five thousand dollars of which was paid him in advance to commence operations. Kurker is now carrying on the war, and his first skirmish occurred while we were in Taos, within two miles of the town in which we were sojourning. He is a man of daring and reckless disposition, who has himself suffered from the villainy of the Indians, and he now hunts them as much in revenge for the injuries they have done him as in the prospect of emolument.

The battle which forms the subject of the present sketch occurred close under the black mountains of Taos, in the valley of the same name, near to a small town called the "Ranch" [Rancho de Taos]. Kurker with about fifty men, was here encamped, when a party of thieving Apachus crept upon them in the night and stole a number of their horses. The Indians were not aware that Kurker's party were prepared for war, but supposed they were stealing from an encampment of traders, who would not dare to pursue them. The robbery had scarcely been committed when it was discovered, and in a very few minutes more Kurker and his fifty men were in close pursuit of the Indians. Knowing that the thieves would endeavor to escape over the mountains, by ascending a ravine that opened into a valley near the spot where the robbery was committed, Kurker led his men quickly around a bypath up the mountain side, and as the grey light of morning spread over the valley, the pursuers found themselves upon an eminence commanding the ravine up which the Indians were hurrying, mounted upon stolen horses. The marauders numbered about a hundred and twenty, more than double the force of the pursuing party; but although these vagabonds hold the Spaniards in great contempt, they are the vilest cowards when opposed by the Americans. Cunning as they were, they did not discover their danger until fifty American rifles levelled, each with deadly aim, at a separate

victim. The first cry of alarm from the Indians was the
signal to fire, and as the early sun beam penetrated the
ravine, echo started suddenly from slumber, bounding
wildly from cliff to cliff, and away among the distant crags,
like the spirit of fear speeding from death to danger.
Twenty Indians fell from their horses at that fire, some with
a single frightful yell, expiring on the instant, while others
with clenched teeth, and with desperate energy of departing life, clung to the reins, and were dragged about and trod
upon by the alarmed horses. The Indians rode like devils,
and without pausing an instant turned and fled toward the
valley. Some were wounded and fell from the frightened
animals while they were full speed down the ravine. Kurker
and his men followed without reloading their rifles, and
chased the Indians until they emerged from the ravine, and
took refuge within the walls of the ranch.

This town called the Ranch lies at the base of a gigantic
mountain, and is watered by a swift stream that rushes
from the ravine we have mentioned. It contains about three
hundred houses, and these are built compactly together,
forming a wall, and enclosing a large square, in the center
of which stands the church. Into this square the Indians
rushed and endeavored to force their way into the church,
having been taught to believe that the sacred roof is protection against all danger. But Kurker's men felt no disposition to let the savages off so easily, and reloading their rifles
they resumed the attack within the walls of the town. It was
still early morning, and the inhabitants sprang from their
beds in the wildest confusion and alarm. First was heard
the thronging of the Indians into the town—their murmurs
of fear and terror; then the shouts of the pursuers; children
screamed within the dwellings, and there was the report of
firearms, followed by the most fiendish screams and yells
from the victims, over which again rose the loud hurrahs
of the Americans, as wild and savage as the dreadful war
whoop of the Indian. The men seemed to grow delirious
with excitement, and to become inspired with the savage
nature of their enemies. One man after discharging his rifle
and pistols rushed madly among the Indians with his knife,

Rancho de Taos Church, where Kirker and men slaughtered Apaches in first battle of campaign.

and actually succeeded in taking a scalp before he was killed. The fight lasted but half an hour, when the Indians begged for mercy and were suffered to depart.

Kurker's men are mostly robust, daring fellows from Kentucky and Missouri, waggoners, speculators who yielded to the seduction of the Monte Bank [a form of gambling] and were ruined; men of rough, yet chivalrous and romantic natures, who love the wild life they are leading. Their pay from Kurker is a dollar a day and half booty, so their interest as well as their love of excitement leads them to make battle whenever the opportunity occurs. In this battle forty Indians were killed, and of Kurker's party but one American and a half breed. The stolen horses were recovered, and all the other animals in possession of the Indians was taken as booty. Kurker, himself, is brave as a lion, and a man of great enterprise as well as skill in this kind of warfare. Having just commenced operations his force is small, but men were thronging to join him every day, and he will soon be at the head of a powerful army.

Despite Matt Field's observation that men were "thronging" to join Kirker, he was reported to have only fifty-nine men in his outfit on November 21, 1839, when he passed through El Paso on his way to Chihuahua City. The commandant at El Paso del Norte immediately sent a letter to his superiors informing them of Kirker's presence.

"Today," he wrote, "the 21st inst. there came Santiago Querque with 59 men, Shawnees, Americans, Englishmen, Frenchmen and Delaware Indians from the Territory of New Mexico and destined for the capitol of this state [Chihuahua City], where he has entered into a contract with the Society for War Against the Indians."[6]

Kirker's trip south was probably the result of his running low on funds. He was returning to Chihuahua to collect the second payment on his contract with the Society. His first payment was received in August and he kept his force in the field for nearly three months. Each man received one dollar a day, but this item alone amounted collectively to $59 daily, or $1,770 a month, minimum, and not figuring any other expenses at all, Kirker's payroll for that time would amount to $5,500, which also would mean that by this time some of his men were behind on their pay.

Although Jim's agreement was with a private group it was heavily influenced by the political climate, which changed from hot to cold with great rapidity. Anastasio Bustamente, a conservative, and Antonio Lopez de Santa Anna, an opportunist, were going in and out of office, almost in turn, as national president. As they alternated in exile, the various state governments were shattered by an almost total spoils system, which swept men in and out of office with the existing whim in Mexico City. It amounted almost to anarchy but it did have its comical aspects.

One of Santa Anna's great political comebacks was initiated when the French fleet bombarded Vera Cruz, forcing Santa Anna to flee the scene in his underwear. When the shelling died down, Santa Anna went back to pick up his pants and while on this mission had his leg blown off by a stray cannon ball. This made him a hero in the eyes of the Mexican public and he was restored to power, especially after he was successful in getting the French to stop shelling the city. He didn't publicize the fact that he achieved this desirable end only by paying the French 600,000 pesos.

For a time Santa Anna became a national hero whose popularity was exceeded only by that of his leg. This item was solemnly disinterred at Manga de Clavo and reburied with all military honors at the Mexico City Cathedral. The popularity of both Santa Anna and the leg was short-lived, though, for within a few weeks his government was overthrown, the leg dug up and insurrectionists dragged it through the streets at the end of a cord.

State administrations changed as rapidly as did those on the national level and the utter confusion was compounded in Chihuahua City, ruled over by two successive governors with the same name: José Maria Irigoyen, an uncle and his nephew. People, even in those days, couldn't tell which was which, although for purposes of identification the first Irigoyen adopted the name Jose Maria Irigoyen Rodriguez, while the younger became known officially as Jose Irigoyen de la O.

The first Irigoyen was elected second speaker of the governing junta, and the second Irigoyen was elected third speaker in the same election, held January 1, 1839. They then succeeded one another to the governorship within nine months, the second taking over on August 29, 1839. They also had other things in common. Both were lawyers and, what was more important to Kirker, both were supremely interested in seeing that the Apache problem was solved and both were strong boosters of Jim Kirker's methods of pacifying the tribesmen.

Kirker left El Paso about mid-November and reached Chihuahua City shortly before December 1, to learn that Irigoyen de la O. had succeeded the Irigoyen without the O. Fortunately he was just as enthusiastic about the contract with

Kirker as his predecessor had been and readily saw to it that the next payment was promptly made. Further he busied himself to increase the war chest and suggested to Jim that he raise the number in his army to 200.

Taking the governor's advice, Jim began recruiting more men right in Chihuahua City. They pitched their camp in the Plaza de Toros, or bullfight arena, and worked out of this headquarters for several months.

The presence of these ragged foreigners was a constant irritant to the dandified and elegantly costumed professional soldiers of the Mexican military establishment. They grumbled and complained about the hiring of outsiders to perform a job which the Mexican army obviously should be doing. It *was* embarrassing, painfully embarrassing, but not quite so painful as being killed by Apaches so the governor paid little attention. Leader of the complaining clique was Jim's old comrade at Santa Rita, Colonel Justiniani, whose friendship once favored Kirker but who had now turned to support his fellow officers in the shamed military.[7]

Kirker and his followers, meanwhile, ranged over the mountains and deserts of New Mexico and Chihuahua, maintaining constant pressure against their Indian foes and recapturing livestock the Apaches had stolen on various raids against Mexican communities. Kirker and his men were allowed to keep all of this stock they regained as part payment for their services under the contract, regardless of what brands might be burned into the hides. This was a constant irritant and caused a flood of complaining letters from previous owners to the Chihuahua government. One such letter even came from Socorro, where Kirker's men had not long before been feted as heroes. It was written by Antonio Sandoval, a Justice of the Peace, and was addressed to Don Guadalupe Miranda, secretary of government, who forwarded it to the governor. It shows the substance of the trouble and demonstrates the changing attitude of the people toward Kirker and his men.[8]

In the official note of the 14th communicated to me [the secretary] by post from the Juez de Paz of Socorro is the following:

Office of Juez de Paz, Socorro.

Assuming that this prefecture was informed that the American foreigner, Don Santiago Querque last November lifted from the partido of Sabino at Luis Lopes 23 animals and 9 heifers with his company of Shawnee, and the residents of the same department who had knowledge of this since turned out that some of them were damaged, in diligence of finding them [the animals], ran as far as the bosque del Apache where they came upon said commander. At all costs, with arms at hand, he stopped them, laughing at them, because of the small force that accompanied them. ... He was advised that the group were being conducted by 4 residents of Abiquiiu and Algodones [towns near Santa Fe], who were of his own company, and that they made their confession of carrying out this deed, and had declared that one [animal] had died in his own service, and that he, the same Don Santiago, had most of the animals standing around without making any other use of them than the service for which he did the deed, of seizing two animals and one saddle which he admitted were theirs without prejudice to anyone else, hoping that the principal actor [Kirker] would make clear his good or evil intent.

And I transcribe this to you, so that it may be carried to higher information to his excellency to the end that there may be recovered from said foreigner for the damage caused to this jurisdiction and that in consequence, he may be punished with all the force of law for such evil behavior and scandalous proceedings. I have the pleasure of sending you my esteem and consideration. God and Liberty, Barelas, March 21, 1840. Antonio Sandoval. To: Sec. of Government, D. Guadalupe Miranda.

This letter charged that livestock found in Kirker's possession actually belonged to certain Socorro residents; by claiming that the stock was stolen directly by Kirker and his men they could demand it back or receive money for it. Kirker, of course, asserted that he had retrieved the animals from the Apaches and it was the Indians who had stolen the stock, depriving previous owners of the right to regain it. This complication was repeated numerous times, at last so seriously it destroyed Kirker's organization. Meanwhile it was furnishing ammunition for the military to use against Kirker and against the government for collaborating with him.

The disagreement between Colonel Justiniani, spokesman for the disgruntled military, and Governor Irigoyen de la O., was carried over the governor's head by Justiniani to the Minister of War in Mexico City. Justiniani asked that he be declared the supreme commander of all forces and that Governor Irigoyen be restrained from employing foreigners to protect the Department of Chihuahua from Apaches.

The upshot of this move was that Justiniani himself was removed from authority in Chihuahua but his complaint nevertheless eventually brought about the termination of Kirker's contract. Governor Irigoyen died in office and the Minister of War, Garcia Conde succeeded Justiniani as commandant on May 12, and became chief executive of the state on July 6, 1840.

Garcia Conde canceled the agreement with Kirker on the grounds that it was disgraceful to the Mexican Government and "unpatriotic" to employ foreigners to protect its citizens, adding that it would establish a dangerous precedent.[9] Conde would, he vowed, give up his military command before he would countenance foreign mercenaries doing a job which so obviously was the duty of the Mexican Army.

To beef up his defenses, Conde purchased 600 horses in central Mexico. He planned to use these mounts to form cavalry which would chase the Apaches under his own command. He also drew up an elaborate design to establish formal militia at Parral, Guerrero, Balleza, Satevo, Meoqui, Rosales, San Carlos, Bachinivia and Temosachic. To arm these forces, Conde purchased 1028 new rifles, fifty swords, 656 lances and 1400 hand guns.

With this show of burgeoning force Conde announced that he would negotiate from strength with the Apaches and see if there wasn't some basis of understanding to be reached with the enemy. To this end, Conde dispatched Don José Cordero at the head of a committee to see if a preliminary agreement couldn't be reached to discuss a permanent peace.

Cordero learned that the main condition insisted upon by the Apaches before they would even consider coming to any peace conference was the banishment of Kirker, McKnight and the Shawnee warriors forever. It indicated that Kirker and his men must have been doing an effective job but Conde accepted the condition.

There were, however, several other stipulations made by the Apaches before they would agree to a powwow and they are interesting enough to list in their entirety. Here is the Apaches' answer to Conde:[10]

Proposition in order to have Apaches assembled for peace with the department of Chihuahua by invitation which has been made by them at the request of Señor Don José Cordero and some residents in various parts of this Department.

1)  They [the Mexicans] do not again settle the area of the copper mines, and that it be given to them [the Apaches] for their land that they may live there.

2)  That if they make peace, the establishments place them in the limits of New Mexico because they fear it is necessary to take precautions in Chihuahua. [This in effect would mean gerrymandering the northern border of Chihuahua and giving away the whole northern part, including the rich copper mines.]

3)  That Don Santiago Kirker and Don Roberto [McKnight] not return to New Mexico, nor shall the Shawnee be admitted in Chihuahua and its department.

4)  That they [the Apaches] receive 5000 pesos in money annually.

5)   That the sons of Sarquediga be given the lagoon, Lake Guzman, Boca Grande, Alamo Gueso and Sierra de los Animas, that they live there and that they go with all their possessions.

6)   That those captives be redeemed, those that have bled and been sold among us [the Apaches] be set free.

7)   That an accounting be made, and they shall freely sell horses and mules and other moveable things that were taken during the war.

8)   That some Apaches who do not wish peace be separated from the others and be shown a mountain where they may live and may be pursued until they are subjected to order.

This is a copy. Santa Fe, February 28, 1842.

Signed: D. [Donaciano] Vigil.

Conde did abrogate Kirker's contract with the Society and made any such transaction in the future illegal but to conform to the other conditions in the list of pre-conditions to a peace treaty with the Apaches would have been nothing short of surrender. In essence what the Apaches asked was that Chihuahua give up its principal source of revenue, the copper mines, and all of its lakes, which were the most habitable parts. The Apaches would allow them to keep the deserts and Chihuahua City.

No one in his right mind thought that Chihuahua leaders were ever going to give up their rich mines or scarce lakes of water just to talk peace with Apaches. These questions soon became academic anyway, for the Indians resorted to their old raiding, looting, killing and raping as soon as Kirker's enforcers were called off, and all of Conde's horses, lances and rifles were to no avail because he didn't have men who knew how to use them. When the Apaches began killing people in the streets of Chihuahua again, the citizens demanded a meeting of the junta and a memorial was sent to Mexico City asking for the recall of Conde, military reputation and all. President Bustamente reacted to their plea by promoting Conde to national Senator and appointed in Conde's place General Mariano Monterde,

The main street of Guadalupe y Calvo, Chihuahua, Mexico, appeared the same when James Kirker lived here 130 years ago. Never has a wheel of any kind rolled down this street, be it automobile, truck or ox-drawn two-wheeled careta, for it is necessary to top out over an 11,000-foot mountain range to drop down into the village, so carts were useless, as are trucks today. There are absolutely no roads leading to the town today, or ever.

who assumed the double office of Commandant General and Governor of Chihuahua on December 8, 1842.

Meanwhile, after losing his contract with the Society, Jim accepted an offer to go to the mining community of Guadalupe y Calvo, operated by John Buchan and Robert O. Auld for some British interests, and guard that community from Indian depredations.[11] Jim and his men went to this out-of-the-way community in southwest Chihuahua early in 1842 and there Jim learned his new employers were on excellent terms with Her British Majesty's Consul at Mexico City, Ewen C. Mackintosh. For some time Jim had rankled at losing the furs and

mules to the Indians and Governor Perez, but revenge on both
was all he could manage. Now he decided to try a new tack: he
would see if the British government would intercede for him
and force payment of his losses from the Mexican national
government.

Jim collected a number of witnesses, including Pauline
Weaver, Frank Ortiz and James Glenday, who had been with
him when the Indians stole his goods, and departed for Chihuahua City, where they made out long and detailed sworn statements, or depositions, as to what happened. Jim also made a
legal declaration and asked Consul Macintosh to press his claim
against the Mexican government. He included in his petition
the following: "I accompany you certified documents to prove
the truth of my assertions and in order farther to corroborate
the veracity of my statements I beg to refer to you Don Vincente Sanchez de Vergara Deputado al Congreso del Depart-
mento de Nuevo Mexico—General Don Pedro Garcia Conde,
and Teniente Coronel Ponce the officer in command of the
troops sent in pursuit of me."[12] It would indicate that Kirker
was still on pretty good terms with the man who just fired him,
Conde, since he referred to Conde as a corroborating witness.

Jim sought the sum of $32,900, the amount claimed as
having been lost to the Indians but which he maintained finally
ended up in the hands of Governor Perez, or at least most of
it. The immediate point in question, however, was Jim's citizenship. For the British government even to consider assisting him
in the collection of damages, that would have to be established
first. Of course, Kirker had actually forfeited all of these rights
years ago, when he fought with the Americans in the war of
1812 and again when he assumed citizenship of Mexico, perhaps as early as 1825, according to one reference.

Jim was rather clumsy in his presentation, too, for in the
"certified documents" he was referred to time and again as "the
naturalized Irishman," or "the American Irishman," or the
"naturalized Anglo-American." Even in the copy of the permit
issued by Governor Perez, Kirker is termed the "naturalized

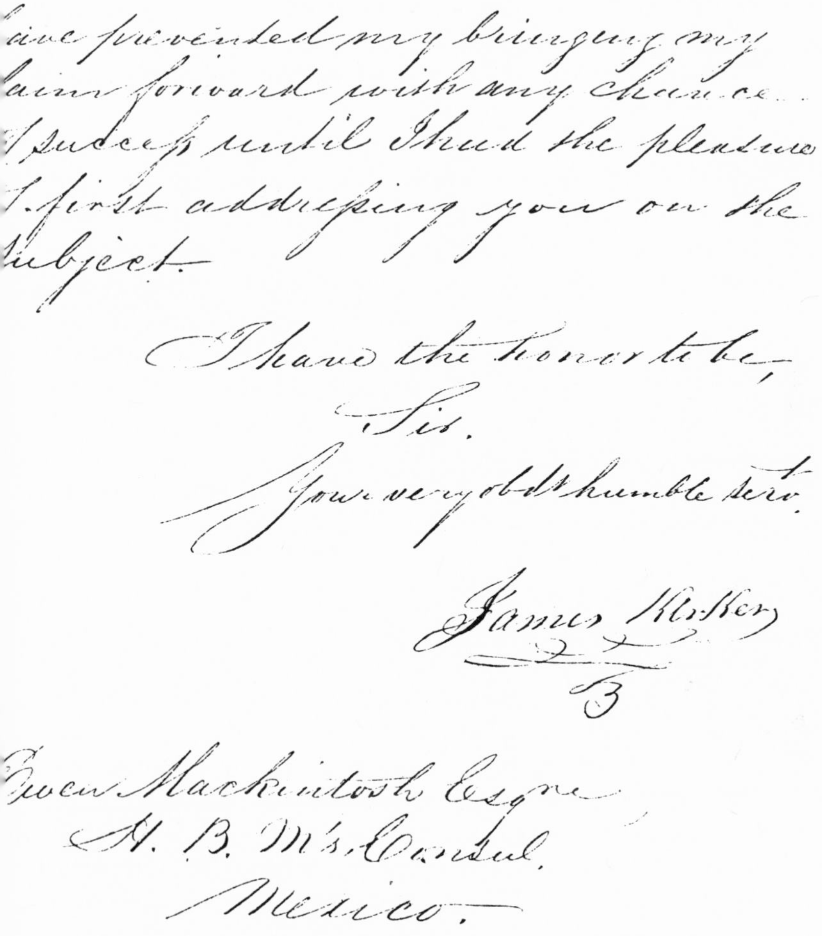

*[Handwritten letter in cursive:]*

...ave prevented my bringing my
claim forward with any chance
of success until I had the pleasure
of first addressing you on the
subject.—

    I have the honor to be,
       Sir.
    Your very obdt humble serv.

        James Kirker

Ewen Mackintosh Esqre
  H. B. M's. Consul,
   Mexico.—

James Kirker's true signature appears above at the conclusion of a letter he wrote from Guadalupe y Calvo, Chihuahua, dated 19 November 1842, to Ewen Mackintosh, H.B.M.'s Consul at Mexico City. Kirker's education and cultural background is made apparent by the fine hand he wrote, one of almost professional quality and certainly an odd talent for a mountain man, trapper and scalphunter. *The original of this letter is in the Public Records Office, London*

Irishman in the Republic of Mexico," so it was scarcely surprising that the Foreign Office instructed Mackintosh to afford him not the slightest assistance because of the contradiction in citizenship. Kirker either had assumed Mexican citizenship, as his permit to trap read or he had lied to Governor Perez about his Mexican nationality solely to obtain the permit. In the first instance the British Government considered him as having forfeited "his right to British protection by accepting citizenship in the Mexican Republic," or in the second instance the Perez license was issued "with the understanding that he was a Mexican citizen." If he wasn't such, then he was outside the law and couldn't expect help from the British government in that circumstance. His petition was denied.[13]

News that the British wouldn't help him press his claim came at about the same time he received another offer from the Chihuahua government to return to Chihuahua City and once more take charge of the anti-Apache activities. Governor and Commandant General Monterde had a whole new deal to offer Kirker and his boys. They were to receive $100 for each Apache warrior's scalp, $50 for the scalp of a squaw and $25 for that of a child. Again it was agreed that the Indian fighters would be allowed to keep all of the livestock retrieved from the Indians, regardless of previous ownership. The scalp money was to be paid directly to Kirker, who would take his share and then divide the balance with his followers.

Jim and his Shawnees were back in business again, once more bivouacked in the bullring with a piece-work agreement which could prove more profitable than any they had in the past.

## NOTES TO CHAPTER XII

1. Gregg's *Commerce of the Prairies,* pp. 202-205; Clyde and Mae Reed Porter, *Ruxton of the Rockies,* edited by LeRoy R. Hafen (Norman, U. of Okla., 1950) p. 148.

2. Francisco R. Almada, *Gobernadores del Estada de Chihuahua,* (Mexico D. F. Imprenta de la H. Camara de Deputados, 1950) pp. 49-82.

3. A printed bulletin, setting out the origins of the society and its aims and methods, plus a call to arms written by Courcier and signed by him was found in 1965 by Robert McNellis, El Paso gun and antique collector, at Ocampo. McNellis provided the author with a Xerox copy, which included annotations and marginalia by town authorities at Jesus Maria in 1838.

4. Kirker interview, St. Louis *Post,* July 10, 1847.

5. This account may also be found in *Matt Field on the Santa Fe Trail,* stories by Field collected by Clyde and Mae Reed Porter, edited by John E. Sunder (Norman, U. of Okla., 1960).

6. This entry, found in *Los Papeles de Chihuahua,* now on micro-film at the University of Texas at El Paso, was discovered and translated by Rex W. Strickland of the history department.

7. Francisco R. Almada, *Gobernadores del Estata Chihuahua* (Mexico D.F., Imprenta de la H. Camara de Deputados, 1950). Dr. Almada treats extensively in this book of Indian affairs and the difficulty encountered with the Mexican military. He sorts out the Irigoyens and establishes the various administrations, interim and otherwise, of the multitude of governors of Chihuahua, changing almost every month during one period of Kirker's activities. Dr. Almada, incidentally, was once governor of Chihuahua himself.

8. Letter item #6003, State Records Center and Archives, translated by Dr. Myra Ellen Jenkins, senior archivist, and Jacquelyn Hillman, assistant.

9. Almada, *Gobernadores,* pp. 92-3.

10. Copy of original in New Mexico Archives, Santa Fe.

11. Francisco R. Almada, *Guadalupe y Calvo* (Chihuahua, Los Tlleres Tipograficos del Gobierno de Chihuahua, 1940) p. 36; and Rio Grande *Republican,* October 26, 1889.

12. Kirker letter, Public Record Office, London, FO 204/79/ 1 105, p. 207-8.

13. Inter-Foreign Office Communication, Consul Mackintosh, October 3, 1842, FO 204/79/2 108.

# CHAPTER XIII

C HIHUAHUA CITY in the 1840s was the metropolitan center of the Southwest for freighters and mountain men, and many came through there in search of relaxation and entertainment at one time or another. From this growing reservoir of manpower, Jim was able to augment his little army with additional recruits. James Hobbs, one of the visitors there, later wrote a book about his early days[1] and in it said there were more than a hundred frontiersmen in the outfit he himself came with, of which about seventy were Shawnee and Delaware Indians.

"We would fight certain tribes . . . for the fun of the thing," wrote Hobbs, "and for common humanity, even if we were not rewarded for every scalp."[2]

Many men of Jim's original band drifted away. They didn't often stay long at the same thing before departing for greener fields—men like Stephen Meek, who had gone back to Independence to hire out as a guide for an Oregon-bound wagon train.[3]

The fabled Spybuck was still hanging around Chihuahua City, big as life and thrice as ornery, even though he had been reported killed by Apaches the fall before.[4] George Wilkins Kendall, owner of the New Orleans *Picayune,* had reported

Spybuck's death both in his newspaper and in a book he published in 1844 about the Texan invasion of 1841. But it wasn't so; Spybuck had simply enjoyed another little brush with the Apaches between jobs with Kirker and in 1843 he was again second in command of Jim's brigade.

The first job after collecting a new batch of operators and bedding them down in the bullring came along within a few days, when a war party of Apaches attacked a mule train belonging to J. Calistro Porras, a millionaire Chihuahua merchant. Porras was a quiet, gentlemanly trader who sent trains to St. Louis regularly on buying trips, as well as over the Sierra Madres to Guaymas and Mazatlan. At the latter ports, his trains met the ships docking there from the eastern coast and Europe. Porras' Guaymas and Mazatlan train usually consisted of about eighty mules, loaded with paniers stuffed with merchandise for the home trip across the mountains.

That summer of 1843 the train nearly made it all the way back to Chihuahua City but a dozen or so miles short of home a band of Apaches struck it, took everything and killed all but one of the crew. The sole survivor came running into Chihuahua City and finally quieted down sufficiently to tell in detail what had happened. Porras immediately sought out Kirker and offered Jim the mules and half of the merchandise if he could overtake and punish the thieves. Added to the government's bounty on scalps, this campaign could earn a fortune so Jim took his force on the trail. He and Spybuck picked up the sign at the site of the attack and within four miles came upon a dead mule, abandoned and lanced by the Apaches when it gave out. The pack saddle had been removed from the dead animal and the 300 pounds of sugar transferred to one of the other mules. The trackers moved steadily onward for the rest of the day.

By dark they reached the campsite the Indians had used the first night after the attack. It was littered with coffee, rice and sugar which was gathered up and sent back to Porras. Kirker and his men were gone by sunup, and by noon they came across another ten mules that had fallen by the wayside and had been lanced to death. Jim and the men stripped these of their cargo, caching it nearby, and pushed on.

On the third day, Spybuck signaled a halt from his lead position and stealthily scouted the hostiles' camp less than a mile ahead. He returned to report to Jim that the opposing party consisted of forty-three warriors. After three days they had imagined themselves out of danger, and since the cargo contained a great number of imported liquors the Indians had decided to camp and indulge in a spree. It was a fatal decision.

Eighty-six infiltrators under Kirker and Spybuck entered their camp when they were all in a drunken stupor and slit the throats of every Apache. The Shawnees scalped them by cutting a neat circle at the crown of each head, then sitting down with their feet resting on the shoulders of the dead enemy; they grabbed a handful of hair, leaning back and pushing forward with their feet until there was a loud *Pop!* The scalps were then brought to Spybuck, who sprinkled them with salt to preserve them and tied the hair to a scalp pole.

While the Shawnees prepared the scalps, Jim went out and rounded up all the horses and mules he could find. With forty-three they got from the dead Indians, they had in excess of 100. Jim then directed his attention to the wide selection of liquors. He opened up a considerable amount of it and invited his men to a giant bash. He knew they would get into the booze sooner or later, so he decided to take a day or so off and get it over with. The mountaineers were soon as drunk as the men they had just killed and they remained that way throughout the rest of that day and part of the next. After the all-day binge, they spent another day sleeping it off. Next morning Kirker called a council.

As a former war chief of the Apaches, Jim knew of a large village within a three-day march, beside a lake, and inhabited by at least 1000 Apaches. Here was a fortune in hair. He asked them if they wanted to go on and attack the village by the lake. They said they would.[5]

Kirker directed some of the men to cache the Porras merchandise and some of the others he set to rounding up the mules and horses. A corral was built, the animals driven inside and a substantial guard was left with the stock. Jim meanwhile had sent Spybuck ahead to scout. Kirker's total number of effectives, not counting those left behind on guard detail, was 150, more than enough to pull off a surprise attack on an Indian village of this size.

Jim and the men hit the trail and after a couple of days were rejoined by Spybuck. He had located the village but hadn't taken the time to reconnoiter it completely so he and Jim went back together to inspect the situation in detail. They circled the village, except the small portion fronting the lake. It was built at the bottom of a saucerlike formation, surrounded on three sides by gently rising high ground and on the other side by water.

After their reconnaisance the two scouts returned to the main body. Jim ordered the horses moved about two miles to the rear, into a ravine, and arranged for a half-dozen men to remain there and guard them. The rest of the company, now slightly more than 140, he led cautiously to the rim of the hills overlooking the Apache village.

It was just at sunset and the variously colored lodges spread out in the heart of a pine grove gave the whole view a carnival aspect. The lake, they could see, was about six miles across and the water was calm as a mirror. There was little or no sound in the twilight.

After the sun went down, the Kirker men watched a war party of about seventy-five braves return to the village from the direction of Sonora, west, and as they walked around the edge of the lake, scalps could be seen dangling from their belts. They also carried hogsheads and jugs of liquor, captured during their latest raid. The men withdrew a couple of hundred yards and Spybuck informed them that the best plan would be to wait until the Indians had time to get drunk and dance most of the night away.

Provisions were brought out and the men had a quick meal. They then lay down to sleep until the guard should give the call at three in the morning. When the call sounded, the men arose, refreshed by sleep and formed into two companies, one led by Kirker, the other by Spybuck. About that time, Spybuck returned from another look at the village with word that all but three or four in the village were dead drunk.

Kirker led his company to one side of the camp and Spybuck took the other side, each man posting himself until Kirker whistled, which would be the signal to charge. Dawn was just breaking by this time. Kirker had a special whistle, which he was to blow when everything was ready, when the men were to rush into the camp, yelling, shoot all they could with the first discharge, then finish the job with knives and tomahawks.

One member of the company was Andy, the huge Negro, who had loaded a musket with buckshot and was stationed next to Hobbs, who was second in command of his detail, under Spybuck. Hobbs claimed that he had given Andy specific instructions not to fire until he heard Kirker whistle but when an Indian suddenly came out of one of the lodges near Andy the black man blazed away, almost tearing the savage in two. Andy was kicked over backward by the gun's explosion, the barrel ripping out of the stock.

Alarmed, the Indians began to stir, and both parties rushed into the fight without any other signal.

Hobbs had his eye on two Indians who were sleeping a few feet away from where he was when the attack started and he rushed them. He leveled his rifle at one, while the other Indian, on all fours, crawled between his legs and rose up with Hobbs still straddling his neck. He finally managed to slip off and the Indian ran far enough away to get off an arrow. Hobbs was fast enough with his rifle to put a slug in his shoulder and ruin his aim, and the arrow fell harmlessly at his feet. While all this was going on, the Indian Hobbs initially was aiming at had gotten away through the other side of the tent.

Spybuck shot the man and tomahawked the women and children in another tepee containing three squaws, while vari-

ous other hand-to-hand encounters were being fought all over
the village. The Shawnees fought like devils, hoping to take
enough scalps to go back to Missouri and retire. They were
using their knives and tomahawks as their principal weapons,
while the Americans, firing both rifles and revolvers, were pushing a great number of Apache braves into the lake and pursuing
them across the valley.

Many of the Apaches made it to the nearest mountain and
found refuge there, while another large number rushed into the
lake and were drowned. The Shawnees gave up chasing them
and sought out a huge corral containing nearly a thousand
horses and mules, as well as mustang ponies.

Cochise, chief of this band, recognized Kirker as the leader
of the attacking force against him. When Cochise reached a
mountain top with a few of his tribe he turned back to look
upon the havoc wrought by the white men. While looking on
the ruins he recognized Kirker gazing at him.

Cochise asked the mountain man what he meant by leading this attack—was he not their war chief? Had they not
treated him as a brother always, avoiding attacks on the mines
and *conductas* while he was guarding them? Was he no longer
their friend?

Cochise turned to continue his flight with his few friends,
declaring in a loud voice that Kirker was the last white man he
would ever believe in. At these words, Hobbs said, he was
watching Kirker's face. Hobbs could tell Jim "felt the rebuke
keenly, but allowed the broken hearted chief to escape."

Kirker then quickly turned to business. He ordered Hobbs
to take twenty men and go at once to the place where they had
all of their horses and mules corralled. He was afraid the Indians might regroup and try to retake the precious animals. This
Hobbs did, uniting both herds of horses and they started the
trek back to Chihuahua City at once, leaving many of the men
behind to clean up various small chores.

The Shawnees finished collecting scalps and many of the
others were gathering up things about the camp. It was about
this time that Spybuck noticed the Apaches had killed the

half-breed Mexican who had guided them to the original site of the massacre.

"Here," said Spybuck, "scalp that fellow."

"No," was the reply, "he is our guide."

"No difference," answered Spybuck, "he is dead now; he won't know it; and his scalp is worth as much as any."

So the guide was scalped. This incident probably is the origin of the story that Jim Kirker augmented his Indian-scalp supply with those of Mexicans when he needed the money.

## NOTES TO CHAPTER XIII

1. Captain James Hobbs, *Wild Life in the Far West,* p. 82.

2. *Ibid.*

3. Stephen Hall Meek, *Autobiography of a Mountain Man,* (Pasadena, edited by Arthur Woodward, Glen Dawson, pub., 1948) p. 7.

4. Kendall, *Sante Fe Expedition,* pp. 56-59.

5. Hobbs' account, the source for most of the information on the Porras expedition and the Apache hunt which followed, doesn't give the name of the lake, but it probably was Lake Guzman, in the northwest part of Chihuahua.

# CHAPTER XIV

JIM KIRKER'S victory over Cochise's Apaches produced a totally unexpected dividend: the rescue of a large number of Mexican women and children who had been prisoners of this band. Kirker's men also liberated 300 sheep and goats so Jim told the freed captives that they could drive the animals back to Chihuahua City and keep them.

While these flocks were being rounded up, Gabe Allen and a couple of men with him happened upon the remains of what once had been a flourishing community, by this time reduced to a heap of ruins. Quite evident were the foundation stones of a church, complete with a large cross made of lignum vitae, a tropical American tree of hard wood.

Nearby were the remains of a smelting furnace, a huge pile of cinder slag and some dross of silver and copper. While looking into the hollow portion of a ceramic cup at the site, Gabe found a nugget of gold weighing about ten ounces. This discovery sent the rest of the men flocking to the ruins and soon they picked up other, smaller, bits and pieces of the precious yellow metal. A messenger was sent immediately to Jim, notifying him of this find, and when he came on the scene he called a council to determine their course of action, whether they should stay and look for more gold or return to Chihuahua City at once to claim their scalp money, sell off their captured livestock and negotiate with Porras for their share of the retrieved merchandise. Kirker pointed out that even though much of the livestock had been started out ahead, it would be slow work getting them down the trail. He thought they must start at once to be safe, for he predicted the Apaches would soon return with all of the warriors in that part of the country seeking revenge. In short, Jim called the meeting only to urge his point of view rather than to consider any other course, for he was convinced that if they were to get back with their skins they should leave within an hour. This certainly was no time to surrender to gold fever. The others, seeing the common sense in his remarks and respecting his knowledge of these Indians, agreed to start off at once, leaving behind their visions of treasure but each promising some day to return.

Three days later they reached a spot where Parras' merchandise had been cached. They dug it up and early the next morning loaded it on mules and hit the trail for Chihuahua City, with Jim Hobbs detailed to guard nineteen captive Apache women. While he was taking them to a waterhole to drink one succeeded in breaking away and made good her escape on one of the better horses. The rest were then placed on the most decrepit and slowest horses of the remuda and there was no more trouble with them.

At San Andreas the train stopped to rest for a couple of days. Jim took the opportunity to send a messenger ahead to notify the governor of their success and of their approach. Three days later when Jim, his men and their loot and captives rounded a bend in the Sacramento River valley road, they heard the music from a full brass band. When the caravan of hunters and Indian fighters rounded the bend to gaze upon the plain lying between them and Chihuahua City, they were amazed to behold thousands of townspeople, led by the governor, approaching to escort them in a formal welcome to the city.

The governor made a welcoming speech and then inquired

into the specifics of their victory. Spybuck ordered up a mule carrying all the scalps.

"How many are there?" asked the governor.

"One hundred and eight-two," said Spybuck, explaining that many other Apaches had drowned in the lake before they could be scalped. Spybuck pointed to the women captives and notified the governor that they had eighteen more "walking scalps."[1]

Once back in the city, Kirker arranged for the returning Mexican women and children to go to their homes throughout Chihuahua and to divide up their sheep and goats. He sent Spybuck to the governor's mansion to turn over the scalps. While counting them Spybuck included the eighteen Apache women whose scalps were still on their heads. The governor refused to consider these scalps and Spybuck offered to remove them at once so they would qualify. The governor hastily agreed to count them just as they were.

Victory feasts were held throughout the city, including the governor's mansion, and the men were feted as heroes. Jim was rewarded by Albert Speyer, an Austrian-American trader, with a fine new suit of clothes of the latest St. Louis cut and the men were invited to drink, free, in all of the cantinas. Meanwhile Kirker and Spybuck settled their accounts with the merchant Porras, amicably and returned to the bullring, where most of the men were sleeping off the effects of the great celebration. Kirker then accompanied Gabe Allen to the Chihuahua mint, where the director, an Englishman named John Potts, informed them that the ore specimens they found in the abandoned village assayed at about twenty-five percent gold.

Things were simply going too well and Jim waited for the reversal in fortune that he felt was due. It wasn't long coming, in the form of a sorrowful explanation by the governor that he didn't have enough money to pay them for the scalps they had turned in. He had only about $2000 in the public treasury, a little more than ten percent of what they had coming. When Jim told his men of this unpleasant turn of events they were on the verge of rebellion, with Spybuck urging that they attack the governor's mansion and take what was due them. Jim finally persuaded them to wait awhile, promising that he would organize a party to go back to the gold mine they had discovered in the ruins.

Another crisis came a day or two later, though, when the governor reneged on his promise once more. This time Kirker couldn't control his fellow hunters. The livestock taken by Kirker's legion from the Apaches was corralled some distance away from the bullring, where the horses and mules were kept on pasture. It wasn't long until the original owners began showing up with their brands and claiming the animals, and again they hinted broadly that Jim's men, not the Apaches, had stolen the animals. This was too much, so Jim and a delegation called on the governor again. Hobbs quotes Jim as saying to his excellency:

"Governor, you know when you made the agreement, that the animals recaptured by us from the Indians was liable to be claimed by various owners, but you promised it should be ours. Otherwise what pay do we get for risking our lives in recovering these mules and other property? If your government is so weak and rotten that you can't sustain yourselves, and keep your promises, then let us know it."

The governor, torn between his word and the pressure of his constituents, chose to go back on his promise.

"It is their property," he said lamely, "and the law gives it to them; therefore, they can take it, though I am sorry that any of the animals should be claimed, after your party has done so nobly."[2]

When Jim returned to the bullring, he told the men what the governor had said. Spybuck, furious, stamped, beat his breast and shook his fists. He called the Shawnees and Delawares together and told them to keep their arms at hand at all times. They were either to get paid or they would fight. Spybuck mounted his horse and rode to the pasture to see how many of their horses and mules had been made off with. He found one

Mexican driving off a horse, which he claimed. Spybuck knocked the man out of the saddle with his tomahawk, then turned on the throng gathered to take the horses and warned them that they had better not, that they should leave or he would kill them. They left. In a short time they showed up at the governor's palace, complaining even more bitterly about their rights.

The governor called for a general mobilization. The next morning between six and eight hundred troops were assembled around the governor's palace—and they had cannon. Learning of this, Spybuck rode his horse into the bull ring and went to where he kept his gear. There he stripped off his buckskins, down to his G-string. He put some feathers in his hair, painted his face half black and half red, drained a bottle of whiskey and leaped back on his horse. He rode rapidly toward the governor's mansion, followed by his Shawnee and Delaware warriors. Bringing up the rear was a worried Kirker, who went along, according to Hobbs, "to prevent any collision or open rupture."[3] Jim's family lived in Chihuahua and he was a naturalized citizen of that state so he hesitated to remonstrate to the extent of open warfare.

Upon reaching the plaza, Spybuck passed contemptuously through the Mexican troops, walked through a file of soldiers guarding the governor's door and pushed the sergeant of the guard out of the way. He crashed through the door and into the governor's office, with Kirker and Hobbs trailing along behind.

Spybuck strode to where the governor was seated at his desk and towering above him asked if the governor intended to keep his agreement. Otherwise, Spybuck informed him, his black eyes blazing, the governor would not long remain on earth to do anything and he had better get his affairs in order to die.

The governor stammered out some sort of weak denial, promised Spybuck anything he wanted and the Shawnee turned on his heel and walked out, Kirker and Hobbs still behind him.

At dawn the next morning, Spybuck and his warriors had

cut out their share of the horses, were all packed and ready to leave. As they rode away, Spybuck glanced at Kirker and said, "Mr. Kirker, if you want to stay in such a country as this, you can do so, but I am taking my portion of the animals, and [leaving]. Tomorrow, or the next day, the governor will come down on us with eight hundred troops, and then we can't do anything but submit to his infamous treachery."[4]

Spybuck led his men through the streets of Chihuahua City, driving their livestock, past the governor's palace, and out of town. Nobody made a move to stop them. Kirker accompanied them to the edge of the city, where Spybuck turned to bid Jim farewell.

"There is only one thing," said he, "that I regret upon leaving here, Captain Kirker."

"What is that?" Kirker asked.

"That I am leaving without the governor's scalp."

Spybuck then stuck his heels into the ribs of his mount and urged him up to the head of the column, in the direction of Bent's Fort. There, about three weeks later, Spybuck and the others averaged about $2500 each for their share of the horses and mules.

Jim and the few men who remained with him received only a few dollars above the $2000 they had been paid by the governor and the others were allowed to claim their horses and mules without reprisal from Jim and his followers. In humiliation Jim returned with only a handful of his closest followers to Corralitos Hacienda.

His withdrawal from action again opened the door to the Apaches and during the next two years the Indians literally ran wild throughout Chihuahua and New Mexico, slaughtering Mexicans the length and breadth of Chihuahua and Sonora. Angel Trias, a former prefect of Chihuahua City, assumed the duties of governor on August 24, 1845. One of his first acts was to send a runner for Jim, asking that he once more gather together his Indian-fighting crew and help them defend their towns from rampaging Apaches. Trias was desperate, and for good reason, for the Apaches had not only brought the government to a standstill but practically life itself.

Why Jim accepted another deal from a government which had thrice before reneged outrageously and humiliated him in the bargain, is difficult to understand. However, he was a citizen and his adopted country was in trouble. Besides, Trias upped the payment for a scalp to $200 each. But what good was that if they didn't intend to pay?

Regardless, Jim Kirker once more brought his crew of scalp hunters together, and once more they headed out to tame the Apaches. The first encounter was at McKnight's old home town of Galeana, where he slaughtered 160 Apaches, men, women and children. George Frederick Ruxton, a young Englishman who visited Mexico at about this time, wrote that Kirker tricked the Apaches into the massacre, providing them with whisky and acting as though he intended to parley with them.[5] The Indians, said Ruxton, came into Galeana unarmed. When the Mexican residents saw Kirker and his men approaching the city, they set upon the defenseless Apaches themselves and did most of the slaughtering. Here Ruxton was reporting only from hearsay and it is difficult to credit. Apaches at that time were never unarmed, especially if they were going into the enemy's camp. Another thing is that for Kirker to *send* them whisky by messenger, as Ruxton claims, would have made the Apaches suspicious. Under no circumstances would the Apaches, who had only recently asked that Kirker and his people be expelled from Chihuahua and New Mexico because they were feared like the scourge, be walking into a meeting with them drunk and defenseless. The Apaches were astute and cunning warriors, not given to stupidity.

Ruxton did see one thing, though, himself, and that was the portals over the Chihuahua City church with its front covered with scalps, for once again Kirker and company were welcomed into the capital with bands playing and natives rejoicing. During the fiesta celebrating the victory, church authorities draped Apache hair over their edifice. Ruxton says:

Opposite the principal entrance, over the portals which form one side of the square, were dangling the grim scalps of one hundred and seventy Apaches, who had been most treacherously and inhumanly butchered by the Indian hunters in pay of the state. The scalps of men, women and children were brought into town on procession, and hung as trophies in the conspicuous situation, of Mexican valor and humanity!

Regardless of Ruxton's opinion of the Apache slaughter, Kirker was the only man who could lead a force against the Indians and win. When the celebration was finished Kirker was called before the new governor and given a proposal.

Governor Trias offered Jim a full commission as a colonel in the Mexican Army, with the proper documents to prove the authenticity of his rank and commensurate compensation. Knowing that there must be some covert reason for this seemingly handsome offer, Jim asked time to think about it. He returned to his hacienda at the Corralitos and on the way, or just after arriving, he learned that American armies, mostly from Missouri, were marching on their way to take over New Mexico and Chihuahua.

Later, when word came that they were approaching El Paso del Norte after capturing Sante Fe Jim realized what the Mexican government expected of him and he was faced with an immediate decision. There was little doubt that many of his friends, and brothers and sons of his friends, would be marching with the Missouri volunteers. He would have to face them in the Mexican army—if he accepted the proffered commission, and if he didn't he would have to leave the country, or go to prison, or face a firing squad. It was a bitter choice to make as his family would remain in Chihuahua as a possible hostage if he were to throw in with the Americans. There must have been a good deal of soul-searching but Jim and a half-dozen of his Shawnees and Delawares slipped out during the night and headed for El Paso del Norte.

He first dropped down to Sacramento, where he knew the Mexican military was digging in to defend their capital city. There he spent a day scouting the defenses, then turned north and traversed the high country toward the Missouri forces.

If Jim could intercept the American army he could give valuable information, could just about assure the conquest of Chihuahua City, which would even his old score with that government. Yes, Don Santiago Querque would collect that $32,900 owing him.

The interest, too, would be considerable: the Mexicans would be forced to pay the debt by losing their city.

## NOTES TO CHAPTER XIV

1. Hobbs, *Wild Life in the Far West,* p. 93. The author suspects, on the basis of other evidence, that Hobbs wasn't there at all, but got the material for this part of the book from Gabe Allen, who was.

2. *Ibid.,* p. 97.

3. *Ibid.,* p. 98.

4. *Ibid.,* p. 99.

5. George Frederick Ruxton, *Adventures in Mexico and the Rocky Mountains* (New York, Harper and Bros., 1848) pp. 158-9.

# CHAPTER XV

W AR with Mexico had become a part of "manifest destiny" the day Texas was admitted into the United States of America on March 1, 1845. After that, the administration of President James K. Polk tried to avoid the conflict by offering $5 million for New Mexico and another $25 million for California. The secret agent Polk sent with this offer, though, let it leak out and a furious Mexican public arose and overthrew the government that would even consider listening to such an offer.

President Polk then ordered General Zachary Taylor to advance from the Nueces River to "positions on or near the left bank of the Rio Grande." This blocked the Mexican Gulf port of Point Isabel, which the Mexicans promptly burned, removing their forces to Matamoras. The United States Navy then threw up a blockade at the mouth of the Rio Grande and kept harassing the foe, hoping for an incident sufficiently important to warrant a declaration of war.

In the late spring General Taylor finally managed to have a skirmish with the Mexican cavalry and word was sent to Washington, where on Saturday, May 9, Polk began to prepare an address to Congress, asking for a declaration of war. He worked all day Sunday on the address and on Monday afternoon presented it to the House of Representatives, which declared war on Mexico by a vote of 174-14 the same afternoon. The next day the Senate voted, 40-2, for a fight. Polk had the authorization he sought.

In declaring war, Congress also voted for a call for 50,000 volunteers and a budget of $10 million to back them. About the middle of May Missouri Governor John E. Edwards called for volunteers to join an expeditionary force to Santa Fe with the First Dragoons under Colonel Stephen W. Kearny. Instructions were to form companies at the various county seats, then rendezvous at Fort Leavenworth where they would be mustered into service.

The first company to organize was Company A of Jackson County, formed at Independence, where a young wagonmaster, Samuel G. Bean, was hanging around between trips. He decided to make his next trip to Santa Fe under the auspices of the United States Army and enlisted under Captain David Waldo, who was a medical doctor. Bean's was the third name on the roster, and his company was the first to reach Fort Leavenworth, so it might be said that Sam, six-foot-four, was the third man to heed the call to colors. Company A arrived at Fort Leavenworth on June 5 and by June 18 seven other companies had arrived, from Jackson, LaFayette, Clay, Saline, Franklin, Cole, Howard and Callaway counties, forming the First Regiment of Missouri Volunteers.

On the same day the men elected all but their general officers by secret ballot. Private Alexander William Doniphan, a lawyer from Clay county and a member of the state legislature, was chosen colonel and second in command to Colonel Kearny. Doniphan had been a brigadier general in the 1838 campaign against the Mormons in western Missouri.

Ten men were selected from each company to form an advance detachment of eighty hunters and butchers, who were to range ahead and provide fresh meat whenever possible. They were commanded by Thomas Forsyth, the son of Jim Kirker's old friend of the same name. Forsyth's hunters hit the trail also on June 18, driving 800 head of cattle and carrying a 100-wagon supply train.

Kearny's total command consisted of 1658 men. There were 856 in the First Regiment of Missouri Volunteers, 300 regulars, 250 members of two companies of light artillery, 107 Laclede Rangers attached to the First Dragoons, and 145 men in a lone battalion of infantry to be used for occupational duty. All the others were mounted, mostly on their own horses, and at Leavenworth they practiced cavalry tactics twice daily.

The main body of the Army of the West left Fort Leavenworth on June 26, 1846, traveling in a southwesterly course designed to intersect the Santa Fe trail, along which 414 wagons of the traders' caravan from Independence would be picked up.

Albert Speyer, suspected of hauling guns and ammunition to the Mexican army, had pulled out on May 22, just a few days after the Missouri call to arms. He wanted to get out of reach of Kearny's forces—and did, with an additional thirty-odd wagons of general merchandise. Other traders had been moving out since early June, with Sam Owens and his group departing Independence on June 13, a short time before Owens' daughter Fanny sprang her husband from jail by changing clothes with him. Her husband was a lawyer named John H. Harper and he was in jail for killing a man he thought was making love to his Fanny, who was only fifteen years old and something of a nymphet. Owens was a highly regarded merchant and it probably was something of a relief for him to get away from his troubles with his daughter.

Kearny and his command overtook the traders within a few days and the whole outfit arrived on July 29 at Bent's Fort. Here they spent three days resting and then left on August 2 for Santa Fe, which they captured on August 18 without firing a shot. This victory was made easy mostly because James Magoffin, a Chihuahua merchant and friend of Kirker's, bribed Governor Manuel Armijo before the American troops arrived. Armijo was Mrs. Magoffin's cousin, which no doubt made the transaction easier.

Colonel Kearny received word that he was a brigadier general while still at Santa Fe. One of his first moves after gaining that rank was to send several companies out to try to make peace with the Indians. He then instructed Colonel Doniphan to march south, through El Paso del Norte, and link up with General John E. Wool at Chihuahua City. Kearny himself struck out on September 25 with a small force to reach California.

The merchants meanwhile had gone on south to a valley along the Rio Grande called Valverde, where there were pasture and water enough to hold their animals. They set up a semi-permanent camp there to await the arrival of Colonel Doniphan and his men. While so encamped they were visited by the Englishman Ruxton, coming up from Mexico City. He bore a letter from Chihuahua's Governor Trias inviting the American traders to proceed to El Paso, where they would be "allowed the advantages of that market, free from molestation."[1]

Ruxton didn't mention carrying the letter, but he gave a good description of life in camp. The company was formed in a square corral of wagons, making a "formidable" fort, and the "wild-looking Missourians" lounged about in front of their shanties and tents, cooking before campfires and practicing target-shooting. Ruxton said the camp was "strewn with bones and offal," while the men were "unwashed and unshaven, were ragged and dirty, without uniforms, and dressed as, and how, they pleased." He said they were "listless and sickly looking," and sat in groups playing cards when not "swearing and cursing, even at officers." After slandering the flower of Missouri, Ruxton did grudgingly admit that these men "were full of fight as a game-cock. 'Every man on his own hook' is their system in action; and trusting to, and confident in, their undeniable bravery, they 'go ahead' and overcome obstacles."

The men, fearing a trick, did not go ahead into El Paso and on December 12 Colonel Doniphan arrived. He appraised the situation, then sent a messenger to Santa Fe, asking that ten pieces of artillery be sent to him at El Paso. On December 14 Doniphan took up the march south, sending Major William Gilpin on ahead with 300 men, followed two days later by 200 more under the command of Lieutenant Colonel Congreve Jackson. Colonel Doniphan then took up the line of march on December 19 with all the rest of the men. These contingents were thus spaced so that foraging for the animals would be easier.

All three sections of Doniphan's command marched night and day across the ninety miles of Jornado del Muerte, or Journey of Death, which they made in less than three days. The rear guard overtook the advance detachments on December 22 at the little town of Dona Ana, where they were able to buy food for the troops and forage for the animals.

At dawn on December 24, the entire command moved out of Dona Ana and made about fifteen miles that day, camping Christmas Eve near the site of today's town of Mesilla. A warm sun rose over the Organ Mountains on Christmas morning, cheering the Missourians with the brightest and warmest Christmas most of them had ever seen. In celebration of the birth of Christ the Doniphan men sang *Yankee Doodle* and *Hail Columbia,* punctuating the music with pistol and rifle shots.

On Christmas Eve a large number of horses and mules had gotten loose so Colonel Doniphan left behind a fairly large number of men to gather them in and then proceed south. The rest of the troops marched their horses on down the Rio Grande, celebrating Christmas with the best material at hand. Liquor was not supposed to be sold on the march but every soldier knew how to tell a trader's wagon with Christmas spirits for sale—the white canvas covers pulled halfway back was a secret sign between the teamsters and the volunteers.

Flankers were out, skirting both sides of the Rio Grande, and a vanguard was a considerable distance ahead, searching out a suitable campground. This was found at a place called Bracito, on the east bank of the river, near today's Vado, New

Mexico. The train was strung out for several miles, so the men straggled in a few at a time, unsaddling their horses and allowing them to roll in the water while they looked for firewood.

Most of the tents had been discarded in New Mexico when they had worn out, so most of the soldiers were spreading their blankets on the ground. The camp had good water and grass, but wood was scarce. Some of the men went off hunting for ducks, geese, turkeys or other game for a Christmas dinner, certain signs indicating it should be plentiful in this vicinity.

The men had captured a Mexican horse, a fine animal, and they came before Colonel Doniphan to ask how they could determine which of them should possess it permanently. Five of them had come upon the horse at once, so Doniphan decided he and some of his officers would have a game of *loo,* popular at that time, and each would represent one of the enlisted men. The winner would turn over the horse to the man he represented.

Colonel Doniphan and four of his staff had just squatted down to play the game of *loo,* when Lieutenant James DeCourcy, Doniphan's adjutant, pointed beyond a clump of cottonwoods and remarked, "Dust is rising some down to the south." The colonel kept a chary eye on the dust as he played his cards and finally asked DeCourcy to ride down and determine *exactly* what was causing the swirl of dust.

DeCourcy was racing back into camp within a matter of minutes, shouting: "The enemy is upon us!"

Assembly was blown and the sound reached many of the men a mile or so away, some looking for wood or game, while others were carrying buckets of water. All dropped their burdens and grabbed arms, assembling under whatever flag was nearest.

Bracito, where the men were camped, was located west of a pass in the Organ Mountains, dividing the Organs from the White Mountains really, as the name changed at this point. (The White Mountains are called the Franklins today.) The Mexican army comprised about 1300 men, 514 of whom were

regular dragoons from Vera Cruz and Zacatecas, 800 infantry
and cavalry volunteers from El Paso and Chihuahua, with four
pieces of artillery. There were at least two Mexican women with
the Mexican troops, both serving in the artillery.

The regular dragoons were a colorful lot, outfitted with
blue pantaloons, green coats trimmed in scarlet, and tall shako
caps plated in front with brass. From the tops of these waved
a plume of horse hair, or buffalo tail. Their lances and swords
gleamed brightly in the sun, slanting into their tawny faces from
the west.

The Americans were skimpily dressed, many without
shoes. Their feet were covered with makeshift footwear made
from deerhides in Santa Fe and Albuquerque and purchased
with personal funds, as none had yet received any pay. Some
of the soldiers were even down to their underwear, covering
themselves with whatever rags or skins they could pick up. At
the blowing of assembly only about 400 men were in camp. The
balance were either bringing up the rear from Dona Ana with
the lost horses and mules, or out hunting game or firewood.

A lone Mexican lieutenant rode rapidly toward the Missourians' lines, bearing a black flag with a skull and cross-bones
sewn on it in white. He stopped a few hundred feet in front of
the American lines, and Colonel Doniphan sent out an interpreter, Tom Caldwell, to speak with him. The Mexican officer's
name was Lara and he explained to Caldwell that the Mexican
General Ponce de Leon "summons your commander to appear
before him."

Caldwell replied, "If your general desires peace, let him
come here."

"We will break your ranks and take him then," boasted the
Mexican lieutenant.

Caldwell was wheeling his horse around by this time,
shouting back over his shoulder, "Come on then and take him."

The Mexican officer waved his black guidon and shouted:
"Curses be upon you! Prepare for a charge! We neither ask nor
give quarter!"

A trumpet sounded from the Mexican lines and the Vera Cruz dragoons charged the American left, where all but sixteen theoretically mounted men were on foot. The Mexicans hoped to reach the American commissary wagons and baggage train but were repulsed with a loss of four or five men.

The Chihuahua infantry, comprising the major force, was on the American right, where there were less than 200 United States troops. These had previously been instructed by Doniphan to hold their positions in a standing position until the Mexicans advanced and fired the first volley. The Missourians were then to fall forward onto the ground and remain in a prone position until the Mexican soldiers drew up to within sixty yards of their positions. Then they were to rise up suddenly and fire a carefully aimed first volley.

The Mexican infantry started the advance and while still several hundred yards away they let go with their first rifle fire. The Missourians fell on their faces. The Mexican soldiers were sure their aim had been so accurate that they had killed them all. Their charge picked up speed and without reloading they came trotting up, yelling, "Bueno! Bueno!"

When these men came within a sixty-yard range, the whole American right wing rose up from the ground like a covey of deadly quail and blasted the close-order Mexican ranks with a volley of Yager balls. Each of these was directed by a frontier rifleman, and few went wide of the mark.

The havoc was surpassed only by the surprise, both of which were so great the Mexican line melted and faltered to a stop. Soon, the Mexicans were running toward El Paso, discarding weapons, provisions and everything else that might impede their flight.

Meanwhile, the Howard County Missourians repulsed a concerted offensive that resulted in the capture of a six-pound brass howitzer, the only one of four pieces the Mexican artillery was able to bring into action. Sergeant Callaway and a handful of men swung the cannon around and began firing into the ranks of its previous owners.

The whole Mexican army soon was in flight, some trying to escape through a pass in the mountains. Captain John W. Reid and some volunteers, including Sam Bean, chased them through the pass for a short distance, then returned to camp.

The Mexican army lost seventy-one killed, more than 150 wounded, among the latter their general Ponce, who was picked off with a rifle shot by Thomas Forsyth, who, with four or five other mountaineers, coolly walked forward, aiming and firing at Mexican officers only, virtually wiping them out. Ironically, both Forsyth and Ponce were friends of Kirker.

Racing frantically southward, the Mexican troopers discarded everything that got in their way—their ammunition, baggage, wine, provisions, blankets, lances, rifles and uncounted stands of colors.

All during the battle, a group of Apaches was lined across the rim of the mountains, watching the two nations in combat, no doubt taking in the contest to see which side to join when it was over. They seldom lost an opportunity to join the winners.

The field was dotted with packages of food and wine, dropped by the fleeing soldiery. John T. Hughes, a Missouri schoolmaster and one of Doniphan's men, wrote that "Gourds of the delicious wines of El Paso were profusely scattered over miles of surface."[2]

With the wine and other items, the men celebrated Christmas in much finer style than they ever expected. "These supplied our soldiers," wrote Hughes, "with a Christmas bouquet. The whole affair resembled a Christmas frolic. This night the men encamped on the same spot where they were attacked by the Mexicans. Having ate the bread and drank the wine which were taken in the engagement, they reposed on their arms, protected by a strong guard."

Only seven of the Missourians were wounded and none killed. One man was shot in the belt buckle and thought he was done for. His name was David Swan, and he ran all the way to bathe in the water of the Rio Grande, only to come hoorahing back when he learned that all the bullet had done was dent his buckle and knock out his wind.

Dusk settled over the camp, and Doniphan started to take up the game of *loo* again, but it was then learned the horse for which they were playing had run off during the battle.

In the twilight, sentries noticed a tall, buckskinned figure silhouetted against the setting sun. The man was standing on the west bank of the Rio Grande, looking down from a rim high above the river and into Doniphan's camp. The officers called to him and he asked permission to enter. It was given. When he moved forward, it was noticed he was followed by four companions, all Indians, but not Apaches. They were Jim Kirker and his faithful Shawnees.[3]

Meredith T. Moore, a private in Captain M. M. Parson's Company F, gave the best description of Kirker's arrival:[4]

He was dressed as a frontiersman of his day—fringed buckskin hunting shirt and breeches, heavy broad Mexican hat, huge spurs, all embellished and ornamented with Mexican finery. He was mounted on a fine horse, which he regarded with great affection and to which he gave the most careful attention. In addition to the Hawkins [Hawken] rifle, elegantly mounted and ornamented with silver inlaid on the stock, he was armed with a choice assortment of pistols and Mexican daggers. He said he had been living some years in Mexico in the service of the governor, who had contracted to pay so much for each Apache scalp he might take. In hunting down these Indians he had employed a force of 30 or 40 Delawares. Some time before the war was declared between the United States and Mexico, the Governor of Chihuahua owed him $30,000 for Indian scalps, he said; and instead of paying him and his Delawares, they were thrown in prison. Most of the Indians had returned to their own country, but he, with those he could find, had set out for the American Army. Some of the Delawares went home by way of Santa Fe; others remained with the Army and went home by way of New Orleans. . . . Kirker was absolutely fearless; he was a fine rider, well accomplished in the daring horsemanship affected by the old trappers and plainsmen of the time, such as leaning over the saddle so far his long hair would sweep the ground with the horse at full speed. He knew all the trails in northern Mexico, and where water could be found along them. He spoke the Spanish language well, also a number of Indian languages; he proved a valuable acquisition to the army. . . . Kirker came to the army directly from his home at Coralitus [Corralitos].

Colonel Doniphan and others of his staff expected another battle before entering El Paso but Kirker assured them there wouldn't be, saying there would be no more battles with that particular army, for it no longer existed. Most of the men, he said, would not stop until they came to the Presidio Carrizal. or perhaps even Sacramento, where—in either case—they would be reorganized to augment the forces then busy digging in on the bluffs.

Kirker's prediction proved correct, as was every bit of advice he gave Colonel Doniphan during the entire military campaign. Doniphan, however, was inclined to mistrust Kirker, doubt his true intent and even question his ability at the onset. It was only as time went on that Doniphan realized he had gained a most valuable ally.

## NOTES TO CHAPTER XV

1. Connelly, *Doniphan's Expedition,* p. 276.

2. Hughes's diary is published in Connelly's *Doniphan Expedition,* from which the details of this campaign are taken.

3. Frank S. Edwards, *A Campaign in New Mexico with Colonel Doniphan,* London, 1848, cited in Connelley's *Doniphan Expedition,* p. 424; Marcellus Ball Edwards, *Marching with the Army of the West,* Ralp P. Beiber, editor, (Glendale, Clark, 1936) p. 237.

4. Connelley's *Doniphan's Expedition,* p. 388.

# CHAPTER XVI

ONTRARY to what he expected, Jim Kirker found he knew few of the young Missourians, for it had been more than twenty years since his last visit to St. Louis and most of the volunteers were not even that old. An exception was Tom Forsyth, whose father had been a regular customer at Jim's store. The Forsyth son was about forty years old now, much closer to Jim's age than were the rest of the men.

Forsyth and Jim weren't afforded much time to reminisce, however, for Tom was dispatched the day after Christmas to Santa Fe, carrying news of the victory at Bracito and urging the immediate dispatch of Major Meriwether Clark's artillery to bolster American forces for the contemplated invasion of Chihuahua City.

Kirker marched south with Doniphan, first camp being made at a brackish lake some eight miles north of the present city of El Paso, where the men were called to arms twice during the night, only to learn there was no danger. The next morning they reached what was known as the Great Pass, a gorge in the mountains which no longer exists. Here, at about noon, they encountered a deputation of El Paso citizens bearing a white flag. They besought Colonel Doniphan to show clemency toward all citizens and to protect their property in return for the surrender of their city, which he agreed to. That constituted the capture of El Paso del Norte.

The men were bivouacked south of the plaza but suffered from wind-driven sand, which got into their eyes, their nostrils, their mouths and their food, and were shortly moved into houses near the plaza. Residents were assured that the quartering of troops, the purchase of food, provender and supplies would all be legally contracted and paid for through the quartermaster department. Samuel Combs Owens, the Independence trader, carried with him a ready and large supply of cash, which he advanced to the quartermaster for immediate payment, so it was not necessary to resort to the issuance of script.[1]

Kirker's first job was to help in the search of El Paso homes for hidden guns and ammunition, which was begun on December 29; when it was completed on New Year's Eve more than ten tons of powder and lead had been uncovered. A few days after the New Year Jim was chosen to lead a hunting party up the Rio Grande, consisting of Captain David Waldo, a young Scottish engineer from Company B named Corporal Lachlan Allan Maclean, who was also an artist and mapmaker, and an un-named Mexican friend of Jim's, probably a member of the Ponce family. They were out about ten days and upon returning reported great sport. They also told of chasing small bands of Mexicans encountered here and there.[2]

The Americans, meanwhile, were literally having themselves a ball, for the *bailes* and *fandangoes* were in constant progress, attended by great numbers of young ladies eager to take care of their guests's wants and desires. Hughes wrote in his diary that attending all of the dances was an "abundance of fair senoritas of the place whose charms and unpurchased kindness almost induced some of the men not to wish to return home." Hughes told also of so much gambling taking place in the streets that Doniphan had to forbid it to keep the public thoroughfares free of obstruction.

An unusual accident occurred one night at the Frenchman's, a two-story saloon and hotel on the southeast corner of the plaza, a favorite gathering place for the Missourians. Two lieutenants got drunk there and became embroiled in a vicious fight. Lieutenant Robert Barnett of Company B stuck his bowie knife completely through the throat of Lieutenant R. A. Wells, Company F, with the blade protruding about an inch out of the back of his neck. Barnett, in a panic now, pulled the knife out and called the medics. Wells was not cut in any vital organ or blood vessel and lived, becoming so intrigued in his wound and subsequent treatment that he took up medicine, practicing at Jefferson City, Missouri, and later in Montana.

Remarkable medical cases seemed to abound among these rough soldiers. One volunteer from Company F, named Samuel Cogburn, came down with the measles during a snowstorm. He leaped out of bed and jumped in a snowbank, stuffing snow in his mouth and rubbing it under his arms. It killed him.[3]

Another Samuel, last name Maxwell, was a blacksmith and farrier. He was one of those who wanted to remain permanently in El Paso and when he heard that the men had voted to go on and attack Chihuahua City he was shoeing a horse. He dropped the horse's hoof in consternation and began talking against the decision. He spoke without stopping for two solid weeks, talking himself to death, and was buried in El Paso.[4] Many of the men suffered no illness worse than lovesickness but sometimes this cost Doniphan the services of important individuals. The interpreter, Thomas J. Caldwell, quit his job and returned to Santa Fe to join his sweetheart and raise a family. He owned a store in that city with his partner, Samuel Wethered.

Caldwell was replaced by James L. Collins, a former justice of the peace at Boonville, Missouri and a one-time associate of Sam Owens in the Santa Fe trade. Collins had made his first trip west in about 1826. Redheaded, peppery and abrasive, he was called The Squire. He was loud and raucous, a propensity which caused him to be arrested at El Paso del Norte a few days before the Battle of Bracito. He was taken to Chihuahua City for trial on charges of treason against his adopted country, but managed to escape with the help of another Missourian, a man named Pomeroy, who threw a rope over the prison wall.[5]

Tom Forsyth returned from his trip to Santa Fe to bring back more astonishing news then he had gone up with: the Indians and certain native leaders in northern New Mexico had revolted against the American authorities, resulting in the assassination of Governor Charles Bent on January 19. The rumors preceding the event had delayed Colonel Sterling Price from sending the artillery requested by Colonel Doniphan earlier. Forsyth said order had been restored, however, and the cannons were on their way. The four six-pounders and two twelve-pounders arrived in El Paso del Norte on February 1, after battling a blizzard for the last 150 miles.

Despite the arrival of artillery, Colonel Doniphan was hesitant about advancing on Chihuahua City. His orders had been "to join General Wool" in that city but General Wool was bogged down before Santa Ana's armies and it appeared Wool might never reach Chihuahua. Kirker urged him to capture the capital, guaranteeing victory and outlining both the strategy and tactics to bring it about, causing the *Niles' Register*—the *Time* magazine of that day—to publish the following observation: "The news of the insurrection in New Mexico had produced irresolution in our ranks and persuasion of Kirker alone induced our army to move forward."[6]

Kirker's constant heckling and cajoling finally persuaded Doniphan that the logical move was to advance before the morale of the army was destroyed with easy living offered by the fleshpots of El Paso, so the army moved out on February 8, headed south toward Chihuahua City, taking with it five prominent malcontents of El Paso as hostages. The most important of these was Father Ortiz, the Catholic priest who had been caught conspiring against American occupational forces.

The next day, February 9, Jim Kirker selected a special detachment of eight men to accompany him on an advance scouting party. The first man Jim selected was Forsyth and the others, too, were experienced in the lore of the wilderness. Their

Thomas Forsyth, a scout and buffalo hunter with Doniphan who shot General Ponce de Leon in the Battle of Bracito. Both he and his father, who was Indian Agent to the Sauk and Fox Indians, were customers at Jim Kirker's store in St. Louis. *Courtesy of the Missouri Historical Society*

first obstacle was the Presidio of Carrizal, the only major fortification standing in their path to Chihuahua City. Normally this old Spanish fortification was inhabited by about 400 people, but intelligence reports had it that the Mexican government had recently augmented its strength by four companies of infantry, artillery and cavalry.[7]

Kirker's tiny force carried no provisions and after four days of scouting, they were forced to kill and eat one of their mules to keep from starving. Just as they were eating their first meal in three days, they were joined by Lieutenant George R. Gordon, on patrol with fifteen men, including Jim Collins and another interpreter named Henderson.

Kirker had been perplexed over how only eight men were going to take fortifications supported with artillery and several companies of troops but with an additional sixteen men he felt much more confident. They marched on Carrizal and captured it simply by rushing the gates and catching the inmates by surprise. It was not so heavily reinforced as rumor had led them to believe. The additional troops had pulled out hours before Kirker and his men arrived.[8]

Meanwhile Colonel Doniphan was forming the merchant traders into a combat battalion and on February 12 a vote was held with Sam Owens being elected major, being the oldest and most experienced of the caravan members. A native of Green County, Kentucky, Owens was forty-seven and beset with what his friends called "family problems."

Edward J. Glasgow, a younger veteran of the Santa Fe trail, was selected as one captain and Henry Skillman, later to play an important part in the history of El Paso, Texas, was captain of the other company. Skillman was a native of New Jersey, raised in Kentucky.

Doniphan's command now numbered just under 1000 men, and they reached Carrizal on Thursday, February 18, where they joined Kirker and the other men who had taken the town several days earlier. The Missourians remained over at Carrizal for two full days, men and animals consuming the supplies Kirker's advance unit had captured for them.

Kirker informed Doniphan that now only two obstacles lay in his path to Chihuahua City: Hacienda Encinillas, owned by Governor Angel Trias, and the fortifications at Sacramento. On Saturday, February 20, Jim took Forsyth and fifteen men with him to scout out these two positions.[9]

Kirker was later joined by Captain Reid and a handful of mounted men, including the artist, Lachlan Maclean. Together they captured Encinillas, which also was reported to have been reinforced. Hughes was a member of this party and he reports that they had to approach the hacienda from the rear, across a three-mile-wide shallow lake.[10]

> Reaching the opposite shore, they saw no sentinel. Therefore they approached nearer. Still they saw no sentry. Cautiously, and with light footsteps, and in the most breathless silence, without a whisper or the jingling of a sabre, and under covering of dark, they advanced a little. They heard the sound of music, and at intervals the trampling of horses. Perhaps it was the military patrol. None knew.
>
> They rode around the hacienda; the walls precluded the possibility of seeing within. No satisfactory reconnaisance could therefore be made. Not wishing to return to camp without effecting their object, the captain and his men, like McDonald and his mad-caps at Georgetown, made a sweeping dash, with drawn sabre and clattering arms, into the hacienda, to the infinite alarm of the inhabitants. They now had possession. The 700 soldiers had started, about an hour previous, to Sacramento. This was a bold and hazardous exploit. They then quartered in the place, which contains several hundred inhabitants, and were sumptuously entertained by the Administrator del Hacienda.

Jim selected two or three Shawnee and Delaware scouts to accompany him and went south to make a detailed study of the enemy position at Sacramento, returning on Saturday, February 28, with a diagram of the latest positions and a report that there were 4000 Mexican soldiers facing them.

Jim imparted this information to Colonel Doniphan and his staff, then stretched his legs and sought out a sutler's wagon for a drink of brandy. There he met Collins and Sam Owens. The latter, usually jovial and talkative, was morose and silent. He had just received word by the latest mail that the husband of his fifteen-year-old daughter had been recaptured in Arkan-

sas and was being brought back to Independence to stand trial
for the murder of the man suspected of having an affair with
his child wife. Sam had talked the case over with Colonel
Doniphan, a leading Missouri lawyer, and the latter had agreed
to defend the man provided they returned in time.[11] Owens
went to his tent a short time later, walking unsteadily, as he had
been drinking constantly for the last three or four days, ever
since the delivery of the mail on February 20.

Jim and Collins bought themselves a bottle of *aguardiente*
and sat down to kill it while talking over old times. It wasn't
long until the liquor had made Collins inordinately brash and
he made a remark which aroused Jim's ire, probably about his
cousin David's surrendering to a war party of Comanches and
leaving ten companions on their own to face hundreds of Indians. This cowardice of David's had rankled in Jim's memory
for more than twenty years and time in no way dimished his
shame every time he thought about it.

Collins continued with his blathering and finally, without
noticing Kirker was growing angrier, suggested that cowardice
probably ran in the Kirker family.

Kirker leaped on Collins, as "that meant a fight to the
death," wrote an eyewitness, Meredith T. Moore. "Colonel
Doniphan heard of the difficulty and prevented a duel. He told
them the Mexican army would be encountered within a day or
two, and that their courage or cowardice could be tested on the
field of battle—that nobody doubted the bravery of either—that
he could not have his men killing one another in the very
presence of the enemy. They agreed to postpone their meeting
until after the battle with the Mexican army had been fought.[12]"

While Kirker and Collins slept that night, snoring their
disdain at each other, Sam Owens stayed up, thinking, fretting.
Shortly before sunup, he laid out a dazzling white suit of duck,
some white cotton gloves and a beautiful red cravat. Sam
wanted to be dressed fit to kill the next day. At dawn he was
up shaving, combing and brushing his hair, carefully dressing
himself. Not far off, one of Owens' old employees watched this

unusually fastidious preparation with great interest. He later told Josiah Webb, a friend of Sam's, that Owens "shaved and dressed himself with care, saying he did not know what might happen. If killed in battle, he wanted to be clean shaven and fitly dressed." The man told Webb further that Owens "courted death, owing to family troubles, as he knew of no more honorable or desirable death than to die in battle."[13]

Meanwhile Jim slept on, not knowing that his hatred for Collins would indirectly be the cause of Sam Owens' death.

## NOTES TO CHAPTER XVI

1. Connelley, *Doniphan's Expedition,* p. 92, quoting from Hughes's diary, January 13, 1847.

2. *Ibid.,* p. 386, fn.

3. Connelley, p. 556, fn. 78.

4. *Ibid.,* p. 396, n. 102.

5. *Ibid.,* p. 91-2.

6. *Niles' Register,* Vol. LXXII, No. 11, May 15, 1847, p. 172.

8. Marcellus Ball Edwards, *Journal,* Ralph Beiber, editor, Southwest Historical Series, Vol. IV, p. 252.

9. Connelley, p. 101, entry in Hughes's diary for Saturday, February 20, 1847.

10. Connelley, p. 405, Hughes's diary. According to Hughes, those taking part in the attack were, besides Kirker, Captain Reid, C. C. Human, W. Russell, J. Cooper, T. Bradford, Todd, I. Walker [a Wyandot Indian], L. A. Maclean, C. Clarkin, Long, T. Forsyth, Tungitt, Brown, W. McDaniel, J. P. Campbell [a beef contractor for the army], T. Waugh, J. Vaughn, Boyce, Stewart, Antwine, A. Henderson and F. C. Hughes.

11. Doniphan was defense attorney for William H. Harper, husband of Owens' young daughter, the following November, and after obtaining a change of venue to Platte County, Mo., Doniphan was successful in getting Harper acquitted. Accounts of the affair appear in the Missouri *Republican,* June 1, 1846, and the St. Louis *New Era,* June 1, 3, 12, 1846, as cited in Waugh's *Travels,* p. 110, and also *History of Jackson County, Mo.,* p. 641.

12. Connelley's *Expedition,* p. 416, fn. 108.

13. Josiah Webb, Southwest Historical Series, p. 274.

# CHAPTER XVII

T HE 400 covered wagons hiding the American army rattled and weaved along the road to Sacramento. They proceeded in columns of four parallel lines, spaced fifty yards apart, with the artillery in the center, two rows of wagons on each side. In advance of the whole were the cavalry companies of the first and second battalions and the Chihuahua Rangers.

"By this arrangement," wrote Major William Gilpen in his official report, "giving compactness to our force and effectually concealing our numbers, the whole army could be deployed in battle order to the front, rear, or on either flank, the wagons at the same time forming a corral sufficiently large, if necessary, to envelop and protect it."[1]

The road down which they were passing would split apart about eighteen miles this side of the capital, one branch passing around some high bluffs and sloping land to the right, while the other went to the left. The two parts of the road came back together again about six miles farther south after skirting the high ground.

The highest part of the bluff was at the eastern end of the plateau, or on the Americans' left, and the heights reached some sixty feet above the plain upon which the Missouri army was approaching. The ground sloped downward from the bluffs to the west, or the Americans's right, for about two miles and about another two miles beyond that was an abandoned *torreon,* or circular fort, made of adobes crumbling with age.

The newer and more traveled branch of the road angled across a dry creek bed to the right, then climbed slightly over a lower portion of the plateau and about a mile farther south began a descent which led to a junction with the left branch of the road. The older, or left, fork of the road meandered around to the east of the bluffs, following a little valley, and took about another two miles to reach the juncture behind the rise at the hacienda headquarters.

In these heights, rising as a sort of island between the old and new roads to Chihuahua City, the Mexicans were gathered to make their stand. "Upon this formidable line of defenses," wrote Major Gilpin, "was deployed the Mexican army. On their extreme left, and in front of the redoubt of the main road, was 1000 cavalry, drawn up in four masses, two on the right hand and two on the left of the road. In the redoubt was infantry. In the first fort immediately on the right, two 10-pound, two six-pound pieces of artillery and six musquetoons [a large caliber musket, short barreled and used by cavalry]. These pieces of artillery are all of brass, drawn by eight mules each, served by 300 artillerymen, and supplied from 10 large wagons and many pack mules loaded with ammunition. Along the trenches in the intervals of forts were 2100 infantry; in their rear and in the camp, 800 rancheros, mounted infantry . . ."[2]

Two larger cannon were placed on the promontory facing north, which commanded both the old and new approaches to the mesa. The entire position was in the best military tradition, manned with a total of 4224 Mexican troops under the overall command of Major General Jose A. Heridia. Garcia Conde, architect of the defenses, was in command of the cavalry only. General Mauricio Ugarte was leader of the infantry, while the now General Justiniani commanded the artillery. Chihuahua's governor, Angel Trias, was leader of the state volunteers.

The Mexican general staff sat their horses on the highest portion of the bluff watching the Americans approach. The Mexican army was arrayed before them, brilliantly uniformed, standing in rows under flapping regimental colors and guidons. Prayers had been said, the troops properly blessed, the clergy assuring them they were God's chosen and held his benediction. The priests then walked out of the war arena and joined the hundreds of spectators who had traveled from Chihuahua City on horseback, in shiny black buggies and in coaches, to see the excitement. They had brought with them baskets of food and jugs of wine to enjoy while they watched the battle from high rims, crags and hills—well out of reach of pistol, rifle, or even cannon.

Mexican officers studied the American army carefully with their telescopes. Flankers rode wide on each side, scouts in buckskin. Near the center and at the head of the cavalry rode several officers, one of whom attracted the immediate curiosity of the Mexican viewers. He was dressed all in dazzling white and the Mexican officers guessed that he was the supreme commander, for why else would he wear such a costume? The man in white actually was only a slightly obese trader recently elected major of the freighters' battalion, Sam Owens.

The figure farthest out at the Mexicans' right as the American army approached was a massive buckskin figure on a horse which these excellent judges of horseflesh could see was an unusually fine animal. This was Jim Kirker, riding all alone, to the east of the wagon columns.

The day was warm, the sun a little south of west. Perspiration oozed from under Jim's low-crowned sombrero and ran down the sides of his long angular jaw, dripping at his chin, the result of last night's whisky. His horse picked its way through the rock-strewn mesquite. In the tortures of a hangover, Jim was working up a monumental hate, not at the Mexicans but at a particular redheaded Irishman named Jim Collins.

The wagon columns surprised the Mexican generals by making a gigantic, wheeling turn to the west before coming into range. The officers, watching in amazement as the columns of Missourians continued on west, interpreted this to mean that the United States troops were desperately trying to avoid a fight, that they were frantically trying to reach the old *Torreon* and there make a stand, Alamo style, to the last man.

General Heridia had placed a thousand cavalry under the foot of the bluffs, backed up by another thousand foot soldiers, to charge the Americans head-on when they came close enough.

"In the meantime," wrote Major Gilpin, "the enemy, embarrassed by the change of direction in the American column, and finding their position useless, withdrawing from every point, formed upon their second line. This line consisted of 13 redoubts of infantry, forming a continuous chain along the crest of the bench flanking the main [new] road, terminating in the fifth redoubt for the cannon at the southwest corner of the highland, where it commands the ford to Sacramento."[3]

Meanwhile Colonel Doniphan had sent out a detachment of laborers with picks, shovels and several span of mules to fill a crossing over the dry creek bed. Within minutes they had dumped rock and sand into the depression and topped it off with flat stones to make the wagon crossing almost easy.

Surprise of the Mexican general staff at the Missourian turn to the west changed to amazement when they saw Doniphans's forces turn once more and head south, beyond the filled *arroyo*. Amazement became consternation when the Americans swung another ninety degrees and pointed due east, up the rising slope and directly toward the Mexican position from the west, advancing on the Mexican flank.

Out from between the columns came the mounted riflemen. The two Missouri battalions pulled up and dismounted, leaving every seventh man to hold horses. The Second Battalion took up positions at the extreme left under Major William Gilpin, while the First Battalion under Lieutenant Colonel D. D. Mitchell, mounted on a white horse, moved to the extreme right. In the center was the artillery, commanded by

Major Meriwether Lewis Clark, who was personally in charge of the six cannon, and Captain Richard Hanson Weightman, commanding the two twelve-pound howitzers, mounted on special carriages to charge with the cavalry behind teams of Kentucky horses, trained personally by Weightman.

The 400 wagons, manned by the Traders' Battalion under the command of Major Owens and Captains Glasgow and Skillman, were wheeled into two mammoth corrals at the rear, to form a sort of fortification to which the Americans could fall back for a last-ditch stand if necessary.

Weightman meanwhile unlimbered his two howitzers, his men leaping to the ground to check over their teams, making sure harness and chains were secure for the charge they planned to make with the cavalry when ordered.

The Mexican artillery opened with a few futile rounds and at this Weightman's voice sounded over the din: "Form battery, action front, load and fire at will," and the American artillery answered.[4] The enemy was about 900 yards away and the artillery from neither side was effective. The two Mexican ninepounders, facing the extreme right of the American lines, opened up on the Missourians but the copper balls struck the ground 200 yards in front of the line and became completely visible after being slowed down with the first bounce. The men were able to anticipate the course of the balls so well that they could dance around and dodge between them, with even the horses leaping and spreading their legs to let them go by.[5]

With each round, though, Justiniani was adjusting his range so that he was soon striking the corralled wagons and hitting some of the horses. One ball broke the legs of Company G horse-holder, Private Ami Hughes.

Kirker noticed with concern the increased effectiveness of the enemy battery set up in the southern redoubt. This was the battery he had worried about and one that must be silenced if heavy carnage was to be avoided. This could make the difference between victory and defeat.

Jim stood once more in his saddle to locate the black

leather cap on top of flaming red hair, finally spotting Collins with Captain John W. Reid's company of cavalry. Now, Kirker said to himself, was the time to put his plan in action, for the good of everybody—except perhaps Collins. Or Kirker. Jim wheeled his bay and rode around behind the infantry column, spurred to a trot and was loping by the time he came up beside Collins. Jim shouted loudly enough above the din for those many yards away to hear, including Meredith Moore, private of Company F, from Cedar City, Missouri:

"Let's you and I see who can get into that Mexican battery first!"[6]

Jim pointed to the second redoubt on the right where the cannon were fast getting the range of the American forces. At almost the same time, Colonel Doniphan gave the order for the cavalry to charge.

Collins looked around at Kirker, but made no reply. He pulled his leather cap down tightly on his head, "drew his sword and buried the rowels in the flanks of his horse and was away for the battery at full speed."[7]

Kirker and Collins raced almost side by side toward the enemy lines, which spurred Captain Reid to follow. Within seconds John P. Campbell, the meat contractor, Sam Owens and Private Joseph Marshall, Company D, were also running their horses to catch the leader, Kirker. These six men charged the two nine-pound guns guarded by at least a company of infantry in dug-in stone breastworks.

Kirker was first to reach the redoubt, then Collins, both emptying their pistols in the faces of the cannoneers, and then came Sam Owens, his snow-white suit glistening in the sun. "Owens and his horse were killed almost at the redoubt," said Private Moore. As soon as the troubled man struck the ground, a score or more of Mexican soldiers came out from the redoubts and ran him through with lances, stripping his body of the white suit and even removing his footgear.[8] It was a death Kirker had meant for Collins.

This insane charge, instigated by Kirker out of his hatred

for Collins, ironically saved the day for the American forces, according to Moore, who said:

> Owens and his horse were killed almost at the redoubt, and the others turned to the left and ran along the Mexican front past several redoubts, drawing the fire of the entire Mexican line unhurt. That action saved the lives of the Americans. . . . The order to charge came after these men were under way, and the whole line leaped forward. From some cause never rightly understood, DeCourcy [Doniphan's adjutant] rode down the line shouting, "Halt, Captain Parsons! halt, Captain Parsons!" DeCourcy was drunk, and should have been promptly shot . . . Colonel Doniphan seeing the confusion arising from DeCourcy's action, galloped down the line shouting the order to charge, but many did not hear him because of the rattle of Mexican fire drawn by Kirker and others. . . . A storm of indignation and wrath was rising and would have broken in a minute, for the troops were not regular soldiers, disciplined to strict obedience. Each man thought for himself, knew what he was there for, and realized that his life depended upon the defeat of the Mexican army. But in a moment, as with a single movement, all were away with yells that startled the Mexicans, who had no time to reload flintlocks just discharged at Kirker and the others before the whole American line was over the redoubts.[9]

It is obvious not only that it was Kirker's strategy to approach the Mexican army from the west and up the gently rising slope but also that Jim unwittingly set in motion a tactic which handed the American forces an easy victory; even though that tactic was originally designed to get Jim Collins killed, or maybe Jim Kirker too. The only man killed in the entire American army that afternoon was Sam Owens, and every indication points to his death as having been a sort of suicide. There were eleven wounded. In view of DeCourcy's drunken behavior Kirker's charge may have saved Doniphan's men from disaster, too.

Whatever other results this "insane charge" had, it most certainly relieved the bad feelings between Kirker and Collins, for after returning to the American ranks the two seemed, if not overly friendly, at least not enemies.

One of the most surprising events of the aftermath—or perhaps it isn't, considering military jealousy—is the fact that this charge by Kirker and the others is not mentioned in a single official report by any of the officers, including Doniphan. Many are cited for bravery, but not these men. They were not even given credit, hint or slightest mention in the official dispatches. All of the accounts come from private diaries, journals and interviews. This could not have been accidental negligence. The officers must have been ashamed of the conduct of some of their own and under no circumstances would admit the victory was actually won by a handful of scouts and traders not officially in the service.

DeCourcy's egregious blunder is likewise omitted, as his superiors and fellow officers covered up his strange actions. Neither was DeCourcy's drunkenness ever reported officially nor was he court-martialed, which only may go to show the army hasn't changed much in the 125 years between Kirker's charge and the buried scandals of Vietnam.

Doniphan came out of the battle a hero. Frank Edwards, with Captain Weightman's artillery company, says that when the charge began Colonel Doniphan fell to his knees, "covered his face with his hands, and almost groaned out, 'My God! They're gone! The boys will be killed.' "[10] This, of course, was one more item not included when Doniphan sent his officers' reports on the battle a few days later, on March 4.

Poor Sam Owens was laid to rest with a high requiem mass in the Catholic cathedral on the plaza. He was buried in a black suit bought for him by his Chihuahua City partners, James and Robert Aull.

George Rutledge Gibson, of the quartermaster department, said the ceremony was "imposing," that "they said every prayer, performed every genuflection, and tried every trick they knew to get him safely into heaven, but the most potent charm was the $600 which they charged. . . . This took him through purgatory at once and no doubt landed him safe."[11] Owens was then buried in the cemetery located near the bullring.

Sam may still be turning over in his grave though, over that $600 laid out unnecessarily. Somebody made a mistake. Sam was a member of the Cumberland Presbyterian Church back in Independence.

## NOTES TO CHAPTER XVII

1. Connelley's *Doniphan Expedition,* pp. 428-9.

2. *Ibid.*

3. *Ibid.*

4. Frank S. Edwards, *A Campaign in New Mexico with Colonel Doniphan,* London, 1848, cited in Connelley's *Expedition,* fn. pp. 424-25.

5. *Ibid.* p. 425.

6. M. T. Moore, quoted by Connelley, following both a verbal and written interview, note, 108, p. 416, Doniphan's *Expedition.*

7. *Ibid.*

8. Lieutenant Marcellus Ball Edwards, *Journal,* p. 264; Webb, *Adventures in the Sante Fe Trade,* pp. 274-5. Edwards wrote: "They approached the very ditch of the battery that seemed lit with flame and smoke. It was here the career of the unfortunate Owens was cut short, he having received two shots and two lance wounds, and Captain Reid's horse two balls in the thigh . . ." Webb says: "Colonel Owens kept on, charged a redoubt alone, and with his pistol fired on the Mexicans, who returned the fire, killing the Colonel's horse, which fell on him. And the Mexicans left their defenses and killed and stripped him of his valuables, and returned . . . the body was found not a rod from the embankment thrown up for defense."

9. Moore account to Connelley, *Expedition,* pp. 418-19.

10. Frank S. Edwards, *A Campaign in New Mexico with Colonel Doniphan,* cited in Connelley's *Expedition,* p. 427.

11. George Rutledge Gibson, *Journal of a Soldier Under Kearny and Doniphan,* edited by Ralph P. Bieber, Glendale, 1935, p. 354.

# CHAPTER XVIII

COLONEL DONIPHAN made his grand entry into Chihuahua City on March 2 to the strains of *Yankee Doodle* and *Hail Columbia,* two songs which had already served him well as Christmas carols, and he was immediately faced with the question of what he should do now. One-year enlistments were nearing their end and many of the non-enlisted personnel were heading back to Missouri, including Major John Campbell, the beef contractor, and his able assistant, Thomas Forsyth. Their job was done, and Campbell's original 800 beeves had been consumed long ago.

News of General Zachary Taylor's victory at the battle of Buena Vista reached Chihuahua City on March 18, and two days later Doniphan dispatched Jim Collins as an express to Taylor, congratulating him on his victory and asking what Doniphan's orders were now. Meanwhile Doniphan called his officers together for a council of war. Some wanted to return immediately to St. Louis, others to Santa Fe. Some liked the girls and the wine right where they were, but Major Gilpin led the largest group of officers, those who wanted to continue down to Mexico City and capture the national capital. He suggested there was $800,000 in the Chihuahua mint and that this would be enough to finance the expenses for such an adven-

ture and then some. One detachment, under Lieutenant Colonel Congreve Jackson, did go as far as San Rosalia, some three
days to the south, but was ordered back.

Another council was held and Doniphan, exasperated at
so many opinions, settled the whole matter by banging his fist
on the table and exclaiming, "Gentlemen, I'm for going home
to Sarah and the children."

On April 23, Collins returned and the information he
brought fitted right in to Doniphan's plans. The Missourians
were ordered to proceed to Saltillo, where they would be mustered out and sent home.

Kirker, like the others, had received no pay during this
period, although it had been agreed he was to receive the same
compensation as a colonel for the duties he was rendering Doniphan. He decided to go along to Saltillo, where he expected to
be officially mustered out and paid up along with the rest.

Upon arriving at Saltillo they were received with pomp,
reviewed by General Wool, who suggested they all re-enlist for
another year. There were no takers. General Wool said in that
case, they would have to walk seventy-five miles farther, to
Walnut Springs, near Monterey. Here they were greeted by
General Zachary Taylor, who also reviewed them and when the
subject of mustering out was raised said they would have to go
on to New Orleans and report to General Sylvester Churchill,
the inspector general, who would muster them out of the command and issue their discharges and pay. So Jim followed along
as they boarded the ships *Murillo* and *Republic* at Brazos
Island on June 9 and docked at New Orleans on June 15.

The appearance of these famous heroes from Missouri
came as a shock to the residents of New Orleans who had
prepared to receive a spit-and-polish, 100-percent uniformed
force of military men. Thousands of spectators lined the docks
and jammed the streets to welcome the first authentic batch of
heroes to come out of the Mexican conflict. Instead the men
who stumbled off the boats were dirty, bearded and the ones not
in rags were in their underwear.[1]

Of the officers and men to arrive in New Orleans, Kirker was one of the few to be singled out for a special story in the New Orleans *Picayune,* which had carried a couple of stories concerning his adventures a half-dozen years earlier. It said: "We are happy to announce to the citizens of New Orleans, that Don Santiago Kirker, late Colonel of the Mexican service, and celebrated for his feats of daring against the Indians, but during the present war, better known as spy, interpreter, &c., of Colonel Doniphan's command of Missouri Volunteers, is now in this city and leaves for the west in the *Clarksville,* this day. [June 26, 1847]."

This was the good news about Jim but he soon learned the bad news that he would not receive any pay for himself or his handful of Delaware and Shawnee scouts because he was considered the same as members of the Traders' Battalion, who wouldn't be paid either. The army's position was, explained General Churchill, that Colonel Doniphan did not have the authority to muster in additional forces.[2]

Since he had come this far, Jim decided it would be to his advantage to take the *Clarksville* on up to St. Louis and go back to Santa Fe by the overland route. Again when the ship reached St. Louis it was Kirker whom the reporters sought out. The *Clarksville* docked at St. Louis on July 3, 1847, and a reporter was waiting to interview Jim for a story which appeared in the St. Louis *Reveille* on July 5:

> We had a long felt desire to meet Kirker and sure enough, we encountered him the day before yesterday. His history is a most remarkable one. If ever a man has un-Irished himself, as far as appearance goes, it is Don Santiago— otherwise Mister Jim! He is dark as night, and upon occasion can look quite threatening. His exploits against the savages, while under the pay of the Chihuahua government, are well known. We regard him as one of the most interesting among the mountain men. He will be in St. Louis but a day or so longer.

Col. Charles Keemle, or "Gray Eagle" to the Indians of the Upper Missouri, was a long-time acquaintance of James Kirker and probably was author of the Kirker biographical sketch which appeared on July 10, 1847 in the *St. Louis Saturday Evening Post and Temperance Recorder*. Keemle owned this newspaper when the story appeared, selling it just one week later, and continued to print it from his shop for the new owners. *Courtesy of the Missouri Historical Society*

Jim must have been anxious to get back to his family in Chihuahua, especially to learn if they had suffered because of his defection from Mexico to the United States. However, there were other reporters to talk to Jim. One wrote a rather long

interview, long especially for that day, when most papers were
only four pages in size and most stories only a short paragraph.
It appeared in *The St. Louis Saturday Evening Post and Temperance Recorder,* dated Saturday, July 10, 1847.[3]

Jim's many friends and acquaintances in St. Louis and
Santa Fe must have considered it a good joke that his biography
should appear in a publication devoted to abstention, for ab-
stemious Kirker never was. Keemle owned the *Post* at the time
Kirker's story appeared but sold it one week later. There is little
doubt that Keemle wrote the article himself for the author
mentions having known Colonel Kirker twenty-five years earlier and that "the visit of Col. Kirker among us seems like a
dream." Keemle is the only man in the newspaper business at
that time in St. Louis who would have known Jim back in the
days when he ran a grocery on Water Street, above the Team
Boat Ferry.

An engraving of Jim's likeness accompanied the story,
which was also an unusual touch in 1847 journalism. The biography follows.

James Kirker is a native of Belfast, Ireland, where he was
born on the 2nd December, 1793. On the 10th June, 1810,
the subject of our sketch arrived in the city of New York,
where he resided until the breaking out of war in 1812, at
which time he went on board the privateer *Black Joke,* and
served on the coast of Brazil till 1813. The vessel in which
he served was at length captured by the British ship *Lion,*
and he was soon exchanged for the crew of the *Java.* He
returned to New York in the American ship *William,* commanded by Capt. Davis.

In 1817, then in his 24th year, Mr. Kirker arrived in St.
Louis, and remained in this city until the spring of 1821,
when he joined the mountain company of General Ashley
and Major Henry, and departed for the upper Missouri
region.

The defeat of General Ashley by the Arickeras, which
soon after followed, led to the expedition of General Leavenworth in 1822. The company of Ashley and Henry were

ordered to form a junction with Gen. Leavenworth at the Arickera village. Mr. Kirker with others, accordingly descended the Missouri to that place. Owing to some disagreement which took place between Mr. K. and the leaders of his party, he left their company, and joined the force under General Leavenworth, with whom he subsequently returned to this city.

In 1824, Mr. Kirker again left the haunts of civilization, and repaired to the Mexican country on a trapping expedition. For some time he was quite fortunate, as well in the recovering of an impaired state of health, as in his success as a trapper. Eventually, the products of his enterprize were seized by Governor Narbone of Santa Fe, without any excuse or apology, and future labors of the kind forbidden. Mr. Kirker then repaired to the copper mines of Mr. Robert McKnight, where he remained for a period of eight years, trapping the Rio Gila every winter.

In 1835, the subject of our sketch obtained a license from the Governor of Santa Fe, Don Alvino Perez, to trap and trade with the Apache nation of Indians for one year. He set out with 18 men, and was, for a time, highly successful in pursuit of his enterprize. Previous to the expiration of his license, however, the Supreme Government hearing of his success, sent an order to Gov. Perez for his arrest, and decreed the confiscation of his property, alleging that the Governor possessed no authority to grant such a license to an alien and a heretic. Perez accordingly proclaimed Capt. Kirker an outlaw—though it was obvious that he had broken no law whatever—seized his property, and offered $800 for his arrest, dead or alive.

Thus compelled to abandon the country, Capt. K. repaired to Bent's Fort, on the Arkansas, and remained there until after the death of Perez, who fell a sacrifice to mob violence, in the streets of Santa Fe, in 1836.

As soon as Armijo had assumed the reins of power, he invited Captain Kirker to return to the province, which invitation was soon after accepted.

About this time news was received in Santa Fe that the mining operations of Cuicier [sic] & McKnight, in the state of Chihuahua, had been broken up by the Apache Indians. Capt. Kirker at once resolved to go to the protection of his old friends. He raised, at his own expense, a party of 23 men, several of whom were Shawnee Indians—one of them the noted Shawnee chief, Spy-Buck—and marched into Apache country, near the scene of hostilities. Coming upon an Apache village containing 247 persons, this little party attacked it, killed 55 warriors, took nine female prisoners, drove off 400 head of stock, and totally destroyed the village. In this engagement the assailing party lost one man killed and eight wounded. The rest, only 14 strong, conveyed their wounded, prisoners and stock to the small town of Socorro, in New Mexico.

The fame of this victory reaching Chihuahua, Capt. Kirker was invited by the governor of that state to head a party of 50 men against the Apaches, who at that time were very troublesome to the Mexicans. He acceded to the proposition, and was allowed the pay of a colonel, although his non-citizenship did not permit the grant of a colonel's commission.

From the period just named, until the breaking out of the war with the United States, Col. Kirker remained in the service of the Mexican Governor, constantly warring against the Apaches, escorting Government trains, &c. While in the service of the State of Chihuahua, he estimates the number of Apaches killed by himself and command at 487, and in all this time his own loss only reached three men killed.

As soon as the Governor of Chihuahua received intelligence of the contemplated invasion of his state by the Americans, he sent for Col. Kirker, and offered him a bona fide Colonel's commission, and many other inducements to get him to take command in the regular service against the invaders. Without giving a direct reply, Kirker resolved at once to join the American arms, and to this end he was prompted by the solicitation of the Magoffins, and other traders, who were then prisoners. Accordingly with four followers he quitted Chihuahua, and after a journey of 17 days through the wilderness, fell in with Col. Doniphan's command at Valverde on the very night succeeding the battle of Bracito. Col. Doniphan and his command were overjoyed at meeting with so efficient and valuable an ally, and at once availed themselves of his aid as guide and interpreter.

As soon as it became known at Chihuahua that the slayer of the Apaches had joined the army of the invaders, "Don Santiago Kirker" was pronounced an outlaw, and the neat little sum of $10,000 was offered for his head. Neither at Sacramento, however, nor subsequently at the City of Chihuahua, nor at El Paso, nor on the entire march through Durango to Saltillo, did any one appear to request the favor of the prize. "Don Santiago" still wears it, as its semblance here presented—taken the present week by the unrivalled daguerreotypist, Easterly, and engraved by that excellent artist Ware—testifies. It is an excellent head, and worth every cent of the price set upon it by his excellency, the run away Governor of Chihuahua.

After so many years of absence from St. Louis, the visit of Col. Kirker among us seems like a dream to those who knew him as a citizen of St. Louis a quarter of a century ago. He is still the free, kind hearted acquaintance, yet years of peril, privation and exposure have done their work in altering his outward mien: while his long association with the Mexicans and Indians has so changed his accent that few would suspect him of being a son of the Emerald Isle. Col. Kirker is a highly intelligent man, and his experience he has acquired by his intercourse with the semibarbarians of the West, has pre-eminently qualified him to aid the public service at this crisis. We understand that he immediately leaves this city for the mountains—whether in a public capacity we have not been informed.[4]

The facts as given in this interview, with the exceptions of certain specific dates, were probably essentially accurate, as Keemle was completely familiar with those aspects dealing with early St. Louis and the Arickara campaigns, since he, too, was there. Internal evidence indicates the writer had known Jim since the early St. Louis days.

That doesn't mean that Jim gave *all* of the facts, by any means. His Mexican citizenship is never mentioned, nor did he speak of either of his two wives, or the families he had both east and west.

## NOTES TO CHAPTER XVIII

1. Connelley, p. 492.

2. This caused hundreds of the men who served in these outfits to complain bitterly. Captain Edward Glasgow, whose son, William, would attend West Point and become a general, wrote his feelings down and they were typical: "The Traders' Battalion has been treated badly by the government, for although it participated in the battle and its major, Samuel C. Owens, was killed in the engagement, none of us received any payment or pensions, the excuse given for the refusal being that Doniphan had no legal authority . . ." Connelley's *Expedition,* p. 398.

3. The biographical interview appeared on July 10, 1847, and was so credited when it was reprinted on November 20, same year by the Santa Fe *Republican,* but no copy of this issue of The *Post* is extant. There is one for the following week, July 17, 1847, in which there is mention of the previous week's story on Kirker. This is Vol. 1, No. 14, and is in the MHS collection, St. Louis.

4. Thomas M. Easterly, mentioned as the daguerreotypist, was the first to establish a rogues' gallery in this country. He was born at Brattleboro, Vt., in 1809, and died in St. Louis, March 11, 1882. He came to St. Louis in 1847 from Liberty, Mo., and refused to adopt the photographic process, remaining a daguerreotypist until the end of his life. Joseph E. Ware, the engraver of Kirker's likeness, was a young wood and metal engraver in St. Louis, reported by Alonzo Delano in his *Across the Plains and Among the Diggings* (New York, Wilson-Erickson, 1936) p. 70, as from Galena, Ill., and author of the *Emigrants' Guide to California,* 1849, in collaboration with Solomon P. Sublette. Alonzo Delano reports that Ware died of cholera along the California trail in July of the same year, but Dale L. Morgan, in correspondence dated August 28, 1969, says, "Actually the man in question was one Thomas Waring of Hannibal, Mo. Ware was still in his trade as an engraver, etc., in St. Louis through 1851." According to an advertisement in the St. Louis Directory for 1851, Ware also acted as a draftsman and agent for U.S. patent applications. Ware is not listed in any St. Louis directories after 1851.

# CHAPTER XIX

J IM was back in New Mexico in the fall of 1847. On November 20 the Santa Fe *Republican* reprinted the biographical sketch that had appeared in the St. Louis newspaper on July 10, and on Christmas Day the *Republican* carried the following notice:

### JAMES KIRKER
This distinguished mountaineer and Indian slayer, had opened a Hotel in the lower part of town, where we trust he may receive a liberal share of the Patronage, as no man is more deserving of it.

However highly regarded Jim might be in Santa Fe, however deserving of patronage, he was an outlaw in Chihuahua, where Governor-General Trias still offered a reward of $10,000 for him, dead or alive, for the part he played in the American invasion. This made things difficult from a domestic standpoint, for Jim's family was still in Chihuahua and he could not even visit there without risking his life.

He didn't remain in the hotel business long; within six months he was back fighting Indians for what seemed to be a particularly inept U.S. Army. For some time the Jicarilla

Apaches, sometimes allied with the Utes, were raiding settlements along the frontier border between Colorado and New Mexico, and Captain S. A. Boake was sent against them with a command of fifty men, leaving Santa Fe on June 14. When these Indians turned and fought back, Captain Boake and his men literally ran away. Boake claimed he was "too ill to fight."[1]

Major W. W. Reynolds realized that if the Indians were to be pacified at all, it would have to be by Indian fighters, not regular soldiers who were in the army because they couldn't do anything else. Consequently he employed Jim Kirker, Old Bill Williams, Levin "Colorado" Mitchell and Robert Fisher, all experienced mountain men, to provide the knowledge and courageous example needed by inexperienced troops in any confrontation with hostiles.

They left Taos with Reynolds' company on July 8, totaling 150 men to combat approximately 400 Apaches and Utes in the San Juan Mountains at Cumbres Pass. The Indians were dug in and waiting for the fight, which came on July 23, and the Indians were thoroughly whipped, Williams received a bad wound in the elbow but Kirker and the other mountain men came through the battle without a scratch. They were not given a single line of credit in the official report of Major Reynolds to his superior, General Price. Again it is necessary to turn to civilian sources to learn that it was the service of the old Indian fighters which indeed brought victory, as reported in the Santa Fe *Republican* for August 1, 1848, but these seasoned men must have been well paid for going in and doing the army's work.

Old Bill Williams was helped back to Taos by Kirker when the fighting was over and there Old Bill had his shattered elbow set. Kirker dropped back down to Santa Fe, where he found some sufficiently pressing reason to depart the southwest for a hurried trip to Belfast, Ireland, and back. Perhaps there was a death in the family and an estate was to be settled. Possibly his mother had died, for Jim's father had died in the spring of 1812 and his will, probated on May 25, 1813, left Jim certain property upon the death of his mother, "*if he comes home for it.*"[2]

No details of Jim's journey have been discovered, except that the round trip must have set some kind of record for that day. Jim could not have left Santa Fe much before August, 1848, due to his campaign with Major Reynolds against the Indians, and on the following January 29, 1849 he was reported back in St. Louis and getting ready to cross the plains as a scout for a wagon train of midwest gold seekers bound for California. The story, appearing in the St. Louis *Weekly Reveille* (published by Kirker's old friend, Keemle) read:[3]

### ARRIVAL OF KIRKER

Mr. James Kirker, of New Mexico and Chihuahua celebrity, is in town, having just returned from a visit to his family in Ireland. Mr. K. is making preparation to pilot to California a party of gentlemen from Cincinnati. He takes the Arkansas route, and from his acquaintance with the country, and the respect which his name inspires among the Indians of the plains and mountains, his party may expect a speedy and quick trip.

At about the same time the newspapers were filled with stories of a cholera epidemic in St. Louis. The steamboat *Amaranth* arrived from New Orleans on December 28, 1848 with thirty cases aboard, on January 23 the steamer Alex Scott came upriver with forty-six cases and on the same day twenty-six more dying patients were taken from the steamer *St. Paul.* At the height of the epidemic, 722 people died of cholera in one week in St. Louis.[4]

This disease spread rapidly through St. Louis, via the market places and the water supply. Death, during this epidemic, could result from a bite of uncooked fruit or vegetable or a single drink of water from a contaminated source.

The victim first was overcome with diarrhea and fever, then a violent headache, purging, muscular cramps and unquenchable thirst. The final stages were marked with a drop in temperature and blood pressure, arrested circulation, sunken eyes, hollow cheeks and cool breath. A stricken one could run this whole gamut in less than twenty-four hours, with death most often coming within eight to ten hours after the first symptom.

Covered wagons headed west in the California gold rush of 1849 often picked up cholera as an unseen passenger when crossing through Missouri and the trail west was dotted with thousands of graves of those unfortunates who contracted cholera and died en route.

Jim Kirker successfully avoided contracting the disease while waiting in St. Louis that winter and early spring. Jim drank something stronger than water whenever it was available.

## NOTES TO CHAPTER XIX

1. National Archives, War Department, Record Group 94, Major W. W. Reynolds to Brigadier General Sterling Price, dated Santa Fe, August 10, 1848, received October 16, #460 Price correspondence.

2. Probate Records, Antrim County, Ireland, Ref. PRONI T808/8854, extracted by Conner. The extract reads: "Will 24.4.1812 proved 25.5 1813 of Gilbert Kirker of Carnaghlis, Killead Par. His son Gilbert Kirker the . . . 22 acres . . . Residue to wife Rose Kirker including Wm Jenkins' house, if she dies before end of lease then to son James *if he comes home for it* [italics in original will]. He to pay daughters Rose and Martha 13.0.0 yearly if he does not, then to Rose and Martha and their children; sons-in-law Henry Clemans and Hugh Spears. Executor Gilbert Kirker of Killersees and James Kirker of Drumadaneny. Witness William Kirker, Richard Conly, William Simkin. Probate to wife. *Codicil*—Wm. Jenkins holding to be sold; my claim to my late brother, James, part in our lease of farm to his son William. Witness: W. McMaster, S. Thompson, Robert Thompson."

3. St. Louis *Weekly Reveille,* January 29, 1849.

4. Cholera statistics taken from Vol. III, No. 3, March, 1936, *Glimpses of the Past,* MHS, St. Louis, "Cholera Epidemics in St. Louis."

# CHAPTER XX

EXACTLY when or how Jim Kirker made the agreement to lead the Peoria Pioneers and others across the plains is not recorded. Technically, Jim was employed by forty-two men comprising the company known as the Morgan County and California Rangers of Illinois, whose captain was Joseph Heslep. It was with Heslep that Jim made the arrangements for his employment.[1] No mention of the terms is found in the caravan's accounts but Charles Pancoast, who wrote his reminiscences of the trip, said Jim received a riding horse and $50 down, with the promise of $100 more when the party reached its final destination.[2]

Jim and the Peoria Pioneers took a steamboat from St. Louis for Independence, a principal jumping-off point for the trails leading to Santa Fe, Oregon and other western destinations. On the boat were two brothers, Myron and Eugene Angel, the former a one-time cadet at West Point who quit the Military Academy for an adventure in California, the latter a lawyer in Peoria.[3] Myron later edited newspapers in Placerville, Oakland and other California cities and wrote a third-person account of his journey westward.[4] Myron contended that the Peoria group originally intended to go to the gold mines via the South Pass but that the "treachery" of a steamboat captain forced a change of plans. Myron reported that the captain refused to take them up the river to St. Joseph, landing them at Weston, instead. The men then decided to take the trail via the Arkansas and Gila rivers.

Myron wrote: "On the steamer was Captain William [sic] Kirker, an old mountaineer, who had been guide to Colonel Doniphan in his march through New Mexico a few years previously. He told of gold mines in the Rocky Mountains, far richer than those in California, and a large sum of money was paid him by a collection of Illinois and Missouri people who then made up the company."

This is not quite accurate. Myron and his brother were completely broke and were not originally members of the Peoria party, so it is not likely they would know about Kirker's agreement with the expedition leaders, or if they did they had forgotten. Pancoast, on the other hand, was there and he is explicit, writing shortly after his journey.[5]

The Peoria Pioneer train under Kirker left Independence on May 15, with an exceptionally well-equipped caravan. Dr. Augustus Heslep wrote that the original company was supplied with clothing to last two years, including India-rubber garments for rainy weather, blacksmithing tools, provisions for from six to nine months and extra equipment of all kinds, such as saddles, harness, shoes for the animals, scythes and heavy artillery ropes to pull the wagons by hand wherever necessary.[6]

By the time the train was ready to pull out, though, it had grown to 200 members, "ignorant and learned," wrote Pancoast, "wild and erratic, and staid, sober souls; jubilant good fellows, and crooked, ill-natured Curmudgeons. There were preachers, Laborers, Sailors, and representatives of many other occupations. Among them was a 300-pound pilot. Some of the men were as old as 65 years; others were invalids when they started."[7]

All of this meant that Jim had his hands full. It is one thing to take forty or so men across the plains in ten wagons or less and quite another to take more than 200 people in forty-four wagons. There were many campsites sufficient for the needs of a small number of people but there were not so many to accommodate a party as large as the one Jim now was responsible for. At the end of each day a spot had to be found with sufficient water, fuel and forage for the animals and naturally the larger the party the more difficult this would be. Without thinking or consulting their guide the Peoria company invited nearly everybody they saw.

As if this additional responsibility was not enough, Jim came down with the cholera just as they were leaving and had to fight this illness as well as fatigue and the incapacity of those around him.

"Captain Kirker," wrote Dr. Heslep, "suffered from a slight attack of cholera, yet the old man promptly mounted and, though extremely feeble, sat his horse as staid and erect as the youngest man in the company."[8]

Exerting sheer willpower to suppress his physical agony, Jim rode out the painful symptoms of the disease and his condition was normal within a few days. Meanwhile Kirker's caravan had joined up with a small group of men under Congreve Jackson, Jim's old comrade-in-arms who had been a lieutenant colonel under Doniphan, and they continued on together.

Two or three days later, at a place called Lone Elm, the Kirker expedition came upon a stranded train of emigrants with many of its members suffering from cholera. Jim and Dr. Heslep visited with the stricken men and Dr. Heslep not only treated them but advised a doctor with this train of his method of treatment. The group, known as the Pioneer Train and destined to travel the Oregon Trail, was near mutiny.

Having done all they could to help, the Peoria train turned south at this point, mainly to avoid the hundreds of wagons ahead of them on the upper trail. By this time the trail seemed almost solid with covered wagons, not all of which had white tops. Many were painted yellow, blue or any color at hand, to rain-proof them.

At night the wagons formed into a corral, one behind the other, in either a circle or square. The stock was turned loose on pasture until nightfall, then brought into the circle or square for protection. Tents were pitched about twenty feet outside the wagon corral and it was in these the travelers slept, not inside the wagons as seen so often in the movies and on TV. Incidentally, these were not Conestoga wagons, as they were so often called, those Pennsylvania-made vehicles never having gotten much farther west than Pittsburgh.[9]

Captain Heslep, Kirker and a young man named Larue had a brief brush with Indians one day without serious results.[10] A few days later, on June 1, the expedition halted on the banks of the Little Arkansas River and time out was called for a buffalo hunt. A herd of some 10,000 was crossing their path and about sixty hunters, under Kirker, were organized to see how much fresh meat might be obtained. The men were not experienced, according to Pancoast, who wrote that "Buffalo hunting was new to all except Kirker."[11] Jim divided the group into two parties of thirty men each, instructing one to keep to the east, the other to the west, while the train passed to the north.

"The western party started them," said Pancoast, "and they ran toward the eastern company, among whom was our guide, Kirker."[12] The men grew so excited that one shot himself and another shot his horse in the neck. A third was thrown from his mount and it ran away, never to be recaptured, along with all of his equipment. In spite of the confusion Kirker was able to down two buffalo, and Pancoast's mess, at least, was supplied with fresh meat. "Our boys," he recalled, "brought in twenty pounds of good steak, on which we feasted several times."

Four days after the buffalo hunt, while the train was following the Arkansas River, there was another Indian scare, this time a major one. Near where the present Colorado and Kansas state lines meet, 1500 Arapaho and Cheyenne braves were seen approaching over the sandhills on the opposite bank, many of them covered with bearskins with the fur on the outside and looking to Pancoast like "monsters."[13]

The chiefs in the van as the Indians approached the river waved three white blankets on poles, indicating to Kirker they wanted to come in peace. He had a difficult time keeping the men from firing, especially as the hundreds of Indians began crossing the river and coming up the bank occupied by the Peoria Pioneer train. Kirker suggested that the caravan captain order all the men to fall back into the corral which had been formed to the rear and do nothing unless fired upon. Meanwhile Jim and the other leaders held a council with the chiefs, Kirker acting as interpreter. The Indians said they wanted to trade with the emigrants and this Kirker relayed to the train's leaders, admonishing them not to barter any arms or ammunition.[14] Jim had not forgotten the expensive lessons learned from Ashley's mistakes.

"One man from each mess was permitted to go and trade with the Indians, who formed a line fifty yards away. They traded for moccasins, buckskin coats, and other Indian handiwork for trinkets, looking glasses, Tobacco, Whiskey and toy Paints."[15]

When the trading was over, the Indians offered to run foot races with the whites and a "little bowlegged Illinois Blacksmith" ran several races against the best men the Indians had to offer. The blacksmith won every race easily, taking all the money the Indians had, plus several buckskin articles such as coats, pants and shirts. The Indians were so impressed they thronged around him, slapped him on the back, and shouted *"Bueno!"* They asked the captain if they might not take him along with them and race him against other tribes, an offer that was quickly declined by both the captain and the blacksmith.

One of the chiefs came to Kirker and asked if he, or his medicine man, could do anything for a severe chronic infection of the eyes. Dr. Heslep wrote, "He was brought to me for examination by Captain Kirker, which, as a matter of course,

I gave him [and] also prescribed and put up a quantity of medicine. When done, the confounded dirty, greasy chief perforce turned in and gave me three hearty hugs."[16]

Westward-bound emigrants didn't like Indians even when they were friendly.

## NOTES TO CHAPTER XX

1. *Daily Missouri Republican,* May 24, 1849, one of a series of letters written by Dr. Augustus M. Heslep under the *nom de plume* of "Rambler".

2. Charles Pancoast, *A Quaker Forty-Niner* (Philadelphia, U. of Penna. Press, 1930) p. 185.

3. *History of Nevada,* San Francisco, 1881, reprinted, Berkeley, 1958, pp. 305-6.

4. *Ibid.*

5. Pancoast, *A Quaker Forty-Niner,* p. 176.

6. *The Santa Fe Trail, Letters and Journal of Augustus M. Heslep,* ed. Ralph P. Bieber (Glendale, Clark, 1937) pp. 356-7, fn. 266.

7. Pancoast, pp. 184-185.

8. "Rambler," *Daily Missouri Republican,* July 4, 1849.

9. Joseph T. Kingston, member of the staff of the Pennsylvania Historical Commission, writing in *The Southwesterner,* April, 1963, p. C-3, reports that, "Few, if any genuine Conestoga wagons ever travelled as far as the Mississippi. In fact the western terminus of the great bulk of Conestoga wagon traffic, during the decades 1790–1850 was Pittsburgh, Pa." Kingston wrote that the wagons which crossed the plains "had little really in common" with the Conestoga freighters except a "first glance resemblance in profile."

10. Heslep letter, May 20, 1849, 110-mile Creek, Indian Territory, *Daily Missouri Republican,* July 4, 1849.

11. Pancoast, *A Quaker Forty-Niner,* p. 187.

12. *Ibid.*

13. Pancoast, 192.

14. *Ibid.* p. 193.

15. *Ibid.*

16. "Rambler," Greenhorn Village, July 8, 1849, *Daily Missouri Republican,* September 12, 1849.

# CHAPTER XXI

J IM KIRKER led the band of gold-seekers to the site of today's Pueblo, Colorado, which consisted then "of three deserted Log Cabins," according to Pancoast. There the expedition camped for several days to make wagon repairs and build a ferry boat large enough to take the wagons safely across the Arkansas River. The ferry was in the form of a raft, made by placing hollow-log canoes abreast about two feet apart and nailing planks across.

While the work was progressing a violent storm came up, smashing wagons and blowing down tents. Terrorized animals stampeded through the camp. Fortunately no one was hurt and the next morning, after gathering together what horses were left, a fairly large party took out after the lost stock. They were personally "led by Kirker, who was so expert that he could follow the trail at a gallop."[1] The men returned about nine o'clock that night, "half starved" but bringing back all but two of the cattle.[2]

Kirker told the leaders of the expedition that if all they were looking for was gold they could find it along Sangre de Cristo Creek, and about fifty men were sent out to prospect.[3] "Some was found," wrote Dr. Heslep, "but not sufficient to justify detention. The question of the existence of valuable mines at that point is settled by examination. There is no gold of consequence, notwithstanding our private advices of the fact."[4] Later events were to prove Heslep wrong and Kirker right, and years afterward Myron Angel, writing his autobiography for the *History of Nevada,* blamed their mistake on the prospectors' "being entirely ignorant of the occurrence of gold, or how to obtain it."[5]

Eight members of the Peoria company, discouraged after the "failure" to find Colorado gold, turned back from Pueblo to the United States. They were murdered by Indians on the plains a few days later.[6]

With the stock all rounded up, repairs made and the ferry built, Kirker began crossing wagons and goods over the Arkansas Tuesday morning, July 10, and by the next day they had made it to the Greenhorn River, where a tiny village was growing up around a trading post.[7] Here a Delaware Indian proposed to several of the gold-seekers that he would take them over the short route to California within thirty days for $50 and a good horse. Against Kirker's emphatic advice some eighty members decided to follow the Indian. He deserted them within a couple of weeks, they became lost and, divided into two groups of about forty each, according to Pancoast, one headed south down the Colorado River while the other left the river, bearing north. The party headed south finally made it to California after undergoing extreme hardship but, says Pancoast, "At the time of the relation of the story (to wit, October, 1851) none of the other Parties had ever been heard from."[8]

Less than 150 men were left in the company being guided by Kirker after the departure of the impatient Forty-niners and Kirker started these off on Friday, July 13. On July 26, the caravan passed over a ridge of mountains and came down into a beautiful valley, "covered with fine grass, over which hundreds of horses, cattle and sheep were ranging," wrote Pancoast. This was Kit Carson's ranch, Rayado, and at sundown they approached its headquarters, "a two-story log affair, sur-

*Left:* Petra Kirker, as she appeared as an elderly woman and wife of Sam Bean at Mesilla, New Mexico. *Right:* Sam Bean, Jim's son-in-law. Bean is celebrated as the first marshal of the Arizona Territory, as well as being the older brother of "All the Law West of the Pecos," Roy Bean, the judge and jury at Langtrey, Texas.

rounded by Adobe walls for the purpose of fortification. Inside the walls were several Adobe Houses, and outside a number more, as well as a large Corral and several buildings used as Stables, Slaughter Houses, etc."

Pancoast added that "Carson had about him a dozen or more Americans and Mexicans and about twenty Indians, besides a number of squaws, all to be fed at his table; and judging from the waste we saw around the place, his table was of no mean order."[9]

Carson is described by Pancoast as "superior," and adds that Kit's skin "was dark and he wore long black hair over his coat, giving him much the appearance of a Mexican. He dressed in first class Indian style in Buckskin coat and pants trimmed with leather dangles, and wore moccasins on his feet and a Mexican Sombrero on his head."[10]

Kirker and Carson had known each other for at least twenty-five years and must have had much to talk over. Pancoast says the Kirker caravan was given a "cordial" reception by Kit, who also supplied each of the various messes with a "clever piece of beef," and that "at our first meeting he had little to say; but after supper he sat down by our camp fire, and we found him very garrulous, entertaining us until 11 o'clock with his numerous Indian adventures."[11]

The next night was spent on the Ocate River and at dawn they were preparing to lower their wagons by ropes through Guadalupe Pass. They had the wagons well into the pass that night when they were hit by a flash flood but made it to high ground in time to suffer nothing worse than their "washing done without extra labor."

The train entered the little town of San Miguel del Bado on Saturday, August 4, and the Sabbath was spent visiting the ruins of the old Pecos Pueblo. On Monday, Kirker directed the line of march so that the caravan camped fifteen miles east of Santa Fe, explaining there wasn't pasture for the animals any nearer. The next day, August 7, Jim left the train and rode into Santa Fe. Here he notified Joseph Heslep that he was quitting as guide. There were many in Santa Fe who could guide them on to California.

No reason is given in any accounts extant for Jim's quitting the Peoria party. Santa Fe may have been as far as he intended to go anyway. It may have been because he found his daughter Petra in Santa Fe, where she was living with her freighter husband, Sam Bean. She and Sam had been married on the previous March 11, in the ancient Church of Guadalupe in El Paso del Norte.[12]

It had to be a joyful reunion for Jim and Petra. Jim hadn't seen any member of his New Mexico family since that day early in December 1846 when he went off with a handful of Delawares and Shawnees to join the American cause at Bracito. He still couldn't go back to Chihuahua to see them for there was still that price of $10,000 on his head.

In Santa Fe Jim struck up a friendship with a Dr. Andrew Randall, who was on his way to California with General James Collier, the newly appointed customs collector at San Francisco, en route to assume his duties. The Collier and Randall party waited over in Santa Fe for nearly two weeks, during which time Dr. Randall and Jim became acquainted and spent long hours in the discussion of various topics. Dr. Randall kept a diary and his entry for Saturday, August 18, read:[13]

> During the last eight or 10 days I have had the pleasure of meeting with Captain Kirker, who was waiting the arrival of a Trader from the states, bound for Chihuahua, that he might make some arrangements with him in regard to his family who reside in El Paso.
>
> The company came by the head-waters of the Arkansas and by Taos to visit some reputed gold mines of that region, but they found nothing worthy of attention. Their reputed richness vanished on using the spade and wash bowl. Mr. Kirker gave me a specimen from the Greenhorn of the Arkansas. Mr. Kirker is one of the most intelligent mountain men I have ever seen, gentlemanly in his deportment, and manner, a more intelligent face I have never seen on a mountain man. He would [be an asset in] any circle of society—he has a large claim against the Mexican government—he has never received a cent for his services from our government, for his services to the Army of the West under Col. Doniphan—to whom he rendered important service. He is bitter against Gov. Armijo and confirms the account given of him by Kendall in the 1st Vol. of his account of that expedition, says he was a sheep thief, a liar, etc., etc.
>
> Mr. K. has a daughter (a fine looking woman) by a Mexican woman, some 22 or 3 years old I should think (with whom he stayed), married to an American by the name of Bean, a trader. For account of him, see the following sketch: [Here is attached the biographical sketch clipped from the Sante Fe *Republican,* Nov. 20, 1847.]

Heslep and others with the Peoria train meanwhile obtained new guides and proceeded onward, while Jim awaited the arrival of "a trader from the States"—probably Ceran St. Vrain—who would help Kirker get his family back up to Santa Fe.

## NOTES TO CHAPTER XXI

1. Pancoast, *A Quaker Forty-Niner,* p. 202.

2. *Ibid.*

3. "Rambler," *Missouri Republican,* September 12, 1849.

4. *Ibid.*

5. Myron Angel, *History of Nevada,* p. 305.

6. The *Pennsylvania Inquirer,* September 26, 1849, as cited in Pancoast, p. 202.

7. Pancoast, pp. 203-4.

8. Pancoast, p. 206.

9. *Ibid.*, p. 209.

10. *Ibid.* A Mexican sombrero of this period was not at all similar to the one thought of today. In the 1850's these hats had large, fairly hard brims, but were low-crowned, similar to the headgear worn by *picadors* in today's bullfights. The Mexican "pico" sombrero, with the high crown, associated with Mexico of recent times, did not come in until after the American Civil War, or about 1867.

11. *Ibid.*

12. The date and place of marriage are given by a long-time family friend of the Beans, Mrs. Katherine D. Stoes, writing in the Las Cruces, N.M., *Citizen,* February 17, 1955.

13. Dr. Andrew Randall's Diary is unpublished, but there is a typescript copy of the ms. in the California State Library, Sacramento, which covers only his trip as far as Santa Fe and a day or two thereafter on the departure for California. The final portion of the diary, covering the trip to the coast, has not yet been located.

# CHAPTER XXII

How and exactly why Jim Kirker landed in California late in 1849 or early in 1850 is unknown. What is known is that he was blown "sky-high" in a steamboat explosion on the San Francisco waterfront in the late afternoon of October 29, 1850, following an all-day celebration of California's admission to the Union.

President Millard Fillmore signed the measure making California a state on September 9, 1850 but the news didn't reach the Bay Area until October 18, when the steamer *Oregon* came into the harbor bearing a huge bunting upon which was painted *California is a State.*

A formal celebration was scheduled in San Francisco for October 29. One of the organizers of the great event was George C. Yount, with whom Kirker had trapped back in 1827. Yount's granddaughter, Mary Liza Davis, aged five, was chosen to represent Miss California on the major float in the parade.[1]

Early pioneers, especially veterans of the Mexican War, were invited to participate on that Tuesday and Jim left his headquarters at Oak Spring to attend the festivities. Oak Spring was about three miles south of New York of the Pacific, or Pittsburg as it is called today, and it was there he took the steamboat for San Francisco.

The celebration started at sunrise, when a cannon was fired, and almost immediately exuberant and festive sounds began emanating from all sections of the city. People gathered in varied kinds of costumes to take their place in the procession, scheduled to start at ten A.M.. The parade started almost on time, its line interspersed with dozens of bands, floats, fire engines, Chinese, Freemasons, soldiers, sailors, city officials and consular representatives of many foreign countries.

One float carried a print shop, complete with press in operation, and printers composed broadsides to pass out to the crowds. The principal display was a colossal chariot drawn by six horses, upon which rode thirty children dressed in blue trousers, with belts and shirts of white wool, carrying escutcheons and seals of the different states of the Union and wearing on their heads the famous liberty bonnets of France. In their midst sat a delicate little child, Yount's granddaughter, representing their youngest adopted sister, the thirty-first state.

At the conclusion of the parade, as related by Ernest DeMassey, there was a period of speechmaking in the plaza, and for some reason people sang, by his account, the *Marseillaise.* Then the Chinese began firing off all sorts of pinwheels, firecrackers and gunpowder. DeMassey was somewhat disturbed by this, pointing out prophetically that "firecrackers are not only noisy but extremely dangerous in a city built of dry wood, where one lone spark could really start a large fire."[2]

If DeMassey thought this was noisy, he must certainly have been shaken about five o'clock that evening by what happened at the Central Wharf.[3] Jim Kirker had just gone aboard the new steamboat *Sagamore* and was headed aft to purchase his ticket to return home on the vessel bound for Stockton. With no warning, the *Sagamore* boilers exploded and the force of the blast blew Jim at least fifteen feet in the air. His life may have been saved when his return fall to the deck was cushioned by two dead bodies. Fifty people were killed in the explosion and many of the wounded were taken to the City Hospital. At two o'clock the next morning fire broke out in the wood-frame hospital and in a half hour it was ashes. Some of the patients were severely burned but no additional lives were lost.[4]

An examining board met to take evidence and determine the cause but few witnesses seemed able to give any rational account. One who did was Jim Kirker and he wrote a detailed story of the catastrophe for the *Alta California,* which published his version on October 31, 1850.

> I—James Kirker had just gone on board and was going aft to pay my passage, when the explosion took place, and was thrown some 10 or 15 feet in the air and lit on the bodies of 2 persons (dead). When I recovered my presence of mind and the steam cleared away, I saw as many as 25 persons on the deck who were apparently not hurt, and a great many who were killed or wounded. I saw 2 hanging on the side of the wreck badly wounded and crying for help. I caught hold and pulled them in.
>
> By this time several boats had got along side and were busy picking up people who were thrown in the water. As I was late getting on board, I should think there were as many as 130 people on the upper deck when the explosion took place.
>
> I had been in the Rocky Mountains since 1821, trapping beaver and killing grizzly bears and for the last five years fighting Apaches and other hostile tribes, as well as being Col. Doniphan's guide, spy and interpreter from Santa Fe to Matamoros. So that I have seen some service as well as being in some tight places. But being blown sky-high by a little hot water and so mixed up that I was uncertain how I would come down is more than I have been accustomed to, so in the future I shoulder Old Reality and take Walker's Line, driving tandem, ie., one foot before the other, in preference to traveling on these blow up concerns.

Jim and the Shawnees and Delawares who came to California with him were occupied as hunters of game, not precious minerals, but such hunting also could have been a lucrative business. Meat was scarce in San Francisco at that time, due to the tremendous increase in population, and the best game was found in Contra Costa County where Jim and his men lived at the foot of Mount Diablo.

The original returns for the Federal Census in Contra Costa County for 1850 were lost, but the State of California ordered a special one, made in 1852, wherein Jim and the half-dozen Indians with him are listed as "hunters."[5] They probably would have given the same occupation thirty or so years earlier.

It is said that Jim did some ranching in the Mount Diablo area but there is no Kirker brand entered in the county records, as there are for other ranchers raising cattle there at the time during which Kirker lived in the neighborhood.

Vincent Neri, who was approaching his ninetieth birthday in 1964, told the California Native Daughters at a Pioneer's Picnic in Contra Costa county how his father had worked in the coal mines near Somersville, California, and that he had known Kirker personally. He spoke to his son, Vincent, several times about the strange old man.

"Kirker's business at the time of his death," his father told Neri, "was running cattle in the open range of Clayton Valley."[6]

Whatever Jim's business was, he didn't live long after that census was taken in the autumn of 1852. He died either before the year was out or in the first days of 1853, apparently from natural causes. No notice of the death is to be found in any of the county records at Martinez, the county seat. Jim's demise is, however, referred to in an early history of Contra Costa County, which states that Dr. Samuel Adams took over his place at Oak Spring in early 1853, "after the death of Kirker."[7]

This perhaps indicates that Kirker's property was acquired in settlement of doctor bills following a terminal illness. If this was the case, it is likely that Jim died of cancer, for that was Dr. Adams' specialty. Subsequent owners of the property report that the physician turned the residential structure into a

Oak Springs, California, where James Kirker's house once stood.

Road sign at start of Kirker Pass, near Pittsburg, California.

skunk warren. This provided him with a source of skunk oil, which he thought beneficent in the treatment of cancer.

Jim Hobbs, who was in no way associated with Kirker in those later days, wrote that Jim died of excessive drinking, although he carefully stated that this was only a guess. "He was," Hobbs wrote, "a very hard drinking man, which may have had some connection with his mysterious death, as he was found dead in his cabin at Mount Diablo, California, in 1852."[8]

Even though Jim lived in California less than three years and what he did there is obscured by time, he must have made a strong impression. The pass leading from Walnut Creek to

Kirker's headstone in relation to others in the Somersville cemetery, behind the State Police Barracks.

All that is left of Kirker's headstone is this sandstone remnant jutting from the ground in the Somersville, California cemetery. It was made by his Shawnee and Delaware Indians, who left the country after Kirker was buried.

Pittsburg, intersecting his property, is called Kirker Pass and today's road is still known as Kirker Pass Road.[9]

Near Kirker Pass lies the long-abandoned Somersville cemetery, on a shady knoll behind the California State Police Barracks. It was here, according to the son of an eyewitness, that Jim Kirker was lowered to his final resting place by his faithful Shawnee and Delaware companions. One of the Indians, according to Vincent Neri's account, carved out the brownstone marker, scratching Jim's name on it and placing it over the mound. Only a few inches of the stone extends out of the ground today and no name, or other marking, is discernible.[10]

The good that is so often interred with men's bones must have gone into the ground with Kirker, too. Neri averred that his father said Jim Kirker "was a bad man" and that everybody in the neighborhood was glad when, after the Indians buried him, they mounted their horses and rode down the cemetery hill, headed back east and never again were seen in that part of California.

## NOTES TO CHAPTER XXII

1. Ernest deMassey, "Journal of a Frenchman in the Gold Rush Days," translated by Marguerite Eyer Wilbur, California Historical Society *Quarterly,* Vol. 6, No. 1, March, 1927, pp. 39-41.

2. *Ibid.*

3. Marysville *Herald,* Friday, November 1, 1850, "Terrible Disaster in San Francisco."

4. *Ibid.*

5. A copy of this census, put in typescript by the Daughters of the American Revolution, is in the California State Library at Sacramento.

6. Fred Heitfeld, "Toddy Briones . . . locates Kirker Grave," *The Southwesterner,* Columbus, N. M., Vol. III, No. 11, May, 1964, p. 16. Clayton is listed in Erwin G. Gudde's *California Place Names* (Berkeley, University of California Press, 1962) p. 63, as in Contra Costa county.

7. *History of Contra Costa County,* (San Francisco, Slocum & Co., 1882) p. 484.

8. Hobbs, *Wild Life in the Far West,* p. 81.

9. Gudde, *California Place Names,* revised and enlarged edition, Berkeley, 1962, p. 157.

10. The grave was located by Fred Heitfeld, of Sacramento, after a long search, working with John "Toddy" Briones, of Martinez, who was born in Contra Costa County in 1874, and is considered the unofficial historian of the area. One of his duties as a deputy sheriff over the years was to look after the cemeteries in the county, including the one at Somersville. He as well as Neri attested that this was the site of Kirker's grave but certain identification could not be made without disinterment, perhaps not even then.

# EPILOGUE

When Jim Kirker died he left more heirs than property. He was survived by both of his wives and at least seven children, one of whom was his stepson, Edward Dunigan.

At the time of Jim's death Edward was in the book-publishing and bookselling business at 151 Fulton Street, New York City, with James B. Kirker, the son of Jim by his first wife, Catharine. They both lived with their mother, who had grown quite wealthy, at 175 Henry Street.[1] It is not likely that either of these boys ever knew what happened to their father and stepfather, nor did their mother. Edward was the first to follow Jim in death, expiring of unnamed causes at the age of forty, on September 16, 1853.[2] Edward named his mother and brother as executors of his estate, and left a will which sheds little light on the family business operations.[3] The legal abstract of this document is short.

14 September, 1853: I Edward Dunigan of New York City . . . 1) my executors to pay my affectionate mother Catherine Kirker out of my estate $1800 to repay debt owed her; 2) $500 to charities of the executors' choosing; 3) $5000 to mother; 4) after payment of all debts, all the remainder of

215

my estate to my half brother and present co-partner in
business, James B. Kirker; also three parcels of land in 89th
and 90th streets near Yorkville; also the house and lot at
151 Fulton street; 5) permission to sell or mortgage any or
all real estate given to executors, at their discretion; 6) my
mother, Catharine Kirker, and my half brother, James B.
Kirker, to be executors. Wit.; W. A. Seely and Frederick
L. Seely, 202 Fulton street.
    Attest in open court before Alexander W. Bradford, Sur-
rogate, done 21 September, 1853: James B. Kirker and
Catherine Kirker proved to be the only heirs and next of
kin.

Nearly ten years after the death of his half-brother, James
B. Kirker enlisted in Corcoran's Legion of the Union Army and
was appointed Captain and Assistant Quartermaster on October 20, 1862. He accompanied Brigadier General Michael Corcoran's Legion to Newport News, Virginia, in December.
Though he resigned from the Union Army on June 16, 1863 he
was somehow breveted a major on March 13, 1865.[4]

James continued to operate the book business after the
death of his half-brother, carrying on under the old name of
Edward Dunigan and Bro., at 151 Fulton Street, until 1859, at
which time he moved the business to 599 Broadway. Another
location added in 1861—142 Mercer Street—was probably the
printing plant. There is an extra line inserted in the directory
for 1866: James B. Kirker, Catholic Book Publisher, 599
Broadway, h. 175 Henry st.

James died early in March 1868. The exact date is unknown but his mother, as executrix of his estate, filed letters of
administration on March 7, granted by Gideon Tucker, Surrogate, who ascertained by questioning that "applicant was the
only heir and next of kin of said deceased."[5]

Catharine outlived all of her family, dying an illiterate but
extremely wealthy woman just before March 25, 1870, at which
time her will entered probate. She left money to build a Catholic
church and provided other amounts to further pet projects of
various priests, and the sum of $1750 to a nephew, John M.

*May 1887*

Cantina operated in Mesilla by Sam Bean and his son, Sam, Jr. who is standing in center with white apron. May, 1887.

Coughlin, an accountant at 24 Desbrosses Street, where he lived in a house in the fashionable "new" section of Brooklyn, known as Clinton Hill. In later days he was a merchant.

With the passing of Catharine the last living connection between Jim Kirker and his family in New York was severed.

Meanwhile, during the time Jim Kirker was in California and following his death there, Sam Bean was busy working to bring the other members of the Kirker family up from the El Paso del Norte in Chihuahua, to Mesilla, in New Mexico.[6]

The Beans and some of the Kirker children remained in Mesilla and Las Cruces for the next half-century. Some are living there yet, including Roy Bean, grandson of Sam and Petra. Roberto and Rafael returned to their father's old haunts at the Santa Rita copper mines. Santiago José went into the freighting business in Utah and the family has lost track of him. Dozens of descendants of Rafael and Roberto still live in the Santa Rita region, at the towns of Central, Bayard and Silver

Roberto Kirker, third son of James Kirker, said to have been born at Guadalupe y Calvo. (Records were destroyed previous to Civil War.) Roberto was a miner and deputy sheriff at Pinos Altos, New Mexico.

Rafael Kirker, the second son of James Kirker, with two of his own sons.

Roberto Kirker, one of Jim's many, many great-grandsons living today in the Southwest, where Kirker's descendants nearly outnumber the Apaches. Roberto, shown with a drill he invented, is employed by Kennicott Copper Corporation, Chino Division, in the same Santa Rita Copper mines, once worked by Great-Grandpa Jim. Three other great-grandsons are working in the Santa Rita mines and there has been a Kirker there almost continously since Jim first arrived in 1824.

City. One, still a young man, is named James Kirker and Roberto Kirker was a candidate for sheriff in Grant County in a recent election and holds a patent on a special mining drill used in the Santa Rita operation.

The Beans and Kirkers were considered well-to-do in Las Cruces and Mesilla, with the Beans owning considerable property in both towns, including stores, mills, hotels and gambling halls. Petra was greatly admired for her courageous and direct manner, traits she might have inherited from her father. They still tell a story about what she did to some squatters on her property after the Civil War.

It is said the Beans, favoring the Confederacy, had to flee

to San Antonio when Mesilla was overrun by Union soldiers from the California Column in 1862 and the Bean property was confiscated by the federal authorities. Carpetbaggers bought up these titles for almost nothing and when the war was over they were a source of bitterness and contention.

The Bean home in Mesilla was lost in this manner, according to the story, and when the war was over, Petra and her husband returned. Upon learning that a stranger was occupying her house Petra strapped on two pistols, chased the frightened squatters out and defied any authority to come and take her home away from her. They didn't try, perhaps because of sentiment, perhaps because they remembered her father and decided it was better not to.

The years passed, and Sam and Petra Bean became the oldest old-timers in the El Paso border area. Back in 1903, when they first began squabbling seriously about the Chamizal area that Mexico claimed from the United States because of a change in the flow of the Rio Grande, they called Sam to testify as to where the river ran in 1854. He was the only one still alive who had personal knowledge of the river's course. Sam went to El Paso and testified on April 13 as to its location. On the following October 29, 1903, at four o'clock in the afternoon, Sam came home, laid his head in Petra's lap and died. Only minutes before he had been to the office of the Las Cruces *Citizen,* where he had left them the last of many articles written over the years. It read:

> I like El Paso. I used to live there, and I like to see the giant city of the southwest looming up there. I knew all of the old timers there, and there are a few of them now, but the majority of my acquaintances have passed over the range, or gone to other fields of enterprize. The El Paso News sometimes copies my letters from the Las Cruces Citizen, but when I was in the News office the last time in El Paso, no person recognized me. There were no old timers and I suppose that was the reason. I am not seeking notoriety anyhow; we will meet in the great beyond. Adios—
>                                    SAM G. BEAN

Petra lived for nearly a decade after Sam's death, dying on July 19, 1911. They left three daughters—Margarita B. Ryan, Cecilia B. Buquor and Anita B. Casteneda—and a son Sam F. Bean, of Las Cruces, who was a popular saloon and hotel keeper in the El Paso area for many years.

Old Sam lived long past his time and was, perhaps, the last who could, and did, try to interpret the old times and attitudes for the twentieth century. He testified as to the course of the Rio Grande in the mid-nineteenth century and he also described what it meant to live at that time in many articles for various southwestern publications. He was quick to come to the defense of "old-timers," especially his father-in-law, Jim Kirker, whom many latter-day observers castigated because he was not only a scalp-hunter, but the king of scalp-hunters. Typical is one of Sam's stories in the Rio Grande *Republican,* October 26, 1889.

As there were many harmless, tame Indians in Mexico whose long black hair resembles the Apaches, some of his [Kirker's] friends started a report that he occasionally killed some of them and palmed off the scalps for genuine Apaches. Although he could have done this without detection, if he had been unscrupulous, still no person ever considered the report more than a good joke on Kirker, which he understood and enjoyed as much as anybody.

There are a few who have some idea of the appalling condition of the country twenty and some forty years ago, who know how to appreciate any history pertaining to the early days of New Mexico, but there are not many, and they came here before the railroads and know how to sympathise with the first settlers in their historic struggle for life itself.

Such, however, will not be found among the emigrants that have come here in sleeping cars within the last decade. They view the first settlers with a cold, uncharitable look, as much as to say, "I want no truck with their sort; they are not progressive like us! They belong to another era back in the dark ages." Give them no chance in the battle of life and let them flounder at the bottom of the chasm.—OLD TIMER.

It would appear that Sam Bean held his father-in-law, James Kirker—and all of those like him—in high regard.

## NOTES TO EPILOGUE

1. New York City Directory, 1847.

2. The New York *Post* carried the following: "Fri., Sept. 16, 1853. Edward Dunigan, 40 yrs., brother of James B. Kirker."

3. Liber 108, p. 97 ff., of New York Wills in the Surrogate's Office, New York City.

4. James B. Kirker's complete service record was supplied by Elbert L. Huber, Chief, Navy and Military Service, General Services Administration, National Archives, Washington.

5. New York Wills, liber 177, p. 256, dated March 1, 1856: "I James Kirker, bookseller of the City of New York: I give and bequeath unto my mother Catharine Kirker of the City of New York, all my estate of what nature and whatever kind, whether real, personal or mixed. I nominate and appoint my said mother to be executrix. (Signed): James B. Kirker. Wit.: John Conroy; Jno. A. Keating."

6. Adlai Feather, Mesilla Park historian and former member of the faculty at New Mexico State University, relates that during his research in old files in the basement of the Dona Ana County court house, Las Cruces, he came across numerous documents used in getting Rita Garcia Kirker and her children out of Chihuahua and settled in Mesilla, but that these were later damaged by water and have subsequently been removed or destroyed.

# BIBLIOGRAPHY

## PUBLIC RECORDS

### NATIONAL ARCHIVES, U.S.A.

War Department Records   Letters received, Sec'y War, 0-5(16)1822. April 9, 1822, O'Fallon to Calhoun.

Letters sent, Sec'y War, Indian Affairs Record Group 75, Vol. E. p. 295, July 2, 1822, J. C. Calhoun to Clark.

Letters received, Record group 107, C-77 (17) 1823, July 4, 1823, Clark to Calhoun, enc. Ashley correspondence.

Letters received, Record group 107, C-78 (17) 1823, Clark to Calhoun, enc. Ashley correspondence.

Letters received, Sec'y War, Cass, extract letter from Thomas Forsyth, Oct. 21, 1831, St. Louis, reprinted in U.S. Senate Doc., S. 22A-E7.

Letters received, Record group 94, Reynolds to Price, dated, Santa Fe, Aug. 10, 1848; rec'd Oct. 16, 1848, #460.

### NATIONAL ARCHIVES, BRITISH FOREIGN OFFICE, PUBLIC RECORD OFFICE, LONDON, ENGLAND

James Kirker   to Ewen Mackintosh, H.B.M.'s Consul, Mexico, dated, Guadalupe y Calvo, Aug. 18, 1842, forwarded to B.F.O. Sept. 17, 1842, "Copy of letter from James Kirker and papers relating to certain grievances suffered by him in Dept. of New Mexico." FO 204/79/ 1

James Kirker   to Ewen Mackintosh, dated Guadalupe y Calvo, Aug. 20, 1842, concerning grievances. FO 204/79/ 1

James Kirker   to Ewen Mackintosh, dated Guadalupe y Calvo, Nov. 19, 1842, "Respecting his claim for outrages done against him by Mexican authorities and promises further proof of grievances." FO 204/79/2

Ewen Mackintosh, H.B.M.'s Consul, Mexico, Oct. 3, 1842, "Observations on the case of Mr. Kirker." FO 204/79/ 2.

## MEXICAN ARCHIVES, STATE RECORDS CENTER, SANTA FE, N.M.

Letter, José Joaquin Calvo, dated Chihuahua City, April 19, 1836, to Captain Cayetano Justiniani, Dept. New Mexico, Archive #4676.

Letter, Bernardo Revilla, Chihuahua City, July 11, 1838, to José Joaquin Calvo, #5500.

Letter, Antonio Sandoval to Secy. of Gov't, D. Guadalupe Miranda, dated Socorro, N.M., March 21, 1840, #6003.

Copy, by Donaciano Vigil of propositions by Don José Cordero to Apaches, dated February 28, 1842, Santa Fe, #6704.

## NEW YORK CITY, SURROGATE'S OFFICE, DEP'T. OF WILLS

Liber. 108, p. 97 ff, Sept. 14, 1853.

Liber. 177, p. 256, March 1, 1856.

Liber. 195, p. 207, April 14, 1870.

## ST. LOUIS, MO.

Record of Deeds, City and County, Book L, pp. 75-78, May 23, 1821, John McKnight to James Kirker.

Book I-3 pp. 257-58, June 8, 1841, John McKnight, Jr.—John McKnight.

Book R, pp. 692-93, James Kirker (by Sheriff) to George W. Scott, April 16, 1832.

## PROBATE RECORDS, ANTRIM COUNTY, IRELAND

P.R.O.N.I., T808/8854 extracted by Conner, April 24, 1812.

**DEPARTMENT OF U.S. ARMY** Military service file, James B. Kirker, Captain Ass't. Quartermaster, U.S. Volunteers.

# MANUSCRIPTS

Chisholm, Jesse, Interview with Henry Spybuck, Indian Pioneer History, University of Oklahoma Library, Phillips Collection, Vol. 17.

Papeles de Chihuahua, on micro-film, University of Texas at El Paso, Library, El Paso, Texas.

Randall, Dr. Andrew, Diary, State Library, Sacramento, California.

State Census, Contra Costa County, 1852, State Library, Sacramento, California.

# PERIODICALS

*Dalhousie Review,* July, 1934.

*Engineering and Mining Journal-Press,* Vol. 116, No. 18, Nov. 3, 1923.

*Southwesterner,* April, 1963; May, 1964.


# PERSONAL INTERVIEWS

Blanco, Father, Nov. 15, 1963, Guadalupe y Calvo, Chi., Mexico.

Kirker, Hugh Gilbert, October 21, 1969, Kilcross, Killead Parish, North Ireland.

Kirker, Rafael, Roberto, and José, October 3, 1962, Central and Bayard, New Mexico.

McNellis, Robert, Sept. 21, 1965, Xeroxed Bulletin "Sociedad de Guerra Contra los Barberos."

Strickland, Dr. Rex, Oct. 2, 1968, El Paso, Texas, Juan José Compa, etc.

Voelker, Fred, Oct. 31, 1964, St. Louis, Mo., opinions on Ashley.

Wallace, William, Nov. 10–11, 1962, Hacienda Corralitos, Chi., Mexico, Apaches at Carcaj.


# CHURCH RECORDS

Flotte, Robert, baptismal record, son of Luis Flotte and Refugio McKnight, Church of Guadalupe, Juarez, Mexico, Oct. 30, 1838.

Polinaria(o?) infant son (daughter) of Santiago Querque and Rita Garcia, *libro de entierros* (burial book) August 29, 1859, Catholic Church, Mesilla, N.M.

Bean, Maria Virginia, daughter of Samuel Bean and Petra Kirker, baptismal record, dated July 7, 1854, Mesilla Catholic Church, "Abuelos Maternos: Santiago Kirker and Rita Garcia," grandparents.


# CORRESPONDENCE WITH AUTHOR

Embleton, Miss I., Ulster-Scot Historical Society, Aug. 7, 1963, Belfast, Ireland.

Kirker, E. C., Miami, Fla., Feb. 26, March 15, May 17, Aug. 1, Aug. 2, and Sept. 26, 1963; Jan. 14, June 23, 28, 1964.

Strickland, Dr. Rex, July 17, 1964, El Paso, Texas.

Taylor, Mary, Mesilla, N.M., Jan. 28, 1963; April 30, 1964.

# HISTORICAL SOCIETY PUBLICATIONS

California Historical Society *Quarterly,* Vol. 6, No. 1, March 1927.
Historical Society of Southern California Annual Publication, Vol. 1, Part 3, 1887, Los Angeles.
—Vol. VII, Parts II-III, 1907–8.
—Vol. XVI, Part I, 1934.
Missouri Historical Society *Bulletin,* Vol. III, No. 2, Jan. 1947.
—Vol. III, No. 4, July 1947.
—Vol. V, No. 1, Oct. 1948.
—Vol. V, No. 2, Jan. 1949.
—Vol. XV, No. 3, April 1959.
—Vol. XXI, Part 1, July 1965.
—Publication No. 12, St. Louis, 1896.
Missouri Historical Society *Collections,* Vol. II, No. 6, July 1906, St. Louis.
—Vol. V, No. 1, Oct. 1927.
—Vol. V, No. 2, Feb. 1928.
—Vol. V, No. 3, June 1928.
Missouri Historical Society, *Glimpses of the Past,* Vol. I, No. 7, June 1934, St. Louis.
—Vol. I, No. 10, Sept. 1934.
—Vol. II, Nos. 1-2, Dec.–Jan. 1934–35.
—Vol. I, No. 4, March 1934.
—Vol. II, Nos. 6-10, May–Sept. 1935.
—Vol. III, No. 3, March 1936.
—Vol. V, Nos., 1-3, Jan.–March 1938.
—Vol. VI, Nos. 1-3, Jan.–March 1939.
—Vol. VI, Nos., 10-12, Oct.–Dec. 1939.
—Vol. VII, Nos. 7-9, July–Sept. 1941.
—Vol. IX, Nos. 1-2, Jan.–June 1942.
—Vol. IX, No. 3, July–Sept. 1942.
Missouri Historical Society Review, Oct. 1911.
New Mexico Historical Review, Vol. XXXVIII, No. 1, Jan. 1963.
—Vol. XXXIX, No. 1, Jan. 1964.

# NEWSPAPERS

Baltimore, Md., *Niles Weekly Register,* Vols. 1 through 70, various.
Belfast, Ireland, *Newsletter,* April 25, 1817.
Las Cruces, N.M., *Citizen,* Oct. 29, 1903; Feb. 10, 1955; Feb. 17, 1955; Feb. 24, 1955; Mar. 3, 1955.
*Rio Grande Republican,* Las Cruces, N.M., Oct. 26, 1889.
Marysville, Calif., *Herald,* Nov. 1, 1850.
New Orleans *Picayune,* Feb. 28, 1840; Mar. 2, 1840; June 26, 1847.
New York City *Post,* Sept. 16, 1853.
New York City *Shipping and Commercial List,* March 7, 1817.
Philadelphia, *Pennsylvania Inquirer,* Sept. 26, 1849.

Savage Scene227

Sacramento, Calif., *Daily Union,* Nov. 27, 1867.
St. Louis *Enquirer,* Oct. 20, 1820.
St. Louis *Missouri Gazette,* Jan. 11, 1809; Aug. 5, 1815; Sept. 2, 1817; Oct. 4, 1817;
Feb. 13, 1822; Apr. 4, 1838.
St. Louis *Missouri Republican,* June 1, 1846; May 18, 1847; July 5, 1847; Aug. 1, 1848;
Aug. 15, 1848; Apr. 25, 1849; May 24, 1849; June 9, 1849; July 4, 1849; Sept. 12,
1849.
St. Louis *Missouri Saturday News,* April 4, 1838.
St. Louis *New Era,* June 1, 1846; June 3, 1846; June 12, 1846.
St. Louis *Reveille,* Oct. 21, 1844; July 5, 1847; Jan. 29, 1849.
St. Louis *Saturday Evening Post,* (July 10, 1847;) July 17, 1847.
San Francisco, *Alta California,* Oct. 31, 1850.
San Francisco *Call,* Dec. 9, 1893.
Santa Fe *Republican,* Nov. 20, 1847; Dec. 25, 1847; Aug. 1, 1848; Aug. 15, 1848.

## BOOKS

Abert, Col. John James, *Abert's New Mexico Report, 1846–'47.* Albuquerque, Horn
& Wallace, Publishers, 1962.
Allman, C. B., Lewis Wetzel, *Indian Fighter, The Life and Times of a Frontier Hero.*
New York, The Devin-Adair Co., 1961.
Almada, Francisco R., *Diccionario de Historia, Geografia y Biografia Senorenses.*
Chihuahua, Chi., Mexico, Ruiz Sandoval, S. De R.L., 1952.
*Gobernadores Estado de Chihuahua.* Mexico, D. F., Imprenta de la H. Camara de
Deputados, 1950.
*Guadalupe y Calvo.* Chihuahua, Chi., Mexico, Los Talleres Tipograficos del Go-
bierno de Chihuahua, 1940.
*Resumen de Historia del Estado de Chihuahua.* Mexico, D. F., "Librados Mex-
icanos," 1955.
Alter, J. Cecil, *James Bridger, Trapper, Frontiersman, Scout and Guide* (with which
is incorporated a verbatim copy, annotated, of James Bridger, a biographical sketch
by Major General Grenville M. Dodge). Columbus, Ohio, Long's College Book Co.,
1950.
*Jim Bridger,* 2nd edition. Norman, University of Oklahoma Press, 1962.
*Ashley-Smith Expeditions and the Discovery of a Central Route to the Pacific 1822–
1829.* Harrison Clifford Dale, ed., Glendale, Calif., Arthur Clark Co., 1941.
Atkinson, M. Jourdan, *Indians of the Southwest.* San Antonio, Texas, The Naylor Co.,
1958.
Bailey, L. R., *Indian Slave Trade in the Southwest.* Los Angeles, Westernlore Press,
1966.
Baldwin, Gordon C., *The Warrior Apaches.* Tucson, D. S. King, 1965.
Bancroft, Hubert Howe, *The History of Arizona and New Mexico,* Vol. XVII. San
Francisco, The History Co., Publishers, 1889.
*History of California,* 5 vols. San Francisco, The History Co., Publishers, 1886.
*History of the North Mexican States and Texas,* Vol. XVI. San Francisco, The
History Co., Publishers, 1889.

Bartlett, John Russell, *Personal Narrative of the Explorations and Incidents in Texas, New Mexico, California, Sonora and Chihuahua.* New York, D. Appleton & Co., 1854, 2 Vols.

Beard, Charles, A., Mary and William, *The Beards' New History of the United States.* New York, Doubleday, 1968.

Bell, Major Horace, *Reminiscences of a Ranger or Early Times in Southern California.* Los Angeles, Yarnell, Caystille & Mathes, Printers, 1881.

Billon, Frederic L., *Annals of St. Louis in its Early Days Under the French and Spanish Dominations.* St. Louis (Press of Nixon-Jones Printing Co.), 1886, 2 vols.

Blair, Water and Meine, Franklin, *Mike Fink, King of Mississippi Keelboatmen.* New York, Henry Holt and Co., 1933.

Blackwelder, Bernice, *Great Westerner, The Story of Kit Carson.* Caldwell, Idaho, Caxton, 1962.

Bonner, T. D., *The Life and Adventures of James P. Beckwourth, The Mountaineer, Scout, and Pioneer, and Chief of the Crow Nation of Indians.* New York, Harper and Bros., publishers, 1856.

*The Life and Adventures of James P. Beckwourth,* etc. Charles G. Leland, ed., London, T. Fisher Unwin, 1892.

Brackenridge, Henry Marie, *Views of Louisiana, Together with a Journal of a Voyage up the Missouri River in 1811.* Chicago, Quadrangle Books, Inc., 1962 (first published, Pittsburgh, 1814).

Brewerton, George Douglas, *Overland with Kit Carson, a Narrative of the Old Spanish Trail in '48.* New York, Coward-McCann, Inc., 1930.

Caesar, Gene, *King of the Mountain Men, The Life of Jim Bridger.* New York, E. P. Dutton Co., 1961.

Chapelle, Howard I., *The History of American Sailing Ships.* New York, Bonanza Books, 1935.

Chittenden, Hiram Martin, *The American Fur Trade of the Far West.* Stanford, Calif., Academic Reprints, 1954.

*History of Early Steamboat Navigation on the Missouri River, Life and Adventures of Joseph La Barge.* Minneapolis, Ross and Haines, Inc., 1962.

Cleland, Robert Glass, *Pathfinders,* San Francisco, Powell Publishing Co., 1929.

*This Reckless Breed of Men, The Trappers and Fur Traders of the Southwest,* New York, Alfred Knopf, 1950.

Clyman, James, *James Clyman Frontiersman, The Adventures of a Trapper and Covered-Wagon Emigrant as told in his own Reminiscences and Diaries.* Charles L. Camp, ed. Portland, Oregon, Champoeg Press, 1960.

Conard, Howard Louis, *"Uncle Dick" Wooton, The Pioneer Frontiersman of the Rocky Mountain Region.* (Chicago, W. E. Dibble Co., 1890) reprinted, Columbus, Ohio, Long's College Book Co., 1950.

Connelley, William Elsey, *War with Mexico 1846–1847, Doniphan's Expedition and the Conquest of New Mexico and California.* Topeka, Kansas, published by author, 1907.

Conner, Daniel Ellis, *Joseph Reddeford Walker and the Arizona Adventure.* Donald J. Berthrong and Odessa Davenport, eds. Norman, University of Oklahoma Press, 1956.

Cooke, Philip St. George, *The Conquest of New Mexico and California in 1846–1848.* Albuquerque, N.M., Horn and Wallace, Publishers, 1964.

Copeland, Fayette, *Kendall of the Picayune, Being His Adventures In New Orleans, on the Texan Santa Fe Expedition, In the Mexican War and in the Colonization of the Texas Frontier.* Norman, University of Oklahoma Press, 1943.

Coues, Elliott, *The Expedition of Zebulon Montgomery Pike.* (first published 1810) republished, New York, Francis R. Harper, 1895.

Cutts, James Madison, *The Conquest of California and New Mexico by the forces of the United States in the Years 1846 & 1847.* Albuquerque, Horn and Wallace, publishers, 1965.

Davis, W. W. H., *El Gringo or New Mexico & Her People.* (Reprinted with permission of the Rydal Press, Santa Fe, 1938) Chicago, The Rio Grande Press, Inc., 1962.

Delano, Alonzo, *Across the Plains and Among the Diggings.* New York, Wilson-Erickson, Inc., 1936.

DeVoto, Bernard, *The Course of Empire.* Boston, Houghton Mifflin Co., 1952.

*Mark Twain's America and Mark Twain at Work.* Sentry Edition, Boston, Houghton Mifflin Co., 1960.

*The Year of Decision, 1846.* Boston, Houghton Mifflin Co., 1943.

Dobie, J. Frank, *Apache Gold and Yaqui Silver.* Boston, Little Brown, 1928.

*Don Santiago Kirker,* reprint from Santa Fe *Republican,* Nov. 20, 1847. Annotated by Arthur Woodward. Los Angeles, privately printed, 1948.

Driver, Harold E., *Indians of North America.* Chicago, University of Chicago Press, 1961.

Eastman, Edwin, *Seven and Nine Years Among the Comanches and Apaches.* Jersey City, Clark Johnson, 1879.

Emory, Lieutenant W. H., *Lieutenant Emory Reports* (a reprint of Lieutenant W. H. Emory's *Notes of a Military Reconnaissance*) Albuquerque, University of New Mexico Press, 1951.

Evans, George W. B., *Mexican Gold Trail, The Journal of a Forty-Niner.* Glenn S. Dumke, ed. San Marino, Calif., Huntingdon Library, 1945.

Evans, Nelson W., *Pioneer History,* "A Sketch of Governor Thomas Kirker." Published by author, 1903.

Executive Documents, printed by order of the Senate of the United States, First Session, 35th Congress, and special session of 1858. 1857–'58, Vol. I, Washington, William A. Harris, printer, 1858.

First Session, II Session, 22d Congress, No. 99, 1831.

Falconer, Thomas, *Letters and Notes on the Texan Santa Fe Expedition 1841–1842.* (New York, Dauber, & Pine Bookshops, Inc., 1930) Chicago, The Rio Grande Press, 1963.

Favour, Alpheus H., *Old Bill Williams, Mountain Man.* Norman, University of Oklahoma Press, 1960.

Field, Matt, *Matt Field on the Santa Fe Trail,* John E. Sunder, ed., Norman, University of Oklahoma Press, 1936.

*Prairie and Mountain Sketches.* Kate L. Gregg and John Francis McDermott, eds., Norman, University of Oklahoma, 1960.

Foreman, Grant, *Pioneer Days in the Early Southwest.* Cleveland, Arthur Clark Co., 1926.

*Marcy & The Gold Seekers, The Journal of Captain R. B. Marcy, with an account of the Gold Rush Over the Southern Route.* Norman, University of Oklahoma Press, 1939.

Fowler, Jacob, *The Journal of Jacob Fowler* Elliott Coues, ed., New York, Francis P. Harper, 1898.

Galloway, William Albert, *Old Chillicothe, Shawnee and Pioneer History.* Xenia, Ohio, The Buckeye Press, 1934.

Garrard, Lewis H., *Wah-To-Yah and the Taos Trail.* Ralph Bieber, ed., Glendale, Calif., Arthur Clark Co., 1938.

Ghent, W. J., *The Early Far West, A Narrative Outline 1540–1850.* New York, Tudor Publishing Co., 1936.

Gibson, George Rutledge, *Journal of a Soldier Under Kearny and Doniphan 1846–1847.* Ralph P. Bieber, ed., Glendale, Calif. Arthur Clark Co., 1935.

Gregg, Josiah, *The Commerce of the Prairies.* Max L. Moorhead, ed., Norman, University of Oklahoma Press, 1954.

*Diary & Letters of Josiah Gregg, Excursions in Mexico & California, 1847–1850.* Maurice Garland Fulton, ed., Norman, University of Oklahoma Press, 1944.

Gray, A. B., *The A. B. Gray Report.* L. R. Bailey, ed., Los Angeles, Westernlore Press, 1963.

Gudde, Erwin G., *California Place Names, The Origin and Etymology of Current Geographical Names.* Berkeley, University of California Press, 1962.

Hafen, LeRoy R. and Ghent, W. J., *Broken Hand, The Life Story of Thomas Fitzpatrick, Chief of the Mountain Men.* Denver, Colorado, The Old West Publishing Co., 1931.

Hafen, LeRoy R. and Ann W., *Old Spanish Trail, Santa Fe to Los Angeles.* Glendale, Calif., Arthur Clark Co., 1954.

Hamilton, Holman, *Zachary Taylor, Soldier of the Republic.* Indianapolis, Bobbs-Merrill, 1941.

Hamilton, W. T., *My Sixty Years on the Plains* (from the original edition by E. T. Siber). Norman, University of Oklahoma Press, 1960.

Harris, Benjamin Butler, *The Gila Trail, The Texas Argonauts and The California Gold Rush.* Richard H. Dillon, ed., Norman, University of Oklahoma Press, 1960.

Heitman, Francis B. *Historical Register and Dictionary of the United States Army,* 1789–1903. (Washington, Government Printing Office 1903) reprinted Urbana, University of Illinois Press, 1965.

Hill, Joseph J., *The History of Warner's Ranch and Its Environs.* Los Angeles, Calif., privately printed, 1927.

*History of Contra Costa County, California.* F. J. Hulanski, ed. Berkeley, The Elms Publishing Co., Inc., 1917.

*History of Contra Costa County.* San Francisco, Slocum & Co., 1882.

Hobbs, Captain James, *Wild Life in the Far West, Personal Adventures of a Border Mountain Man.* Hartford, Conn., Wiley, Waterman & Eaton, 1875.

*Holden's Triennial Directory of Belfast, Ireland, 1805-6-7.*

Hollon, W. Eugene, *The Lost Pathfinder, Zebulon Montgomery Pike.* Norman, University of Oklahoma Press, 1949.

Howe, Henry, *Historical Collections of Ohio.* Cincinnati, published by Henry Howe at E. Morgan & Co., 1853.

Hunt, Elvid, *History of Fort Leavenworth 1827–1937.* 2nd. ed., Walter E. Lorence, ed., Fort Leavenworth, Kansas, The Command and General Staff School Press, 1937.

Inman, Colonel Henry, *The Old Santa Fe Trail, The Story of a Great Highway.* New York, The Macmillan Company, 1898.

James, Thomas, *Three Years Among the Mexicans and the Indians.* Reprinted with permission of the Missouri Historical Society. Chicago, The Rio Grande Press, 1962 (originally published 1846).

Johnson, Abraham Robinson, Edwards, Marcellus Ball and Ferguson, Philip Gooch, *Marching with the Army of the West, 1846–1848.* Ralph P. Bieber, ed., Glendale, Arthur Clark Co., 1960.

Jones, Daniel W. *Forty Years Among the Indians.* Los Angeles, Westernlore Press, 1960.

*Journals of Forty-Niners, Salt Lake to Los Angeles.* LeRoy R. and Ann W. Hafen, eds., Glendale, Arthur Clark Co., 1954.

Kendall, Charles Wye, *Private Men of War.* New York, 1932.

Kendall, George Wilkins, *Narrative of the Texan Santa Fe Expedition.* New York, Harper and Bros., 1844.

Kirkpatrick, John Ervin, *Timothy Flint, Pioneer Missionary, Author, Editor, 1780 –1840.* Cleveland, Ohio, Arthur Clark Co., 1911.

Larkin, Thomas Oliver, *The Larkin Papers, Personal, Business and Official Correspondence.* 10 vols. George P. Hammond, ed., Berkeley, University of California Press, 1953.

Larpenteur, Charles, *Forty Years a Fur Trader on the Upper Missouri, The Personal Narrative of Charles Larpenteur.* Chicago, R. R. Donnelley & Sons Co., 1933.

Lavender, David, *Bent's Fort.* New York, Doubleday & Co., Dolphin Books, 1954. *The Fist in the Wilderness.* New York, Doubleday & Co., 1964.

Lay, Bennett, *The Lives of Ellis P. Bean.* Austin, University of Texas Press, 1960.

Leamon, Jacob A., *The Atlas of Adams County, Ohio.* Newark, Ohio, Caldwell, 1880.

Lee, Nelson, *Three Years Among the Comanches, The Narrative of Nelson Lee, The Texas Ranger.* Norman, University of Oklahoma Press, 1957.

Leonard, Zenas, *Adventures of Zenas Leonard, Fur Trader.* University of Oklahoma Press, 1959.

Little, George, *Life on the Ocean, or Twenty Years at Sea: Being the Personal Narrative of the Author.* 3d. edition, Boston, Waite, Pierce and Company, 1843.

Lockwood, Frank C., *The Apache Indians.* New York, The Macmillan Company, 1938.

Longworth's *American Almanac, New York Register and City Directory, 1811–1832.*

Loomis, Noel M., *The Texan-Santa Fe Pioneers.* Norman, University of Oklahoma Press, 1958.

Luttig, John C., *Journal of a Fur-Trading Expedition on the Upper Missouri, 1812– 1813.* Stella M. Drumm, ed., New York, Argosy-Antiquarian Ltd., 1964.

Lyman, George D. *John Marsh, Pioneer, The Life Story of a Trail Blazer on Six Frontiers.* Chautauqua, N.Y., The Chautauqua Press (Charles Scribner's Sons), 1930.

MacMullen, Jerry, *Paddlewheel Days.* Stanford, Calif., Stanford University Press, 1944.

Magoffin, Susan Shelby, *Down the Santa Fe Trail and Into Mexico, The Diary of Susan Shelby Magoffin, 1846–1847.* Stella M. Drumm, ed., New Haven, Yale University Press, 1962.

Marsh, James B. *Four Years in the Rockies; or, The Adventures of Isaac P. Rose.* (Printed originally at New Castle, W. B. Thomas, 1884), reprinted Columbus, Ohio, Long's College Book Co.

Meek, Stephen Hall, *The Autobiography of a Mountain Man 1805–1889.* Notes by Arthur Woodward, Pasadena, Calif. Glen Dawson, 1948.

Meriwether, David, *My Life in the Mountains and on the Plains.* Robert A. Griffin, ed., Norman, University of Oklahoma Press, 1965.

Mills, W. W., *Forty Years at El Paso 1858–1898.* El Paso, Texas, Carl Hertzog, 1962.

*Mines of the Old Southwest, Early Reports on the Mines of New Mexico and Arizona by the Explorers Abert, Aubry, Browne, Cozzens, Emory, Mowry, Pattie, Whipple, Wizlizenus, and others.* Rex Arrowsmith, ed., Santa Fe, Stagecoach Press, 1963.

Moore, Arthur K. *The Frontier Mind, a Cultural Analysis of the Kentucky Frontiersman.* University of Kentucky Press, 1957.

Moorhead, Max L., *New Mexico's Royal Road, Trade and Travel on the Chihuahua Trail.* Norman, University of Oklahoma Press, 1958.

Morgan, Dale L., *Jedediah Smith and the Opening of the West.* Indianapolis, The Bobbs-Merrill Co., 1953.

*The West of William H. Ashley, recorded in the Diaries of William H. Ashley and his contemporaries 1822–23.* Dale L. Morgan, ed., Denver, Colo., The Old West Publishing Co., 1964.

Morrison, Lorrin L., *Warner, The Man and the Ranch.* Los Angeles, privately published, 1962.

*Mountain Men and the Fur Trade of the West,* Vols. I through VII. LeRoy H. Hafen, ed., Glendale, Arthur Clark, 1965.

Mowry, Sylvester, *Arizona and Sonora, the Geography, History, and Resources.* New York, Harper & Bros., publishers, 1866.

Mumey, Nolie, *James Pierson Beckwourth, 1856–1866, An Enigmatic Figure of the West, A History of the Latter Years of His Life.* Denver, Colo., The Old West Publishing Co., 1957.

Myers, John Myers, *Pirate, Pawnee and Mountain Man, The Saga of Hugh Glass.* Boston, Little, Brown and Co., 1963.

Nidever, George, *The Life and Adventures of George Nidever, (1802–1883).* William Henry Ellison, ed., Berkeley, University of California Press, 1937.

Nunis, Doyce Blackman, Jr., *Andrew Sublette, 1808–1853.* Los Angeles, Dawson's Book Shop, 1960.

Oglesby, Richard Edward, *Manuel Lisa and the Opening of the Missouri Fur Trade.* Norman, University of Oklahoma Press, 1963.

Pancoast, Charles Edward, *A Quaker Forty-Niner, The Adventures of Charles Edward Pancoast on the American Frontier.* Anna Paschall Hannum, ed., Philadelphia, University of Pennsylvania Press, 1930.

Parkhill, Forbes, *The Blazed Trail of Antoine Leroux.* Los Angeles, Westernlore Press, 1965.

Pattie, James O., *The Personal Narrative of James O. Pattie,* Philadelphia, J. B. Lippincott Co., 1962 (reprint).

Peters, DeWitt C. (M.D.), *The Life and Adventures of Kit Carson, The Nestor of the Rocky Mountains.* New York, W.R.C. Clark & Co., 1858.

Pritchard, James A., *The Overland Diary of James A. Pritchard from Kentucky to California in 1849.* Dale L. Morgan, ed., Denver, The Old West Publishing Co., 1959.

Public Documents, 30th Congress, 1st Session, Senate Executive No. 1. Washington, printed by Weldell and Van Benthewysen, 1847.

Raht, Carlysle Graham, *The Romance of the Davis Mountains and the Big Bend Country,* Texana ed., Odessa, Texas, The Rahtbooks Co., 1963.

Reid, Mayne, *The Scalp Hunters; or Romantic Adventures in Northern Mexico.* London, Skeet, 1851.

Robinson, Jacob S., *A Journal of the Santa Fe Expedition Under Colonel Doniphan.* Princeton, Princeton University Press, 1932.

Roosevelt, Theodore, *The Winning of the West.* New York, Putnam, 1889.

Ross, Alexander, *The Fur Hunters of the Far West.* Kenneth A. Spaulding, ed., Norman, University of Oklahoma Press, 1956.

Ruxton, George F. *Adventures in Mexico and the Rocky Mountains.* New York, Harper & Brothers, Publishers, 1848.

*Life in the Far West.* LeRoy R. Hafen, ed., Norman, University of Oklahoma Press, 1951.

*Ruxton of the Rockies.* LeRoy R. Hafen, ed., Norman, University of Oklahoma Press, 1953.

Sage, Rufus B., *Rufus B. Sage, His Letters and Papers, 1836–'47.* LeRoy R. and Ann W. Hafen, eds., Glendale, Calif., Arthur Clark Co., 1956, 2 vols.

Salpointe, Rev. J. B. (D.D.), *Soldiers of the Cross.* Banning, California, St. Boniface Industrial School, 1898.

Sandoz, Mari, *The Beaver Men, Spearheads of Empire.* New York, Hastings House, Publishers, 1964.

Scharf, J. Thomas, *History of Saint Louis City and County.* Philadelphia, Louis H. Everts & Co., 1883.

Sonnichsen, C. L., *Roy Bean, Law West of the Pecos.* New York, The Macmillan Co., 1943.

*Southern Trails to California in 1849.* Ralph P. Bieber, ed., Glendale, Calif., Arthur Clark Co., 1937.

Spafford, Horatio, *New York Gazeteer.* New York, 1813.

Stanley, F., *Giant in Lilliput, The Story of Donaciano Vigil.* Pampa, Texas, Pampa Print Shop, 1963.

Stewart, George R., *The California Trail.* New York, McGraw-Hill Book Co., 1962.

Stone, Irving, *Men to Match My Mountains.* New York, Doubleday & Co., 1956.

Storrs, Augustus and Wetmore, Alphonso, *Santa Fe Trail First Reports: 1825.* Houston, Stagecoach Press, 1960.

Sunder, John E., *Bill Sublette, Mountain Man.* Norman, University of Oklahoma Press, 1959.

Templeton, Sardis W., *The Lame Captain, The Life and Adventures of Pegleg Smith.* Los Angeles, Westernlore Press, 1965.

Tevis, Captain James H., *Arizona in the '50's.* Albuquerque, University of New Mexico Press, 1954.

Triplett, Colonel Frank, *Conquering the Wilderness or New Pictorial History of the Life and Times of the Pioneer Heroes and Heroines of America.* New York, N. D. Thompson & Co., 1883.

Thompson and West's *History of Nevada, 1881.*

Tucker, Glenn, *Tecumseh, Vision of Glory.* Indianapolis, The Bobbs-Merrill Co., 1956.

Twitchell, Ralph Emerson, *The History of the Military Occupation of the Territory of New Mexico, from 1846 to 1851.* Denver, Smith-Brooks Co., publishers, 1909.

234 Savage Scene

*The Leading Facts of New Mexican History.* Cedar Rapids, Iowa, The Torch Press, 1911.

Tyler, Sergeant Daniel, *A Concise History of the Mormon Battalion in the Mexican War.* Chicago, The Rio Grande Press, 1964 (first published 1881).

Van Tramp, John C., *Prairie and Rocky Mountain Adventures or Life in the West.* Columbus, Ohio, Segner & Co., 1868.

Vestal, Stanley, *Kit Carson, The Happy Warrior of the Old West.* Boston, Houghton Mifflin Co., 1928.

Victor, Mrs. Frances Fuller, *The River of the West.* Hartford, Conn., Columbian Book Co., 1871.

Wallace, Edward S., *The Great Reconnaissance, Soldiers, Artists, and Scientists on the Frontier, 1848–1861.* Boston, Little, Brown and Co., 1955.

Wagner, Henry R. *The Plains and the Rockies, a Bibliography of the Original Narratives of Travel and Adventure, 1800–1865.* 3rd. ed. revised by Charles L. Camp, Columbus, Ohio, Long's College Book Co.

Ware, Joseph E., *The Emigrant's Guide to California.* Princeton, Princeton University Press, 1932.

Waugh, Alfred S. *Travels in Search of the Elephant: The Wanderings of Alfred S. Waugh, Artist, in Louisiana, Missouri and Santa Fe, in 1845–1846.* John Francis McDermott, ed., St. Louis, Missouri Historical Society, 1951.

Webb, James Josiah, *Adventures in the Santa Fe Trade, 1844–47.* Ralph Bieber, ed., Glendale, Calif., Arthur Clark Co., 1931.

Whipple, A. W., *The Whipple Report, Journal of an Expedition From San Diego, California, to the Rio Colorado, From September 11 to December 11, 1849.* Los Angeles, Westernlore Press, 1961.

Wilson, Benjamin David, *Autobiography* as dictated to Hubert Howe Bancroft. Pasadena, A. C. Vroman, Inc.

Wilson, Irish Higbie, *William Wolfskill, 1798–1866, Frontier Trapper to California Ranchero.* Glendale, Calif., Arthur Clark Co., 1965.

Wislizenus, F. A., (M.D.) *A Journey to the Rockie Mountains in the Year, 1839.* Trans. by F. A. Wislizenus, St. Louis, Missouri Historical Society, 1912.

Memoir of a Tour to Northern Mexico, Connected with the Colonel Doniphan Expedition in 1846–1847, 30th Congress, 1st Session, Senate Misc., No. 26. Washington, Tippin & Streeper, printers.

Wood, Ellen Lamont, *George Yount, The Kindly Host of Caymus Rancho.* San Francisco, Grabhorn Press, 1941.

Young, John P., *San Francisco, A History of the Pacific Coast.* San Francisco, J. S. Clark Publishing Co., 1912.

Young, Otis E., *The First Military Escort on the Santa Fe Trail, From the Journal and Reports of Major Bennet Riley and Lieutenant Philip St. George Cooke.* Glendale, Calif., Arthur Clark Co., 1952.

Yount, George C., *George C. Yount and His Chronicles of the West.* Charles S. Camp, ed., Denver, Colo., Old West Publishing Co., 1966.

# APPENDIX

Following is an account of the Battle of Sacramento, written by John T. Hughes just a few days after it was fought. This communication was addressed to Robert H. Miller, owner, publisher and editor of the *Liberty* (Clay County, Mo.) *Tribune:*

Head Quarters 1st Regt. Mo Vol.
Chihuahua March 4th 1847

Mr. Editor:

Passing over the various interesting events that transpired during our March from El Paso to Sacramento, which I mean to give to the public at some future time, I shall bring you at once to the subject of My communication.

On Sunday, February 28th, a bright and auspicious day, the American Army, under command of Col. Doniphan arrived in sight of the Enemy's encampment, which could be plainly beheld at the distance of 4 or 5 miles. The American Army consisted of the following Corps & Detachments (viz) The first Regiment, Col. Doniphan about 800 men; Lt. Col. Mitchel's Escort, 103 men; Artillery Battallion Capt. Weightman, Major Clarke about 110 Men; with a Battery of six pieces of cannon; & two companies of Teamsters under Capts. Glasgow & Skillman, forming a battalion of about 150 men Commanded by Major Samuel Owens of Independence, making an aggregate force of 1163 men. The Enemy had occupied a rocky eminence near the small town of Sacramento, 15 miles from Chihuahua & fortified its approaches by 23 strong redoubts & entrenchments. Here, in this apparently secure position, the Mexicans determined to make a bold stand & were so certain of Victory that they had prepared Strings & handcuffs in which they meant to drive us, as prisoners, to the City of Mexico, as they did the Texans in 1841—According to the best information I have been able to obtain the Mexican force must have amounted to 3700 men; Most estimates make it 4200— Heredid was the Commander-in-chief of the Mexican Army; Gen Garcia Conde, commander of Calvary; Gen. Mauricio Ugarte, commander of Infantry, & Angel Trias, Colonel, & Governor of the State _____ When Col. Doniphan arrived within a half-mile of the Enemy's fortifications, he left the main road & crossed the Rio Sacramento & made the attack from the West. This was the best point of attack that could possibly have been selected, & the event of the day proves how well it was chosen. In crossing the river the Caravan & baggage train (about 400 wagons in all) followed close upon the rear of the Army. Nothing could exceed, in point of solemnity & grandeur, the rumbling of the Artillery, the Moving caravan, the dashing of horsemen, & the

235

waving of banners from both armies as they met on the rocky plain; for Gen Conde, with about 1000 cavalry, dashed down from the fortified heights to bring on the attack. As he came within about 900 yards of our alinement Major Clarkers Battery of six pieces opened upon them a most destructive fire, producing great confusion in their ranks. A brisk cannonading was now kept up on both sides for the space of 50 minutes, during which time the enemy suffered great loss—our battery discharged 24 rounds to the minute—The balls from the Enemy's battery whistled through our ranks in rapid succession—many horses were killed—Sergeant Hughes, of Capt. Parson's Company had both of his legs broken by a cannon ball.

Gen. Conde now fell back behind the intrenchments & redoubts. Col. Doniphan ordered the adavnce to sound & the whole Army, in the following order, moved on to storm the Enemy "breastworks", (viz) The Artillery Battallion in the Center; The first Battalion on the right wing, commanded by Lt. Col. Jackson, & Lt. Col. Mitchel by request. The three Select Mounted Companies Commanded by Capt's. Reid, Parsons, & Hudson immediately on the left of the Artillery; & the Second Battalion on the extreme left commanded by Major Gilpin. The caravan kept close in rear, commanded by Major Owens _____ Col. Doniphan & his aids, Adjutant De Courcy & Capt. Thompson, acted between the Battalions. Sergeant Major Crenshaw promptly dispatched the orders of the colonel—As we neared the Enemy's redoubts a heavy fire was opened upon us from the different Batteries consisting of 18 guns in all. At this moment Capt. Reid's Company of select horsemen, of which I had the honor to be a member, was ordered to charge the Battery that had annoyed us so much. Nobly and gallantly did Capt. Reid & his little handful of men dash into the midst of the enemy's ranks. They carried the battery and silenced the guns for a moment; but owing to some mistake, a portion of Capt. Reid's men were halted by an order that did not come from the Colonel, & the small squad that had charged the Battery could not hold possession of it—We were beaten back & many of us wounded—here Major Samuel Owens, who had voluntarily entered into the charge was shot by a cannon Ball which instantly killed him & horse both. Capt Reid's horse was shot under him & some gallant young man, whose name I do not know, immediately dismounted & offered the Captain his horse. By this time the remainder of Capt. Reid's Company, Capt. Parsons' Company & Capt. Hudson's Company, & Companies C & B dismounted, Came to our support. Capt. Wright man & Lt. Choteau with two howitzers rose the hill at the same instant & pounded such a heavy fire in upon the enemy that the battery was silenced in 2 minutes & the enemy retreating over the hill. Major John P. Campbell of Springfield was in this Charge & acted most nobly—It is said he killed 2 Mexicans in the fight—Lts. Barnett, Hinton & Moss acted with great bravery during the whole engagement—They were with Capt. Reid in the daring charge upon the battery. Lt. Hinton drove his sword to the hilt into a Mexican's breast. Every Company was now pressing forward & pouring over the entrenchments & into the redouts of the enemy, vieing with each other in the noble struggle for victory. Companies A, B, C, & a part of company D, respectively under command of Capts, Waldo Walton, Moss & Lt. Miller, led on by Lt. Col. Mitchel & Lt. Col. Jackson Stormed a formidable redoubt on the extreme right, defended by 3 pieces of cannon & a great number of well armed men. This Battery had kept up a continual cross firing upon our right during the whole engagement. Lt. Col. Mitchel acted with great gallantry. It is said that Col. Jackson put a mexican to rest with 18 buck-shot through him—Major Clark did important work with his artillery in storming the different redoubts. These plans for storming the Mexican redoubts were well conceived by the Colonel & promptly put into execution by his Adjutant De Courcy & other aids—

Company G, under Capt. H. H Hughes & a part of Company F under Lt. Pope Gorden Stormed a battery of 3 brass six pounders, strongly defended by embankments & ditches filled with resolute Mexicans—Some of them were taken prisoner, while trying to fire the cannon—I saw Capt Hughes split a Mexican's head wide open with his sabre. Companies H & E under Capts, Rodgers & Stephenson on the extreme left fought nobly—They chased the Mexicans like blood-hounds. Maj Gilpin encour aged his men to fight by his own example—he fought gallantly. The rout of the Mexican Army now became general & the Slaughter continued until night put an end to the chase—The battle continued 3 hours. The men returned to the battlefield after dark completely worn out & exhausted with fatigue. The Mexicans lost 300 men killed on the field & a large number & 60 or 70 prisoners, among whom is Gen Quilty. Wounded, perhaps 400, or 500, together with a vast quantity of provisions, several thousand dollars in money, 50.000 head of sheep, 1500 head of cattle, 100 Mules, 30 wagons, 25 or 30 Carts, 25,000 lbs Ammunition, 11 pieces of cannon, mostly brass six pounders, 6 Wall pieces, 100 Stand of arms, 100 stand of Colors & many other things of less note. Our loss was as follows;

Major Samuel Owens, killed by a cannon ball (buried in Chihuahua)

In Capt. Reid's Mounted Company—

A. A. Kirkpatrick (wounded mortally)

J. Sullivan, (Left arm struck by a cannon ball)

James Barns (left arm broke)

J. T Hughes (flesh wound in the left arm)

Charles Haman (slightly in the side)

Thos. McCarty (slightly in front)

Joshua Wolf, of Hudson's Company, slightly wounded

In Capt. Parsons Mounted Company,

S. B. Fleming (wounded in the right shoulder)

Wm Henke (in the right leg)

W. Gorden (in the right shoulder)

Major John P. Campbell slightly in the face.

Lt. Col. Mitchel, Whiskers shaved by a cannon ball—

The Battalion of Teamsters were unable to get into the fight; they are brave boys & would have fought well—There were various other gentlemen, not connected with the army, who fought bravely & distinguished themselves. Among these are Capts Collins our interpreter, & James Kirker, the Indian hunter, & Mr. A. Henderson a very brave man _____.

All the officers & men, as far as I know, nobly and gallantly performed their whole duty. If there ever was any stain resting upon the arms of Missouri it is now completely & forever wiped out by the glorious & memorable Victory of the 28th. Col. Doniphan now has possession of the City of Chihahau! Lt. Col. Mitchel with 150 men took military possession of the city in the name of his Goverment on the first day of March & Col. Doniphan entered the City in triumphal procession with all his Train on the 2nd. The American residents here are all set at liberty except Magoffin & a few others who are said to be at Perál below here. It is Col. Doniphan's intention to continue his march still further down the Country. He will perhaps return home by the Southern route— We hear that Wool & Taylor have joined their forces. This is a proud moment for us! the Battle of Sacremento gave us the capital & the Flag of our Country, the "Stars & stripes", are proudly and triumphantly streaming over the city. As the Colonel entered the capital he fired a National Salute of 28 guns—

Respectfully
John T Hughes

P.S. The Surgeons, T. M. & J. F. Morton, have been assiduous in the discharge of their duties—Col. Doniphan intends giving each of the Companies a piece of Artillery to take home with them—Young Lewis of the Saline Company, if all be true that is said of him, is worth his weight in gold. In the gallant charge Capt. Reid made on the battery of the enemy this youth killed 3 Mexicans with his Sabre. It was in this charge that I received a wound through left arm from a cannon slug—Many other gallant exploits came under my own observation, but for want of time I must omit the names of the actors, & close this imperfect sketch of the great battle of Sacremento—We had about 950 men actually engaged—

J. T. Hughes

Bob. You must excuse this scroll—I am crippled and out of doors on a sand beach & cannot give you a full account of this battle. I will give you a fuller account hereafter —What I have said is badly said & badly written—make it out right if you can read it—be particular with the orthography—I am well except my wound—our boys are well generally—Riley Stout & Russell R. Cox of Clay deserted the Army at El Paso —Chihuahua is a noble city—large as St. Louis nearly—Company C gained laurels in the battle _____ I cannot tell when we will get home. I think we will go on down the country to Saltillo in 2 or 3 weeks—I want to see you all—My compliments to the citizens of Clay—Remember me to all my female acquaintances—

your friend truly. John T. Hughes

We have learned that Governor Armijo is in prison in Zacetacos—Governor Angel Trios has fled from the State of Chihuahua

# INDEX

Adams, Samuel, Dr., 211-12
Albuquerque *Tribune,* vi
Allen, Alfred, 36
Allen, Gabriel (Gabe), *82,* 83, 84, 107, 122, 145, 147, 153 *n.*
Allen, Hiram, 59
Andy (Negro), Indian fighter, 113, 122, 142
Angel, Eugene, 196
Angel, Myron, 196-97, 203
*Apache Gold and Yaqui Silver,* v
Armijo, Manuel, 107-08, 116-18, 156
Ashley, William H., 44, 45-50, 50 *n.,* 51-62, 65-66, 68
Austin, Moses, 24, 26
Austin, Stephen, 24

Baillo, Paul, 72
Baird, James, 24, 36, 37, 43 *n.,* 77
Baldwin, Howard L., x
Barnett, Robert, 167
Bartlett, John R., 112
Barton, David, 26
Bates, Frederick, 68
Baum, Peter, 34, 36, 42
Bean, Joshua, 12
Bean, Phantley, 12, 104 *n.*
Bean, Roy ("All the Law West of the Pecos"), v, 12, *204*
Bean, Roy, grandson of Samuel G. Bean, 217
Bean, Sam F., grandson of Jim, *217,* 221
Bean, Samuel G. ("Old Timer"), son-in-law of Jim, x, 12, 74 *n.,* 104 *n.,* 155, 162, *204,* 205, 206, 207 *n., 217,* 219, 221-22; quoted, 220, 221; death (1903), 220
Becknell, William, 42, 65, 67
Belfast, Northern Ireland, vi, vii, *9,* 10, 13 *n.,* 193-94
Bent, Charles, 168
Benton, Thomas Hart, Senator, 25, 26-27, 28 *n.,* 44, 68, 71, 72
Big Star, Comanche Indian chief, 38, 39, 40
Bixby, W. Kirker, ix, 13 *n.*
*Black Joke* (privateer ship), ix-x, *16,* 17-19, 21 *n.*
Boggs, Thomas, 72
Bolton, Herbert E., quoted, 112-13
Brackenridge, Henry Marie, 35 *n.,* 44, quoted, 55
Brady, John, 25
Brady, Joseph, 30
Brady, Thomas, 25, 30
Brandes, Ray, xi
Briones, John ("Toddy"), 214 *n.*
Brooks, George R., ix
Bryan, Howard, vi
Buquor, Cecilia B., granddaughter of Jim, 221

Cabanne, Jean P., 26
Caldwell, Thomas J., 160, 167
California, 59-60, 81, 104 *n.,* 154, 157, 206; gold-seekers to (1849), 194-95; as 31st state, 208; statehood celebration (Oct. 29, 1850), 208-10; Jim Kirker's residence in, 210-12; Jim

Kirker's grave in, 213-14; California Column, Union Army (1862), 219-20
Calvo, José Joaquin, 95, 97, 99-100, 104 *n.,* 110, 116, 120
Campbell, John P., 179, 183
Carpenter, William, 34, 48, 49, 50 *n.*
Carson, Kit, viii, 59, 73, 74 *n.,* 203-05
Carson, Moses, 59
Casteneda, Anita B., granddaughter of Jim, 221
Chambers, Sam, 34, 36, 42
Charless, Joseph, 26
Chihuahua City, Mexico, 36, 76, 87-90, 120-32, 136, 138-39, 146-47, 151-52, 176; as target for U.S. Army, 153, 167-70; fall of (1847), 183-84
Chisholm, Jesse, 118 *n.*
Chittenden, Hiram Martin, 54, 63 *n.*
Chouteau, Auguste, 24, 26
Chouteau family, 43 *n.,* 45
Churchill, Sylvester, 184, 185
Cisneros, José, xi
Clark, George Rogers, 107
Clark, Meriwether Lewis, 165, 178
Clark, William, General, 46, 47, 48
Clark, William, Governor, 26
Clegg, Joseph, 22, 23, 28 *n.,* 32
Clyman, James, 53, 54-55, 55-56, 60
Cochise, Apache Indian chief, 143, 145
Cogburn, Samuel, 167
Collins, James L. (Squire), 5, 167-68, 170, 171, 183, 184; in quarrel with Jim Kirker, 3-4, 172, 176, 179-80
Compa, Juan José, Apache Indian chief, 94, 103 *n.*
Conde, Pedro Garcia, 130-31, 132, 134
Contra Costa County, California, xi, 211, 214 *n.*
Cook, Thomas, 37
Cooke, Philip St. George, 104 *n.,* 111
*Constitution* (frigate), 15, 19
Copper Trail, 87-90, 96
Corlew, Henry, 71
Corralitos, *see* Hacienda Corralitos
Courcier, Stephen, 71, 77, 78, 79, 81, 87, 112, 113, 116, 120-21
Crockett, Davey, viii
Cuado, Carlos Myette, 37
Cunningham, Charles, 59

Daley, Andrew W., 117
*Dalhousie Review,* 21 *n.*
Davis, Mary Liza (Miss California, 1850), 208, 209
DeCourcy, James, 159, 180, 181
Dempsey, James, 72
DeMun, Jules, 26
Doan, Lucas, 71
Dobie, J. Frank, v
Doniphan, Alexander William, Col., second in command

Missouri Volunteers, 1, 3, 4-5, 8, 155, 157-85 *passim,* 189-90; *see also* Missouri Volunteers
Douglas, Walter B., 43 *n.,* 73 *n.*
Dryden, William, 117
Dunigan, Edward, stepson of Jim, 19, 21 *n.,* 215-16
Dunigan, Peter, 15, 19
Dutton Lewis, 71

Easterly, Thomas M., *114, 115,* 190, 191 *n.*
Easton, Rufus, 26
Edwards, Frank S., 181
Edwards, John E., 155
Edwards, Marcellus Ball, 182 *n.*
El Paso, Texas, 24, 170, 220
El Paso *Herald-Post,* vi
El Paso *News,* 220
El Paso del Norte (Juarez), Mexico, 95, 126, 152, 157, 158, 167, 205, 217; captured by U.S. (1846), 165
Elguea, Francisco Manuel, 76
Embleton, I., ix, 13 *n.*
*Emigrants' Guide to California,* 1849, Ware and Sublette, *115,* 191 *n.*
Emmons, Ira, 71, 74 *n.*
Encinillas, *see* Hacienda Encinillas

Feather, Adlai, x, 222 *n.*
Field, Joseph M., 50 *n.*
Field, Matthew C. (Matt), v; quoted, 6 *n.,* 122-26
Field, Ruth K., vi
Fink, Mike, 34, 48, 49, 50 *n.*
Fisher, Robert, 193
Fitzpatrick, Thomas, 53, 59
Flint, Timothy, 79
Flotte, Louis, Sr., 43 *n.*
Forsyth, Thomas, Major, 32, 35 *n.,* 51, *52, 53,* 65, 67, 155, *169*
Forsyth, Thomas (Jr.), 155, 162, 165, 168, *169,* 170, 183
Forts
  Atkinson, 57, 61
  Bent's, 101, 102, 106, 113, 122, 150, 156
  Henry, 49, 52, 57
  Kiowa, 58
  Leaton, 119 *n.*
  Leavenworth, 155, 156
  Osage, 72
  Recovery, 58
Fremont, John Charles, 12
Frost, Gordon, 6 *n.*
Furgerson, Jesse, 78, 81

Gibson, George Rutledge, 181-82
Gilpen, William, 158, 174, 175, 177, 183-84
Glasgow, Edward J., 170, 178, 191 *n.*
Glass, Hugh, 53
Glenday, James, 102, 122, 134
Gordon, George R., 170
Gordon, William, 59, 62, 117
Gratiot, Charles, 26
Gregg, Josiah, 117, 118, 119 *n.*
Grey Eyes, Arickara Indian chief, 54, 60, 61

Guadalupe y Calvo, Chihuahua, Mexico, viii-ix, xi, 103 *n., 133*

Hacienda Corralitos, Chihuahua, Mexico, viii, 87, 88, *89, 90,* 103 *n.,* 121, 150, 152, 164
Hacienda Encinillas, Chihuahua, Mexico, 90, 170, 171
Hacienda Sacramento, Chihuahua, Mexico, 5, 7 *n.,* 90, 153, 164, 170, 171; battle of, 174-80, 235-38
Hafen, LeRoy R., x
Hall, Sergeant, 25
Hammond, George P., x
Hammond, Samuel, 26
Harper, John H., 156
Harper, William H., 173 *n.*
Harrington, Mrs. Fred C., Jr., ix
Hays, Carl D. W., x
Heitfeld, Fred, xi, 214 *n.*
Hempstead, Edward, 26
Henry, Andrew, 45, 46-49, 50 *n.,* 51-52, 56-57, 58, 59, 68
Heridia, José A., 175, 177
Heslep, Augustus, Dr. ("Rambler"), 197, 198, 200-01, 201 *n.,* 202-03
Heslep, Joseph, 196, 199, 205, 207
Hextor, Frederick, 37
Hillman, Jacqueline, x
Hobbs, James, 106, 122, 138, 142, 143, 146, 148, 149, 212
Hortiz, Francisco, 97, 122, 134
Houston, Sam, viii
Howard, Alexander, 37
Huber, Elbert L., ix
Hughes, Ami, 178
Hughes, John T., 162, 166, 171, 173 *n.;* quoted, 235-38
Hunt, Wilson P., 54
Hutchinson, William H., v-vi, xi

Indian Tribes
  Apache, 75, 79, 104 *n.,* 108-12, 120-32, 162, 189, 210, 221; as menace for Mexican settlements, 90-100, 103 *n.,* 112-13, 132, 150; as victims of Jim Kirker's scalping raids, v, 136, 138-46, 151-52, 163; U.S. Army attacks on, 193
  Arapaho, 199-200
  Arickara, 54-56, 57, 58, 59, 60-62
  Assiniboin, 49
  Blackfeet, 52, 58, 59
  Cherokee, 70, 97
  Cheyenne, 199-200
  Chiricahua, 94
  Comanche, 4, 38-41, 91, 172
  Coyotero Apache, 94, 98, 99
  Delaware, 113, 126, 138, 148, 149, 163, 203; as companions of Jim Kirker, 7 *n.,* 152, 171, 185, 205, 210, 213
  Fox, *169*
  Hopi, 85
  Jicarilla Apache, 94, 192-93
  Kiowa, *69,* 75, 91
  Lipan, 91, 94
  Llanero, 94
  Maricopa, 81, 91, 94
  Mescalero, 94
  Mimbreno Apache, 75, 94
  Mohave, 80, 81-82
  Navajo, 91, 93, 94, 98, 99, 101
  Opata, 95

  Osage, 38, 45
  Paquime, 90
  Pima, 79, 81, 91, 94
  Sauk, *169*
  Seri, 95
  Shawnee, 10, 102, 106, 113, 118 *n.,* 126, 131, 138, 140, 143, 148, 149, 189; as companions of Jim Kirker, 7 *n.,* 152, 163, 171, 185, 205, 210, 213
  Sioux, 58, 59, 60-61
  Taracone, 94
  Tonto, 94
  Ute, 98, 99, 193
  Wyandot, 173 *n.*
  Yaqui, 95
  Zuni, 81, 91, 100, 101
Irigoyen de la O, José, 127-28, 130
Irigoyen Rodriguez, José Marie, 120, 121, 127
Ivy, John, 37

Jackson, Andrew, viii, 25-26
Jackson, Congreve, 184, 198
Jackson, David, x
Jackson, George C., 59
James, John, 37
James, Thomas, 37-42, 43 *n.,* 70, 73 *n.*
Janos, Chihuahua, Mexico, 76, 87, *88,* 93, *96,* 103 *n.,* 110, 113
Jenkins, Myra Ellen, x
Johnson, John James (Juan), 108-12, 118 *n.,* 119 *n.,* 120
Justiniani, Cayetano, 97, 98-99, 128, 130, 175, 178

Kearney, Stephen W., 155-57
Keemle, Charles ("Grey Eagle"), 19, 21 *n.,* 50 *n.,* 59, *186,* 194; quoted, 74 *n.,* 187-90
Kendall, Charles Wye, 17
Kendall, George Wilkins, 138-39, 206; quoted, 6 *n.*
Kirker, Catherine, widow of Peter Dunigan, wife of Jim, 19-20, 28 *n.,* 95, 215, 216, 222 *n.*
Kirker, David, cousin of Jim, 4, 22, 23, 28 *n.,* 32, 34, 37, 51, *52,* 63 *n.,* 67, 71, 73 *n.,* cowardice of, 41-42, 44, 70, 172
Kirker, E. C., ix, 13 *n.,* 28 *n.*
Kirker, Gilbert, father of Jim, 10, 195 *n.*
Kirker, Gilbert (Jr.), brother of Jim, 10, 195 *n.*
Kirker, Hugh Gilbert, distant cousin of Jim, vii, *9,* 10, *11*
Kirker, James (Jim) (Santiago Querque), biography: birth of, at Kilcross, near Belfast, Northern Ireland (1793), vi, vii, *9,* 10; Scotch-Irish background of, vi-vii, vii-viii, 8-10; arrival in New York City (1810), 14; as privateer, War of 1812, 16-19; marriage to Catherine Dunigan, widow (1813), 19; as New York City grocer, 19-20; arrival in St. Louis (1817), 23; as St. Louis grocer, 32-34, 35 *n.,* 51-52, 63, 65, 71, 72, 187; on expedition to Upper Missouri (1822-1823), 44, 46, 50 *n.,* 51, 62-63; with trade caravans to Santa Fe (1824, 1825, 1826), 67-68, 71-72, 73 and *n.;* as trapper on Gila

River, N. Mex., 72, 73 and *n.,* 79-80, 81-85, 94, 97-102, 188; as Mexican citizen, 72, 95, 191; at Santa Rita copper mines (1828-1836), *75,* 78-79, 87, 90, 94, 95; residences at Janos and at Hacienda Corralitos, 87, *88, 89, 90, 96,* 103 *n.,* 150, 152, 164; marriage to Rita Garcia (about 1831), 95; as scourge of aroused Apaches, 113-14, 121-30; as famous scalper of Apaches, 139-52; as guide and interpreter for Missouri Volunteers (1846-1847), 163-66, 168-73, 176, 178-81, 190; return to St. Louis from Chihuahua City via New Orleans (1847), 184-91; as aid to U.S. Army in attacks on Indians in Santa Fe area (1848), 192-93; on visit to Belfast (1848), 193-94; as Forty-niners' guide from St. Louis to Santa Fe, 196-207; as California resident (about 1850-1853), 208-12; death of, in California (about 1853), 212-14
Kirker, James (Santiago José), son of Jim, 115, 217
Kirker, James, present-day descendant of Jim, 219
Kirker, James B., son of Jim, 20, 21 *n.,* 215, 216, 222 *n.*
Kirker, Martha, sister of Jim, 10, 195 *n.*
Kirker, Petra, daughter of Jim, wife of Samuel G. Bean, v, 104 *n., 204,* 205, 206, 207 *n.,* 217, 219-20; birth (1833), 96; death (1911), 221
Kirker, Polinaria, daughter of Jim, 115
Kirker, Rafael, son of Jim, 115, 217, *218*
Kirker, Rafael, grandson of Jim, 86 *n.*
Kirker, Rita Garcia, wife of Jim, 95, 104 *n.,* 222 *n.*
Kirker, Robert, cousin of Jim, 22, 23, 28 *n.,* 32, 35 *n.,* 74 *n.*
Kirker, Roberto, son of Jim, 115, 217, *218*
Kirker, Roberto, great-grandson of Jim, *219*
Kirker, Roberto, present-day descendant of Jim, 219
Kirker, Rose, née Anderson, mother of Jim, 10, 195 *n.*
Kirker, Rose, sister of Jim, 10, 195 *n.*
Kirker, Thomas, 2nd governor of Ohio, cousin of Jim, ix, 10, 12, 13 *n.,* 23
Kirker Pass, near Pittsburg, California, *212,* 212-13
Knight, William, 111, 117

Labadie, Sylvestre, 43 *n.*
Laclede, Pierre, 24
LaGrand, Alexander, 67
Las Cruces, New Mexico, 217, 219, 222 *n.*
Las Cruces *Citizen,* 104 *n.,* 220
Laughlin, Richard, 78, 81
Leaton, Benjamin, 111, 112, 119 *n.,* 122
Leavenworth, Henry, 57, 58, 59, 60-63

Lewis, Meriwether, viii
Lewis and Clark expedition, 26, 45
Lisa, Manuel, 43 *n.*, 45
Lost Peg-leg mine, 80-81
Lucas, John B. C., 26

McDonald, Angus, 59, 62
McDonough, Michael, 37
Mackay, James, 73 *n.*
Mackintosh, Ewen C., 101, 103 *n.*, 133-34, *135*
McKnight, John (Sr.), 25, 29, 30, 36, 37-43, *69*, 70, 71
McKnight, John, adopted son and nephew of John McKnight (Sr.), *69*
McKnight, Robert, 24, 34, 37, 43 and *n.*, 70-71, 72, 88, 131, 151; as prisoner in Mexico, 25, 36, 42, 90; at Santa Rita copper mines, 77, 78-79, 81, 87, 112, 113, 116, 120-21
McKnight, Thomas, 25, 29, *31*, 32, 35 *n.*, 70, 72, 74 *n.*
Maclean, Lachlan Allan, 166, 171
McNair, Alexander, 26
McNellis, Robert, 137 *n.*
Madrid, José Dolores, 102, 122
Magoffin, James, 156, 189
Marmaduke, Meredith Miles, 67, 73 *n.*
Marshall, Joseph, 179
Maxwell, Samuel, 167
Meek, Stephen Hall, 138
Melendres, José Marie, 102, 122
Merklen, Harold, xi
Mesilla, New Mexico, x, 158, *204*, 217, 219, 220, 222 *n.*
Mesilla Valley, New Mexico, x, 43 *n.*
Mewes, Mary E., ix
Mexican War, 152, 153, 183, 189-90, 208; beginning of, 154-55; *see also* Missouri Volunteers
Mines, William, 37
Missouri Fur Company, 43 *n.*, 54, 59, 62
*Missouri Gazette,* St. Louis, 26; quoted, 46, 50 *n.*
Missouri Volunteers, 3, 8, 152, 155-85, 189-90; formation of (May-June, 1846), 155; Santa Fe captured by, 156; battle of Bracito, 159-63, 165, 167, *169;* Jim Kirker as guide and interpreter, 163-66, 168-73, 176, 178-81, 190; El Paso captured by, 165-66; Presidio Carrizal and Encinillas captured by, 170, 171; battle of Sacramento, 174-80; Chihuahua City occupied by (March, 1847), 183-84; arrival in New Orleans for mustering out (June, 1847), 184-85; *see also* Mexican War
Mitchell, D. D., 177
Mitchell, Levin "Colorado," 193
Monterde, Mariano, 132-33, 136
Moore, Meredith T., 7 *n.;* quoted, 6 *n.*, 163-64, 172, 179, 180
Morgan, Dale L., x, 57, 78, 191 *n.*
Mormon Battalion, 104 *n.*, 111
Mount Diablo, California, 211, 212
Mullins, Janet E., 21 *n.*

Narbona, Antonio, 72, 77, 78, 85, 188
Neri, Vincent, 211, 213-14, 214 *n.*
*New Mexico Historical Review,* vi
New Orleans, Louisiana, 184-85
New Orleans *Picayune,* v, 138-39; quoted, 6 *n.*, 122-25, 185
New York City, 14-15, 19-20, 22
*Niles' Register* (newspaper), 168
Nunis, Doyce B., Jr., vi, xi
*Nymph* (brig), xi, 22

Oak Springs, California, 208, 211, *212*
O'Fallon, Benjamin, 47, 57, 58
One-Eye, Comanche Indian chief, 39, 70
Ortiz, Francisco, 97, 122, 134
Ortiz, Ramon, Father, 43 *n.*, 168
Ottley, Allan R., xi
Owens, Samuel Combs, 156, 166, 167, 170, 171-72, 172-73, 176, 178; death, 179, 180, 181-82, 182 *n.*

Pancoast, Charles, 196, 200, 202; quoted, 197, 199, 203-04, 205
Parsons, M. M., 163, 180
Pattie, James Ohio, 76, 77, 78, 79, 81
Pattie, Silvester, 76, 77, 78, 79, 81
Patton, George S., Jr., 95
Peacock, James, 7 *n.*
Peoria Pioneers, Forty-niners to California, 196-205, 207
Perez, Albino, 100-02, 107-08, 134, 136, 188; quoted, 97-98
Pike, Zebulon Montgomery, 66, 76
Pilcher, Joshua, 54, 58, 59, 61, 62
Ponce, Mariano, 90, 97, 100, 101, 102
Ponce de Leon, General, 160, 162, *169*
Pope, William, 78, 81
Potter, Benjamin, 37
Potts, Daniel T., 50 *n.*
Pratte, Bernard, 26
Presidio Carrizal, Chihuahua, Mexico, 164, 169, 170
Price, Sterling, 168, 193
Pryor, Nathaniel, 78, 81

Rancho de Taos, New Mexico, 123, *125*
Randall, Andrew, Dr., quoted, 206
Reid, John W., 162, 171, 179, 182 *n.*
Reid, Mayne, v, 6 *n.*
Reilly, Bennet, 59-60
Revilla, Bernardo, 104 *n.*, 116, 117
*Rio Grande Republican,* quoted, 221
Robidoux, Michel, 79
Rogers, John, 70
Rogers, Will, 70
Roosevelt, Theodore, quoted, vii-viii
Rose, Edward, 53, 55, 59, 61
Rowland, John, 117
Rowland, Thomas, 117
Russell, Edmund, 81
Russell, William, 26
Ruxton, George Augustus Frederick, 6 *n.*-7 *n.*, 151, 157; quoted, 152

Ryan, Margarita B., granddaughter of Jim, 221

Sacramento, *see* Hacienda Sacramento
*Sagamore* (steamboat), vi, 209-10
Sage, Rufus B., quoted, 106
St. Louis, Missouri, 70, 185, 194-95; early Irish immigrants in, 22-23; description of (1817), 23, 24-25, 28 *n.;* politics in (1817), 25-27; early economic conditions in, 29-34, 65-68; Jim Kirker as grocer in, 32-34, 35 *n.*, 51-52, 63, 65, 71, 72, 187; Santa Fe Trail beginning at, 68; Jim Kirker's biographical sketch in newspaper (1847), quoted, 187-90
St. Louis *Enquirer,* 25; quoted, 44
St. Louis *Saturday Evening Post and Temperance Recorder,* 21 *n.*, 50 *n.*, 57, 59, 73 *n.*, 74 *n.*, *186*, 187-90
St. Louis *Weekly Reveille,* 50 *n.;* quoted, 185, 194
St. Vrain, Ceran, 97, 207
San Francisco, California, celebration of state's admission to U.S., 208-10
San Francisco, *Alta California* (newspaper), quoted, 210
Sandoval, Antonio, 128; quoted, 129
Santa Anna, Antonio Lopez de, 126-27, 168
Santa Fe, New Mexico, 77, 96, 107-08, 117, 122, 165, 168, 192, 193, 205-07; expeditions to (1812, 1821), 25, 34, 37-43; Santa Fe Trail to, 65, 68; trade caravans to (1824, 1825, 1826), 67-68, 71-72, 72-73, 73 *n.*, capture of, by U.S. Army (1846), 152, 156
Santa Fe *Republican,* 50 *n.*, 193, 206, quoted, 192
Santa Fe Trail, 59, 65, 68, 170
Santa Rita copper mines, New Mexico, 73, 75-77, 78-79, 81, 86 *n.*, 87, 94, 97, 100, 112-13, 116, 120, 217, *219*
Scott, Hiram, 59
Scott, John, 26
Shearer, William, 37, 42, 71
Shreve, Benjamin, 34, 36, 42
Skillman, Henry, 170, 178
Sledd, Joshua, 71
Slover, Isaac, 78
Smith, Jedediah, 53, 56, 57, 59
Smith, Ralph A., vi
Smith, Thomas Long (Peg-leg), 80, 107
Socorro, New Mexico, 113, 116, 128, 129, 189
Somersville, California, xi, 211, 213
Sonnichsen, Leland, v
Spencer, John W., 107, 122
Speyer, Albert, 147, 156
Spreen, Orville, ix
Spybuck, half-breed Shawnee chief, 102, 106-07, 113, 118 *n.*, 122, 138-44, 147, 148-50, 189
Spybuck, Henry, 118 *n.*
Stadler, Mrs. Ernst A., ix
Stanley, Elisha, 71, 74 *n.*
Stephens, Aaron, 55

Stephenson, Hugo, 43 *n.*
Stevenson, Hugh, 71
Stoes, Katherine D., 104 *n.*,
   207 *n.*
Storm, Colton, xi
Storrs, Augustus, 67, 68, 71
Strickland, Rex, Dr., x
Stryker-Rodda, Harriet, ix
Sublette, Solomon P., 191 *n.*
Sublette, William, 53, 59, 82
Swan, David, 162-63

Talbott, Levi, 49, 50 *n.*
Taos, New Mexico, 43, 81, 84,
   193, 206
Taylor, Mrs. J. Paul, x, 43 *n.*,
   104 *n.*
Taylor, Zachary, 154, 183, 184
Tecumseh, Shawnee Indian chief,
   10
Tindall, Elizabeth, ix
Trias, Angel, 150-51, 152, 157,
   170, 175, 192

Turley, Stephen, 73

Valencia, Tomas, 102, 122
Vanderburgh, William Henry, 59
Voelker, Frederick E., ix, 74 *n.*

Waldo, David, 155, 166
Wallace, Bill, *89, 90,* 103 *n.*
War of 1812, 15-19, 45, 67
Ware, Joseph E., 190, 191 *n.*
Warner, Jonathan Trumbull (Juan
   José), quoted, 78
Weaver, Pauline (Paulino) (Pablo
   Guiber), half-breed Cherokee
   Indian, 97, 101, 102, 104 *n.*,
   122, 134
Webb, James Josiah, 173; quoted,
   182 *n.*
Weightman, Richard Hanson, 4,
   178, 181
Wells, R. A., 167
*Westways* magazine, vi

Wethered, Samuel, 167
Wetmore, Alphonso, 67
White Bear, Comanche Indian
   Chief, 40
Williams, "Old Bill," 193
Wilson, Benjamin David, x, 95,
   96, 103 *n.*, 111, 117
Wilson, James, 37
Woodward, Arthur A., v, x, 6 *n.*
Wool, John E., 157, 168, 184
Wooley, Abram R., 60
Workman, Julian (or William), 84,
   117
Wyeth, Nathaniel C., 102

Young, Ewing, 72
Yount, George C., 74 *n.*, 78, 79,
   80-81, 84-85, 86 *n.*, 208;
   quoted, 83

*Zebulon M. Pike* (steamboat),
   23-24

F
800

McGaw, William Cochran.
    Savage scene; the life and  times of
James Kirker, frontier king.   New
York, Hastings House [1972]
    xi, 242 p. illus. 22 cm.
    Bibliography: p. 223-234.
    ISBN 0-8038-6712-3

    1. Kirker, James, 1793-1852 or 3.
2. Indians of North America--
Southwest, New--History.
3. Southwest, New--History.
I. Title.

F800.K52M3                    917.8/03/20924   [B]
                              76-38962

SUPAT        B/NA A B8-316281                 10/28/77